TransForming ge

Transgender practices of identity, intimacy and care

Sally Hines

First published in Great Britain in 2007 by

The Policy Press
University of Bristol
Fourth Floor
Beacon House
Queen's Road
Bristol BS8 1QU
UK

Tel +44 (0)117 331 4054
Fax +44 (0)117 331 4093
e-mail tpp-info@bristol.ac.uk
www.policypress.org.uk

British Library Cataloguing in Publication Data
A catalogue record for this book is available from the British Library.

Library of Congress Cataloging-in-Publication Data
A catalog record for this book has been requested.

ISBN 978 1 86134 916 3 paperback
ISBN 978 1 86134 917 0 hardcover

Cover design by Qube Design Associates, Bristol.
Front cover image kindly supplied by Getty Images.
Printed and bound in Great Britain by MPG Books, Bodmin.

Contents

Acknowledgements

This book grew out of research that was initially completed in the School of Sociology and Social Policy at the University of Leeds. The project was part of the ESRC research group 'Care, Values and the Future of Welfare' (CAVA). I would like to thank members of the CAVA team for providing a supportive and stimulating research environment. Particular thanks go to Fiona Williams and Sasha Roseneil. Together they provided much inspiration, generosity and support. I am greatly indebted to their input into my work. I would also like to thank Carol Smart, Judith Halberstam, Jeffrey Weeks and Ruth Holiday, who commented on and contributed to my work at various stages. Collegial (and personal) thanks also go to Diane Richardson and Yvette Taylor for support and friendship during my time working in the School of Geography, Politics and Sociology at Newcastle University.

The support of many friends and family members cannot be overstated. Big thanks go to Mark Jackson for his lasting friendship and co-parenting. I am immensely grateful to my parents, Margaret Hines and Barry Hines, who always provide love and encouragement My son, Gil Jackson-Hines, makes it all worthwhile.

I would like to acknowledge the Economic and Social Research Council, who provided research funding, and members of The Policy Press, in particular Philip de Bary for being a supportive editor, and Jo Morton for all her work as production editor

Finally, this book would not have been possible without the people who participated in the research project which is at the heart of this book. I thank all of you for generously supporting this project, and for sharing your stories with such openness, dignity and humour.

Introduction

This book explores a range of gender identities and experiences that fall under the broad umbrella of 'transgender'. The term transgender relates to a diversity of practices that call into question traditional ways of seeing gender and its relationship with sex and sexuality. Used broadly, the concept of transgender is extensive – incorporating practices and identities such as transvestism, transsexuality, intersex, gender queer, female and male drag, cross-dressing and some butch/femme practices. Transgender may refer to individuals who have undergone hormone treatment or surgery to reconstruct their bodies, or to those who cross gender in ways that are less permanent. Transgender has also been referred to as 'gender blending', 'gender mixing', 'gender fucking' and 'gender crossing' (Ekins and King, 1996). In this book 'transgender' is used as an umbrella term to cover a diversity of practices that involve embodied movements across, between, or beyond the binary categories of male and female. My use of the term 'transgender' thus relates to transsexual identities and practices, and those that are articulated from a variety of other (trans)[1] gender positions.

Influenced by transgender community activism and linked to the proliferation of ideas around gender and sexuality from postmodernism and queer theory, transgender gained academic capital in the 1990s. As Whittle comments, this new strand of academic engagement with transgender:

> started from the premise that to be trans was not to have a mental or medical disorder. This fundamental shift was built upon within academia, and enabled trans men and women to reclaim the reality of their bodies, to create with them what they would, and to leave the linguistic determination of those bodies open to exploration and invention. (2006: xii)

In recent years transgender has also emerged as a subject of increasing social and cultural interest in the UK. Popular representations of transgender are apparent in TV drama, sitcom and reality TV, while the 'trans confessional' is a chat-show staple. Tabloid journalists and magazine feature writers increasingly search for trans people for 'real life' stories, and television documentary and broadsheet journalism has focused upon the experiences of both female and male trans people. Transgender characters have had central roles in recent mainstream films, and, on stage, cross-dressing performers such as Eddie Izzard, Lily Savage and RuPaul draw large audiences. While I do not wish to over-prioritise the political significance of such cultural representations – and indeed many barely move beyond stereotypes – cultural representations can give an indication of how minority gender and sexual identities are able to shift to some degree beyond their marginalised status. In 2004, for example, Grayson Perry won the Turner Prize for his multimedia artwork, which explores his transvestite persona 'Claire'. In the same year the most wide-reaching cultural representation of transgender in the UK arose from the reality television show *Big Brother 5*, whose housemate and winner was 27-year-old trans woman Nadia Almada. In and out of the *Big Brother* house, Nadia received extensive television and newspaper coverage, leading *Observer* columnist Barbara Ellen to comment that: "The triumph of a Portuguese transgender woman in the nation's greatest unofficial popularity contest threw up important questions about Britain today. Are attitudes shifting? Is there a greater tolerance and broadmindedness, at least among the nation's youth? [...]" (Ellen, 2004).

For Christine Burns of transgender political lobbying group and educational organisation Press for Change (PfC), Nadia has emerged as an unlikely role model: "I never in my wildest dreams imagined that after all these years it would be a big-breasted golden-hearted Portuguese nicotine junkie who really turned people's ideas about us upside down" (Burns, 2004, www.bigbrother.digitalspy.co.uk). Similarly, Lynne Jones, MP and chair of the Parliamentary Forum on Transsexualism, suggests that Nadia's success in *Big Brother* represents a cultural sea change: "The Big Brother result indicates people haven't got the kind of prejudices that would in the past have prevented them voting for a transsexual housemate. They're just voting for her as a woman in her own right. The fact of her being transsexual is not important" (Jones, 2004, www.pfc.org.uk).

Alongside an academic and a cultural turn to transgender, shifting attitudes towards transgender people in the UK are evident through recent legislative changes brought by the 2004 Gender Recognition Act (GRA). The GRA marks a key shift in attitudes towards transgender people; representing the civil recognition of gender transition in enabling transgender people to change their birth certificates to their acquired gender and to marry. Cultural and legislative developments suggest that gender diversity is acquiring visibility in contemporary society. Moreover, these developments reflect broader social changes around the conceptualisation and the practice of identity. Transgender is thus an arena in which questions of gendered, sexual, intimate and embodied identity and citizenship are being debated, contested and reconfigured within contemporary UK society. This book speaks to such transformations, and explores how transgender people variously understand and experience this changing landscape.

The book explores both Male to Female (MtF) and Female to Male (FtM) transgender practices, and draws on interviews with people who identify as transsexual and those who articulate more fluctuating gender identities. Thus the book addresses a range of transgender positions, differing in degrees of temporality. Empirical material is used to develop arguments and to provide illustrative case studies of points of discussion (see Appendix for a methodological discussion of the research). The book examines how the social structures of gender and sexuality impact upon understandings, practices and experiences of transgender, and the ways in which these issues feed into debates around identity, intimacy, care, social movements and citizenship.

Key themes

This book addresses three central questions: first, why, and how, has transgender emerged as a subject of increasing social and cultural interest? Second, how has transgender been addressed within recent social and cultural theory? Third, what is the relationship between transgender and the theories and politics of social movements that are organised around gender, sexuality and intimacy, and issues of citizenship and recognition? These questions are considered through an examination of the following themes: the ways in which transgender identities are constructed and experienced individually and collectively, the impact of gender transition upon intimate relationships, and the role of transgender support groups and self-help organisations.

Transgender raises questions about the formation of identity, and the extent to which we can shape and reshape individual and collective identities. These matters are central to contemporary debates around gender, sexual and intimate identities and the materiality of the body. The book explores questions of gender and sexual identity formation and categorisation in order to examine the challenge that transgender theory brings to medical discourse, gay and lesbian theory, feminism and queer theory. It evaluates the strengths and limitations of these theoretical fields in relation to transgendered embodied practices, and considers their relevance to the theorisation of shifting forms of gendered identities. Since the 1990s, a divergent range of transgender identities has been articulated by individuals and groups who are moving away from the identity of transsexualism, which had existed as the dominant Western identity category for transgender individuals. Although some writers continue to articulate a transsexual narrative (Prosser, 1998), others (Stone, 1991; Bornstein, 1994; Halberstam, 1998) are working to reshape the meanings of transgender and, in doing so, are problematising normative taxonomies of gender and sexuality. Influenced by the deconstructive narratives of poststructuralism, queer theory and pluralist strands of feminism, the pertinent question within transgender discourse has become: what is the 'right' body? (Halberstam, 1998). The book explores the ways in which these conceptual shifts feed into wider theoretical debates around the meanings of identity, intimacy and care, and considers the challenges transgender projects bring to current debates around social movements, citizenship and recognition. The debate within transgender studies around how identities are formed and the extent to which we are able to re-create our own identities, goes to the heart of contemporary sociological investigations into gender and sexual identity, and is significant for questions of embodied, social and personal identity.

As the book will show, many transgender people consciously explore the possibilities of creating embodied practices that subvert dominant codes of gender categorisation and sexual classification. Furthermore, many of these individuals move beyond the constraints of traditional ways of thinking about transsexualism that have been expressed in terms of the discovery of a hidden, essential self. In contrast to fated models of identity, the book will show that some transgender identity positions offer the possibility of transgressing the fixed binary categories of male and female to different degrees and with varying levels of permanence. The book will suggest that transgender communities are raising new questions about the construction of the embodied individual and pose a challenge to traditional feminist and lesbian and gay discourse. In addressing the formation of collective identities, the book examines the relationship between transgender communities and the history and contemporary organisation of lesbian and gay activism, feminism and queer politics.

This book will suggest that, while some transgender identity positions can be related to postmodern analyses of gender fluidity and correspond with the deconstructive narratives of queer theory, other transgender narratives articulate embodied practices that conflict with ideas of gender mutability. The complexities within these divergent subjectivities have been under-researched within sociological studies of identity and are largely invisible in analyses of intimate social practices and studies of social and collective movements. In examining the ways in which transgender identities are subjectively understood and lived out in the 'everyday' on both an individual and a collective level, the book seeks to develop studies of shifting gender and sexual identities. Additionally, it aims to contribute to the growing field of published literature within transgender studies by developing knowledge about the diversities of transgender experiences.

The structure of the book

The first chapter of the book reviews theoretical approaches to transgender in order to sketch out the conceptual terrain for subsequent discussions. It begins by addressing medical discourse around transvestism and transsexuality. Medical perspectives on transgender occupy a dominant position that has significantly affected how transgender is viewed and experienced within contemporary Western society. Although contemporary medical insights represent a more complex understanding of transgender practices than was offered within founding medical perspectives, there remain serious problems in the correlation of transgender and biological or psychological pathology.

The following sections of the chapter are organised around critiques of medical discourse brought by varied strands of social and cultural theory. First, the chapter considers ethnomethodology, which provided an initial critique of medical perspectives on transgender by locating gender at a social level. Nevertheless, this approach firmly emphasises a binary model of gender, assuming that all individuals fall within either a male or a female gender category. Next, the chapter examines how a medical approach to transgender has been critiqued through lesbian and gay studies and radical feminist writing. Here medical discourse is positioned in relation to heterosexist and patriarchal oppression. Yet lesbian and gay writers and feminist theorists have frequently reinforced the othering of the transgender individual. Pluralist feminism moves away from positioning transgender individuals as deviant, yet the limitations of feminism linger for a contemporary understanding of transgender. As the chapter moves on to explore, poststructuralist and postmodernist feminist work and queer theory are more helpful here in deconstructing the notion of identity as representing a unified essential subject. Further, these theoretical models work to subvert categories of sexuality that inextricably tie sex to gender. However, a lack of attention to subjectivity within poststructuralism and queer theory is problematic for a social theorising of transgender. The penultimate section of the chapter considers how the developing interdisciplinary field of transgender studies speaks to the theoretical models so far discussed. The final part examines studies on transgender in the UK that employ a social network of analysis. My aim here is to contribute to the development of a sociology of transgender.

The second chapter continues to address the theoretical debates that inform subsequent discussions of the book by examining analyses of care and intimacy. My aim here is to map key shifts in thinking around practices of care and intimacy in order to examine how transgender may be situated within this area of work. The chapter first addresses feminist work on care. It then considers studies of same-sex intimacy and addresses work that has examined the concept of care through the theme of friendship. Although this work has brought challenges to the heteronormativity of traditional care research, transgender lives and experiences remain absent from this analytical framework, which rests upon a naturalised binary gender model that recognises only male or female gender categories. The last section of the chapter considers how transgender practices relate to current debates around citizenship and recognition. The subsequent chapters of the book carry through the theoretical arguments set out in Chapters One and Two to analyse issues of transgender identity (in Chapters Three to Five), and intimacy, care and citizenship (in Chapters Six to Eight).

The third chapter explores the construction of transgender identities, first in relation to the ways in which gender is understood and experienced in childhood and then to consider the formation of transgender identities. The next section addresses the role of 'significant moments' within narratives of transgender identity formation. The chapter then considers the notion of the 'wrong body' within medical discourse and practice, and in relation to subjective understandings of embodiment. The following part considers the relevance of analysing transgender identity positions as gender performances and looks at discourses around gender authenticity. The final section of the chapter explores the ways in which transgender identities are linguistically articulated to produce distinct identity positions.

Chapter Four considers narratives of (trans)gender identity. First it explores the similarities and differences between and within these gendered identity positions. Subsequent sections of the chapter consider the relationship between transgender and feminism, and look at the ways in which gender politics are variously articulated by transgender men and women.

The fifth chapter addresses the relationship between gender transition and sexual desire, identity and practice. First it explores how sexuality may be located as a fluid process, and then it examines the ways in which sexual desire, identity and practice are, conversely, articulated as stable factors. The next section considers the links between sexuality and gendered experiences of embodiment, linking back to themes discussed in Chapter Four. The final section of the chapter addresses the relationship between transgender and lesbian and gay communities and considers the links between transgender and queer theory and activism by examining the commonalities and contradictions between different transgender and queer communities.

The next chapter turns to the theme of intimacy by considering the impact of gender transition upon partnering and parenting relationships. The first part explores the ways in which some transgender people maintain intimate relationships through and after transition, and looks at continuities and changes within these relationships. The next section of the chapter looks at the experiences of people whose relationships have broken down through transition and considers the formation of new relationships post-transition. The final part of the chapter explores how gender transition impacts upon parenting relationships.

The seventh chapter further develops analyses of intimacy by considering the impact of gender transition upon relationships with family and friends. The first section considers the process of gender transition within the context of familial relationships. The chapter then moves on to look at the role of friendship within narratives of gender transition and examine the relevance of the notion of 'friends as family'.

Chapter Eight examines practices of care within transgender support groups and self-help organisations, and addresses how individual and collective practices of identity, intimacy and care relate to current debates about citizenship and recognition. The first section addresses the specific care practices provided by transgender communities. The chapter then explores the significance of support groups in relation to the notion of 'shared experience'. The third section looks at the values 'that matter' to transgender people in relation to the giving and receiving of care. Subsequent sections of the chapter examine education as an ethic of care and then address the need to move towards an individual system of care. The next section considers the extent to which transgender support groups fill a gap left by professional care. The final part of the chapter addresses the complexities of involvement in support groups following transition by exploring issues of transgender visibility and assimilation, and debates about transgender citizenship and recognition.

The concluding chapter of the book consolidates points of discussion from the previous chapters and relates back to the theoretical premise mapped out in the first chapter. I suggest that a theoretical model that fuses social and cultural theories of identity is relevant for understanding the emergence and the experiences of contemporary transgender practices. Social theories of identity (Giddens, 1991, 1992; Beck, 1992; Bauman, 1996) are concerned with the historical development of self-identity, while much cultural theory (Weedon, 1987; Butler, 1990, 1993) seeks to problematise and deconstruct identity categories. I propose that bridging these perspectives may account for the complex and processual nature of identity formation and the multiple and fluid elements within identity positions, while also acknowledging subjective accounts that suggest a more determined experience of identity. This book, then, aims to bridge the gap between social theories and poststructuralist accounts of gender identity formation. In drawing upon and contributing to these different theoretical traditions, I have been influenced by calls for a queer sociology (Seidman, 1996; Roseneil, 2000).

Queer sociology examines how power is discursively and materially produced and resisted at a macro level, as well as analysing subjective experience at a micro level. Such a theoretical approach can overcome the disparities between social theories of identity and poststructuralism by signalling a "transformative project of social theory, in which theory functions as an agent of change in the everyday world" (Namaste, 2000: 33). In exploring transgender practices of identity, intimacy and care from a queer sociological framework, this book seeks to highlight the nuances and complexities of 'transgender' as it emerges (and re-emerges), and as it is variously experienced and practised within contemporary UK society.

ONE

Theorising transgender

The aim of the first chapter of this book is to explore how transgender has been approached within different theoretical fields in order to foreground my discussions of gender diversity in subsequent chapters. I begin by engaging with medical models of transvestism and transsexuality. While transgender practices themselves stretch infinitely back in time, the study of transgender is relatively recent, emerging from medical studies around 100 years ago. Medical perspectives on transgender have, however, come to occupy a dominant position that has significantly affected how transgender is viewed and experienced within contemporary Western society. As Ekins and King argue: "[…] medical perspectives stand out as the culturally major lens through which gender blending may be viewed in our society. Other perspectives must take medical perspectives into account whether they ultimately incorporate, extend or reject them" (1996: 75).

The subsequent sections of the chapter are organised around critiques of medical discourse brought by varied strands of social and cultural theory. First I consider ethnomethodology, which provided an initial critique of medical perspectives on transgender practices. Importantly, ethnomethodological studies located gender at the level of the social and analysed how 'common-sense' methods of understanding gender are acted out in everyday exchanges. Yet ethnomethodology emphasises a binary model of gender in assuming that all individuals fall within either a male or a female gender category. The following two sections of the chapter address critiques of medical discourse brought by lesbian and gay studies, and feminism. As I will explore, however, many writers within these fields have reinforced the marginal position of the transgender individual.

The next section considers the ways in which other feminist writers have attempted to develop more progressive perspectives on gender and sexuality. Yet feminism remains problematic for a contemporary understanding of transgender. As Monro argues: "[…] feminism is problematic as a basis for analysing trans in that its locus rests on male–female categorisation" (2000: 36). This critique can also be applied to lesbian and gay theory. As I move on to explore, poststructuralist and postmodernist feminist work and queer theory are more helpful for developing a contemporary understanding of transgender. The following part of the chapter thus explores how stable identity categories have been disrupted through these bodies of thought, which attempt to move beyond the fixed binary models imposed by normative taxonomies of gender and sexuality. Further, these perspectives work to subvert categories of sexuality that inextricably tie sex to gender. I argue, however, that poststructuralist analyses are limited by a lack of attention to subjectivity, which is problematic for a grounded theorising of transgender. In the final section of this chapter, I consider theoretical positions from the developing interdisciplinary field of transgender studies, and examine current work from the UK that seeks to bring a social analysis to transgender. In conclusion, I begin to sketch out a queer sociological model of transgender, which can build on the strengths and overcome the limitations of poststructuralist theory.

The medical construction of transsexuality

Historians of sexuality (Weeks, 1977; Foucault, 1978) have illustrated how medicine began to take an increasingly dominant role in understandings of sexuality during the 19th century. Central to the medical profession's burgeoning interest in matters sexual was the attempt to classify all acts of non-procreative sex. Alongside homosexuality, practices that we now discuss as transgendered were classified as separate categories of sexual behaviour. Before this, cross-dressing and cross-living practices had been discussed as fetishistic practices and through the terms 'sexual inversion' or 'contrary sexual feeling' used to describe homosexuality (Ekins and King, 1996: 80). The naming of transgender practices during the first half of the 19th century produced distinct ways of thinking about transgender individuals. This is not to locate transgender practices themselves as developing during this period. A complete history of transgender is beyond the scope of this book; however, studies have dated the existence of transgender practices to the Middle Ages (Feinberg, 1996). In their various guises, then, these practices stretch far back. What is significant is that during the early years of the 19th century the practices of transgender became specifically classified and conceptualised. The naming of transgender practices produced distinct ways of thinking about transgender individuals.

Hirschfeld's study *Die Transvestiten* (1910) was seminal in distinctly classifying the practice of cross-dressing. Ellis (1928) further separated transgender practices from homosexuality by arguing against the prevalent correlation of same-sex desire and cross-dressing. The work of Hirschfeld and Ellis had two important consequences. First, transsexuality was dissociated from homosexuality and second, transsexuality became separated from transvestism. During the 1950s, the medical practitioner and campaigner for sexual reform, Benjamin, controversially argued for the acceptance of 'sex-change' surgery by distinguishing between transvestism and transsexuality:

> Transvestism [...] is the desire of a certain group of men to dress as women or of women to dress as men. It can be powerful and overwhelming, even to the point of wanting to belong to the other sex and correct nature's anatomical 'error'. For such cases the term transsexual seems appropriate. (Benjamin, cited in King, 1996: 86)

The classification of transsexuality repositioned transvestism as a less significant pursuit, while the transsexual became the deviant proper. According to Benjamin, the biological deficiencies that may result in homosexuality or transvestism were also responsible for the transsexual 'condition': "if the soma is healthy and normal no severe case of transsexualism, transvestism or homosexuality is likely to develop [...]" (1953: 13). Medical intervention was both diagnostic and curative.

King's (1996) case studies of Roberta Cowell and George Jamieson illustrate the different medical attitudes towards transsexual individuals who enquired about surgery in 1950s Britain. Roberta Cowell was 34 years old and from an upper-class background. She had been taking female hormones for three years when she found a plastic surgeon who agreed to construct her vagina. In contrast, Jamieson – whose identity would later change to April Ashley – was 18 and from a working-class area of Liverpool. She received hospital psychiatric treatment and later moved abroad for surgery that was denied in Britain. Access to reconstructive surgery during this time, then, was highly dependent upon social class and social connections. While genital surgery did take place in the 1950s, it was unusual and most surgeons refused to perform these operations, leaving 'treatment' to the field of psychiatry.

As access to surgical procedures became more readily accessible during the 1960s, the term 'transsexual' became restricted to individuals undergoing surgery, while the concept of transvestism was related to practices of cross-dressing. This period also witnessed the growth of research into transsexuality from the fields of sexology (Benjamin, 1966), psychology (Green and Money, 1969) and psychiatry (Green and Money, 1969), which emphasised dysfunctional socialisation as the cause of the transsexual 'condition'. These bodies of work introduced the notion of gender into discourses of transsexuality and, significantly, gender came to be recognised independently of biological sex. As King explains:

> Thus, it was no longer necessary to claim a biological cause of transsexualism in order to legitimise changing sex. If gender is immutable, even though psychologically produced, and if harmony between sex and gender is a precondition of psychic comfort and social acceptability, it 'makes sense' to achieve harmony by altering the body. (Ekins and King, 1996: 94)

The theoretical shifts that accompanied the increasing acceptance of reconstructive surgery effectively strengthened the role of the medical practitioner. Benjamin argued that if surgery were refused, transsexuals would revert to self-mutilation or suicide, while Money argued that medical opinion should dictate public policy and legislation on transsexualism. It was believed that surgery enabled the 'true' self to emerge. Most practitioners aligned with psychological narratives that emphasised dysfunctional socialisation as the cause of this 'condition'. Benjamin and Money were instrumental in developing the concept of 'gender dysphoria', which, from the 1970s, began to replace the term 'transsexual' in medical writing. Gender dysphoria suggests that those seeking hormone therapy or surgery have been born, and so are living, in the 'wrong' body. Some practitioners and commentators (Fisk, 1973) argued that this term had greater scope as it could also be applied to individuals who fell outside the traditional defining characteristics of transsexualism and thus it could allow for a more nuanced understanding of transgender. King, however, suggests that we can read less altruistic motives into the medical establishment's acceptance of the concept of 'gender dysphoria':

> Gender dysphoria widens the area of expertise of interest of the practitioner. No longer is he or she concerned only with a special type of person, the transsexual, but all who suffer from gender dysphoria and potentially this includes not only transsexuals, transvestites and homosexuals but also those who are physically intersexual and indeed, possibly all of us suffer from it in a mild form. (Ekins and King, 1996: 97)

By the 1970s, surgical procedures had become the orthodox method of 'treatment' (Cromwell, 1999). After surgery, people were encouraged to erase their pre-operative identity and to carve out an entirely new one. Medical professionals recommended they move to new locations, adopt new names and invent a past history in line with their new gender. They were advised to keep their transition a secret, even to future partners and close friends, and to avoid contact with other transsexual people so as not to draw attention to themselves (Cromwell, 1999). The development of gender identity clinics in the 1970s was an attempt by some medical practitioners to break away from mainstream medical practice and to adopt a more sensitive system of care. However, as Chapter Three will explore, the concept of gender dysphoria remains the key classificatory term within medical discourse and practice, and contemporary medical perspectives continue along much the same lines as Benjamin's original explanations in the 1950s. As the following sections address, the social and political implications of a biological disposition within contemporary medical discourse and practice has been variously critiqued by different strands of social theory.

Ethnomethodology and the social life of gender

Developed by American sociologist Garfinkel, ethnomethodology was concerned with the 'common-sense' knowledge of everyday life. Its premise was that a focus on the overriding social structures within traditional sociology failed to recognise the meanings and actions of individuals. Subsequently, within ethnomethodological studies, individuals were credited with the agency to make sense of their own interactions and activities. The impact of ethnomethodology can be seen in poststructuralist deconstructions of everyday texts, and the emphasis on 'the things that we do' has influenced the conceptualisation of 'the reflexive project of the self' (Giddens, 1991). Ethnomethodology was an important theoretical development in that it illustrated how conventional sociology took for granted many central aspects of the existing social order, including gender. Its decoding of social concepts and theoretical classifications addressed normative assumptions of gender and, rather than being positioned as a universal and unconstrained concept, gender was located at the social level of individual understanding and activity. The prevalent medical use of the term 'gender dysphoria' and its theoretical underpinnings, which point to a 'true' gendered identity, can thus be critiqued through the ethnomethodological work of Garfinkel (1967) and Kessler and McKenna (1978). Their studies illustrated how medical discourse reinforced dominant notions of gender. As such these reflections represent an early critique of medical perspectives on transgender.

Garfinkel's *Studies in Ethnomethodology* (1967) sought to examine how intersex people articulate their chosen gender within the constraints of societal and medical gendered discourses. Garfinkel employs the phrase 'passing' to refer to the ways in which these individuals achieved status and recognition in their elected gender. In his widely published case study of Agnes, a woman born with female and male genitalia, Garfinkel shows how gender is managed in everyday life by detailing the ways in which Agnes's speech and behaviour bring to light the unspoken 'rules' of gender. This study led Garfinkel to reflect upon the many ways in which gender 'rules' impact upon intersex people: "The experiences of these intersexed persons permits an appreciation of these background relevances that are otherwise easily overlooked or difficult to grasp because of their routinized character and because they are so embedded in a background of relevances that are simply 'there' and taken for granted" (1967: 16).

Garfinkel's deliberations may seem all too obvious from a contemporary reading that, as a result of feminist and poststructuralist work, has a developed and multifaceted analysis of the influences and constraints of gender. At the time, however, the concept of gender largely went unnoticed within dominant medical discourse and academic thought in general. Garfinkel critiqued the pathological assumptions of medical and psychiatric thought, which discussed transgressive gendered identities as "[…] a very rare occurrence. These people are after all freaks of nature" (anonymous American leading psychiatrist, cited in Garfinkel, 1967: 24). His study showed how Agnes exercised agency in her chosen gender, and resisted and managed social and medical stigmatisation. In this way, Garfinkel challenges the medical model that rarely offered a voice to transgender individuals. Further, he attempts to move beyond a fixed 'diagnosis' to resist a single analysis of Agnes's experiences. The significance of this work was that it moved beyond a medical model by bringing the concept of gender into analyses of non-normative bodies.

Kessler and McKenna (1978) built on Garfinkel's work to assert that all aspects of gender are socially constructed. The social construction of gender behaviour was, by this time, largely recognised within social science. Yet it was still generally assumed that 'sex' was a fixed biological determinant. In *Gender: An Ethnomethodological Approach*, Kessler and McKenna (1978) argued that biology was as equally constructed as social behaviour. Thus they distinguish between bodily parts (chromosomes, gonads and genitals) and the social characteristics of masculinity and femininity. While bodily parts were biological, they suggested that viewing them as essentially male or female was a socially and culturally constructed process. This important theoretical development drew attention to gendered embodiment, and problematised the ways in which 'sex' and 'gender' were collapsed in academic discourse. However, like Garfinkel, in the 1970s Kessler and McKenna took it for granted that there were only two possible genders. More recently, though, Kessler and McKenna (2000) have illustrated how medical and surgical procedures work to construct a binary model in the case of intersex children.

Ethnomethodological studies located gender within the social framework of everyday meaning and interpretation, to illustrate how 'gender' is dependent upon subjective meaning and social construction. Yet ethnomethodology is problematic for a contemporary sociological understanding of transgender because of its reliance on a binary model of gender. Although the possibility of moving between the categories of gender is raised, it is only possible to move from female to male or from male to female within this analysis.

> What we did not consider 25 years ago was the possibility that someone might not want to make a credible gender presentation – might not want to be seen as clearly either male or female. It did not even occur to us that within 20 years there would be some people who would want to confront others with the contradictions between their gender presentation and other 'facts' such as their genitals or gender history. In other words, we did not address what has come to be called 'transgender'. Transgender was neither a concept nor a term 25 years ago. Transsexual was radical enough. (Kessler and McKenna, 2000)

Ethnomethodology provided an important critique of the deviant positioning of transgender individuals within dominant medical frameworks. Further, it recognised the social construction of gender, and was attentive to the subjective understanding and negotiation of gender norms. However, ethnomethodological studies have yet to take account of the diversity of contemporary transgender positions and thus, as Kessler and McKenna (2000) recognise, studies of gender diversity from an ethnomethodological perspective remain theoretically limited.

Lesbian and gay history and anthropology

Scholars within lesbian and gay history have frequently adopted an anthropological approach to transgender. Studies during the 1960s and 1970s focused their gaze on non-Western transgender practices, which were interpreted as personifications of homosexuality. For example, in his study *Gay American History*, Katz (1976) devotes a chapter to the history of the Native American *berdache*,[1] which he entitles 'Native Americans/Gay Americans 1528–1976'. Like Katz, Roscoe (1988) positions the *berdache* as gay men. These studies had the political motive of granting gay men a visible history by countering the absence of writing on early gay experiences. They aimed to provide a positive model by showing that, in contrast to Western society, other cultures incorporated gay men as equal and established members of their communities. However understandable this aim, it has neglected the distinct history of gender diversity by assimilating these practices into a homosexual narrative. The positioning of the *berdache* as gay forefathers is also evident in Williams' (1986) study, in which the *berdache* are employed as an illustration of the cultural acceptance of same-sex practices. In contrast, Whitehead (1981) provides an alternative reading of the *berdache* in which she suggests that this culture represents a specific Native American experience of transsexuality. Yet Whitehead's juxtaposition of transsexualism and *berdache* culture is problematic in that, as Williams notes (1986), transsexuality is largely a Western concept. However, Williams' supposition that the *berdache* are gay men rather than transgender individuals is equally questionable in relation to the manipulation of Western systems of classification. As more contemporary accounts have suggested (Califia, 1997), it is highly probable that cultures such as the *berdache* represented neither same-sex nor transgender practices, but instead, demonstrated the existence of an alternative gender or sexual grouping within an indigenous culture of which there is no Western equivalent.

In challenging the appropriation of the *berdache* within these ethnographic studies, Gutierrez's (1989) insights into *berdache* culture portray a life that is far removed from the romantic narratives of Katz, Williams and Roscoe. Rather than symbolising the cultural acceptance of same-sex desire, Gutierrez maintains that the life of the *berdache* was one of social subjugation and punishment.

These historical and anthropological studies mainly focused upon what can be loosely termed male-to-female practices. Katz (1976) was one of the few writers to discuss female-to-male expressions. Paralleling the fixing of a homosexual identity onto gender transgressive Native

American born men, Katz positions expressions of masculinity in Native American born women as representative of a lesbian identity. His discussion of 'passing women' portrays these gender-crossing women as active lesbian feminists, again problematically translating a Western experience onto a local culture:

> The women whose lives are documented here worked and dressed and lived in what were customarily the occupations and styles of men. Most actually passed as men; the evidence suggests they were also attracted to and had sexual and emotional relations with other women. They both passed as men and passed beyond the restricted traditional roles of women [...] These passing women can only be understood within the framework of a feminist analysis. (Katz, cited in Califia, 1997: 150)

The relationship between 'sex', gender and sexuality has been collapsed in medical models of transgender, and through many anthropological studies within lesbian and gay history. While the stress within lesbian and gay work has been upon sexuality, feminist analyses have focused upon gender.

Feminist approaches to transgender

Attacking transgender: a radical feminist perspective

While activists such as Brake (1976) developed important critiques of medical perspectives on transgender, the theoretical notion of gender itself largely remained unchallenged within early lesbian and gay theory. Central to the theoretical work accompanying second-wave feminism, however, was a radical critique of gender roles that was to have a significant impact on discourses surrounding transgender. Second-wave feminism was one of the first academic fields to respond to the growing public awareness of modern Western transgender practices that began in the 1950s (Hird, 2002a). Transgender raises key questions concerning the epistemological status and the ontology of 'sex' and 'gender'. In addition, transgender problematises the relationships between these categories to evoke complex questions about the construction, deconstruction and ongoing reconstruction of both gender and sexual taxonomies. These issues have long been central to feminist thought. On a theoretical, political and cultural level, however, feminism has been largely hostile to transgender practices (Raymond, 1980, 1994; Jeffreys,

1997; Greer, 1999; Bindel, 2004). Transgender women have been seen to reinforce a stereotypical model of *über* femininity, while transgender men have been located as renegades seeking to acquire male power and privilege. In 1998 Whittle posed the following question: "how can feminism accept men with women's bodies (or is that women with men's bodies)?" (1998: 2). Whittle's question remains central to feminist debates, and the controversial relationship between transgender and feminism prevails.

The publication of Janice Raymond's book *The Transsexual Empire* (1980) established a radical feminist perspective on transgender that was to affect the dominant feminist position significantly for successive decades. Raymond locates transsexuality as a patriarchal characteristic and the medical system as an agent of patriarchal oppression. In Raymond's view, the medical establishment was instrumental in the very creation of transsexualism. As I will explore further in Chapter Four, Raymond's understanding is underpinned by a biological approach through which 'sex' is chromosomally dependent and thus secured at birth. From this perspective, 'gender' is seen as the coherent expression of biological sex. Thus the categories of sex and gender are co-dependently positioned. Raymond positions transsexuality as a genetic male practice fashioned by a patriarchal medical system to construct servile women. Her argument is absolute: transsexual women are not, nor can they ever be, 'real' women. "It is biologically impossible to change *chromosomal* sex. If chromosomal sex is taken to be the fundamental basis for maleness and femaleness, the man who undergoes sex conversion is *not* female" (1980: 10, italics in original).

Stone's essay 'The *Empire* Strikes Back: A Posttransexual Manifesto' (1991) was written in reply to Raymond's thesis. Stone asserts that: "Though *Empire* represented a specific moment in feminist analysis and prefigured the appropriation of liberal political language by the radical right, here in 1991, on the twelfth anniversary of its publication, it is still the definitive statement on transsexualism by a genetic female academic" (1991: 283). In 1994 a second edition of *The Transsexual Empire* was published; this update can be read as a response to the developing field of transgender studies and transgender activism: "Things are more complex, and a plethora of terms such as 'transgendered', 're-gendered', 'gender-blending', 'gender bending', 'gender fucking' and 'transhomosexuality' have been added to the lexicon of so-called 'gender dissonant behaviour'" (Raymond, 1994: xxv). The 14 years between the publications had witnessed considerable shifts both in relation to the lived experiences of transgender people and in terms of theoretical discourse, much of which was being developed by transgender academics themselves. Significantly, this period saw the increased visibility and activism of transgender men. Nevertheless, Raymond simply repeats her earlier denouncement of transgender men as "the tokens that save face for the transsexual empire" (1994: xxv).

More recently, Jeffreys (1997) has rekindled the radical feminist tradition of positioning transgender practices as an anti-feminist phenomenon constructed by a patriarchal medical system. Like Raymond, Jeffreys positions transgender practices as anti-feminist: "Transsexualism opposes feminism by maintaining and reinforcing false and constructed notions of correct femininity and masculinity" (1997: 57). Jeffreys' point of focus is transgender masculinity. She cautions that it is "*now* imperative for lesbian communities to pay attention" (Jeffreys, 1997: 57, italics added), and continues:

> The spectacle of lesbians as freaks who really want to be men has returned with renewed vigour from the sexological literature of the 1950s to haunt popular women's magazines and lesbian literature today. Since the identity of 'transsexual' seems to be learned from such sources then we can expect a proliferation of these very damaging practices among lesbians. (Jeffreys, 1997: 68)

In an analysis that collapses the complexities of (trans)gender and sexuality, Jeffreys denies agency to the individuals who choose a surgical route: "The men who choose the self-mutilation of transsexualism come from two degraded categories, those who feel unable to love men in the bodies of men and transsex to become 'heterosexual' women and those who continue to love women and call themselves 'lesbians' after the operation" (1997: 61). In her conceptualisation of transgender female heterosexuality as internalised homophobia Jeffreys is unable to account for the ways in which some transgender women desire men as heterosexual women. Likewise, she fails to take account of the lesbian desires of transgender women. Jeffreys offers a similar sociosexual diagnosis to that of the medical profession she critiques. Here, however, it is not dysfunctional familial socialisation that is brought to bear, but rather, "men's abuse of women" (1997: 61). Her pathologising of transgender people is thus complicit with the medical model she claims to condemn. As gender identity clinics were attempting to develop more sensitive approaches to transgendered clients, then, radical feminist theory served to reinforce the positioning of transgender men and women as deviant outsiders. Raymond's and Jeffreys' approaches to transgender are worth considering at length here as they exemplify how a gender binary understanding is unable to incorporate transgender into feminist theory and politics. Although some feminist writers (Szasz, 1990; Hausman, 1995; Wilton, 2000) continue to reflect Raymond and Jeffreys' critiques, as Chapter Four will explore, other feminist writers have adopted more progressive approaches to transgender, indicating that a feminist framework may be used to theorise divergent gendered identities and expressions that are unfixed to the 'sexed' body.

Feminist reconfigurations of 'sex' and 'gender'

While radical feminists have argued that sexuality is key to theorising gender – thus understandings of gender are developed from experiences of sexuality (MacKinnon, 1982) – other feminist writers have foregrounded gender in theorising the relationship between sexuality and gender, and here experiences of sexuality are determined by experiences of gender (Jackson, 1999). A different approach to the relationship between gender and sexuality has been developed by theorising gender and sexuality as distinct but overlapping categories (Hollibaugh, 1989; Rubin, 1989; Vance, 1989; Sedgwick, 1990). This framework distinguishes between gender and sexuality in order to theorise gender and sexual difference independently. Although this body of work does not explicitly address transgender, it is significant for developing a nuanced understanding of transgender identities in which erotic desire does not automatically fit preconceived binary identities of either gender (man/woman) or sexuality (homo/hetero).

Vance argues that a feminist account of sexuality has to be able to recognise and include difference: "to ignore the potential for variation is to inadvertently place women outside of culture [...]" (1989: 15). For Vance, the recognition of difference relies on examining the meanings given to sexual symbols (for example, images, practices or performances) within sexual subcultures and realising that these meanings are often different to dominant ways of seeing. This perspective enables the consideration of a range of transgender sexualities in terms of their commonalities, specificities and differences, both in relation to dominant culture and to each other. Hollibaugh (1989) and Rubin's (1989) work is also important for the arguments that will be carried through this book. Hollibaugh argues for a feminist analysis of sexuality that embraces difference by examining how sexual desires and pleasures are socially and culturally constructed. Alongside analysing sexuality as an academic issue, she calls for the consideration of the 'lived' embodied experiences of sex in order to examine the meanings of sexual desire and practice. Rubin moves beyond claims for recognition; to make an explicit demand to "denounce erotic injustice and sexual oppression" (1989: 275). Significantly, Rubin shows how the influences of medicine, psychiatry and psychology have encouraged a discourse that individualises sexuality: "These fields classify sex as the property of individuals. It may reside in their hormones or their psyches. It may be constructed as physiological or psychological. But within these ethnoscientific categories, sexuality has no history and no significant social determinants" (1989: 276).

Following Foucault, Rubin illustrates how sexuality is intertwined with historical moments and social systems. Alongside sexual essentialism, Rubin identifies a series of additional constraints on a radical politics of sexuality, including "the hierarchical valuation of sex acts" (1989: 278). Here she draws attention to the ways in which certain sexual practices, such as heterosexual marriage and reproduction, are privileged above others. Her sliding scale of sexual acceptance positions cohabiting heterosexuals at the higher end, closely followed by other heterosexuals. Gay men and lesbians in long-term partnerships are above promiscuous gay men and lesbians, who, in turn, are just above the lowest groups within the sexual hierarchy: "transsexuals, transvestites, fetishists, sadomasochists, sex workers such as prostitutes and porn models, and the lowest of all, those whose eroticism transgresses generational boundaries" (Rubin, 1989: 278). She argues that a sexual hierarchy rewards those at the top with "certified mental health, respectability, legality, social and physical mobility, institutional support, and material benefits" (Rubin, 1989: 279). Conversely, those at the bottom of the scale are "subjected to a presumption of mental illness, disputability, criminality, restricted social and physical mobility, loss of institutional support, and economic sanctions" (1989: 278). Although Rubin's description of the social ordering of sexual practices does not take into account the ways in which marginalised sexual cultures adopt their own systems of values and means of support, importantly she draws attention to the ways in which sexual practice has become a matter of social, political and legal franchise, or, to the contrary, disenfranchisement. Rubin links the hierarchy of sex acts to a Western system of "sexual stratification" (1989: 278). She acknowledges the ways in which feminism has critiqued the systems of gender, class, and racial and ethnic stratification, although she also argues that feminist thought has failed to challenge sexual stratification. Rubin details how the state controls sexual behaviour and practices through the criminalisation of certain sex acts, such as 'underage' sex or prostitution. Similarly, we can see how transgender practices, whether homosexual or heterosexual, are constrained and penalised through these processes as legal constraints affect the citizenship rights of transgender people.

From her premise that sexuality is as much a political as a social issue, Rubin highlights the ways in which feminism has failed to address 'sexual' discrimination. She questions the extent to which feminism is able to develop a theory of sexuality that takes account of the breadth of sexual inequalities; political, social, cultural, legal, economic and ideological. Like Vance (1989), she identifies feminism's conceptual fusion of sex and gender as being inherently problematic. Thus she argues that it is important to understand 'sex' in terms of sexuality (desire, fantasy and practice) as well as in relation to gender. For Rubin, then, a political theory of sexuality can only be attained within an ideological framework that distinguishes between the categories of sex and gender.

Poststructuralist and postmodern feminisms

The central premise of poststructuralism is that discourse constructs meaning. In taking the discursive formations of gender and sexuality as their starting point, poststructuralist feminist analyses have engaged directly with transgender. Butler (1990) draws on Foucault to illustrate how discursive practices create analytical problems within themselves. Adopting Foucault's "genealogical analysis" (1977: 142), Butler shows how the binary categories of 'sex' and 'gender' have restricted feminist understandings. She argues that the idea of 'sex' as constituting the biological male or female body, and 'gender' as referring to the social meanings attached to such bodies, has disabled the more effective understanding of gender as distinct from sex:

> The presumption of a binary gender system implicitly retains the belief in a mimetic relation of gender to sex whereby gender mirrors sex or is otherwise restricted by it. When the constructed status of gender is theorized as radically independent of sex, gender itself becomes a free-floating artifice, with the consequence that *man* and *masculine* might just as easily signify a female body as a male one, and *woman* and *feminine* a male body as easily as a female one. (Butler, 1990: 6, italics in original)

An understanding of gender as separate from sex thus holds the potential for a greater diversity of masculinities and femininities. These ideas can be incorporated into a contemporary understanding of transgender that allows for a multiplicity of embodied gendered identities and expressions. Further, Butler argues that we should be wary of seeing 'sex' as a purely biological characteristic. Rather, sex is as socially and culturally a determined term as is gender. Butler's thesis is that the dominant way of understanding sex and gender as corresponding characteristics is reinforced through the privileging of heterosexuality. Thus heteronormativity maintains a gender binary model:

> Gender can denote a *unity* of experience, of sex, of gender, and desire, only when sex can be understood in some way to necessitate gender – where gender is a psychic and/or cultural designation of the self – and desire – where desire is heterosexual and therefore differentiates itself through an oppositional relation to the other gender it desires. (Butler, 1990: 22)

Butler develops the concept of performativity to address the ways in which the rules of gender are compulsively and repetitively acted out to reinforce naturality: "There is no gender behind the expressions of gender [...] identity is performatively constituted by the very 'expressions' that are said to be its results" (1990: 25). The practices of cross-dressing and drag are employed as examples of how the naturalisation of gender can be challenged through parody – to signpost 'gender trouble':

> The performance of drag plays upon the distinction between the anatomy of the performer and the gender that is being performed. But we are actually in the presence of contingent dimensions of significant corporeality: anatomical sex, gender identity, and gender performance. If the anatomy of the performer is already distinct from the gender of the performer, and both of those are distinct from the gender of the performance, then the performance suggests a dissonance not only between sex and performance, but sex and gender, and gender and performance. (Butler, 1990: 137)

Alongside poststructuralism, the influence of postmodernism on strands of feminist thinking during the 1990s led to an explicit engagement with transgender. As Wright illustrates, postmodernist approaches have emphasised difference as a requisite theoretical tool for the development of feminist theory: "Postmodernist theory provides feminism with an additional framework, enabling it to articulate the diversity and contradictions that spring up not only between various positions but also within various positions" (1997: 179). This model is useful for an analysis of transgender in that it can be utilised to go beyond the prevailing notion of transgender people as a homogeneous group, providing theoretical space for the recognition of distinct transgender identities. Thus a postmodern framework may be employed to depart from the concept of a unitary transgender identity to recognise that difference cuts across and between a diversity of transgender subjectivities. This can be used, for example, to enable the increased visibility of trans men; not only through analysing the specificities of trans male experiences in relation to trans female, but also by exploring particular subject positions *within* trans masculinity.

Many feminist scholars are sceptical about the cultural turn to difference within postmodernist theory, arguing that such a framework is at odds with a feminist analysis (Benhabib, 1994). From this perspective, postmodernism appears to conflict with a politics of identity, which is seen as central to a feminist framework. Postmodernist theory has also been critiqued for its lack of material analysis. Walby (1994), for example, argues that postmodernism fails to take account of the structural forces that affect lived experiences. Flax's (1997) work is useful here in linking common themes between feminist analyses of gender relations and postmodernism. For Flax, feminism's denaturalisation of the construction of gender relations is akin to the postmodern project of theoretical deconstruction; although she proposes that it is necessary for feminism to extend its deconstructive analysis in order to think more carefully about the relationship between biology, sex, gender and nature. Thus feminism needs to move beyond theorising gender as opposition and towards an understanding of gender as a social relation to enable a more complete analysis of difference. While the articulation of women's experiences is of continued importance, Flax believes that such accounts are invariably partial, since "none of us can speak for 'woman' because no such person exists except within a specific set of (already gendered) relations–to 'man' and to many concrete and different women" (1997: 178). Rather, the way forward lies in the recognition and acceptance of multiple and contradictory experiences. Flax's sentiments are important to the arguments of this book in relation to the question transgender poses to the categories of 'man' and 'woman'.

Queering identity categories

Queer theory sustains poststructuralist and postmodern deconstructions of identity categories, and positions gender and sexual identities as fluid and non-affirmative, thus representing a radical departure from all essentialising tendencies. Queer theorists have argued that traditional lesbian and gay theory and politics have been exclusive in their attitudes towards those whose identities fall outside what is deemed to be correct or fitting. In contrast, queer theory has positively embraced difference and has argued against the representation of identity categories as authentic. In viewing all gendered or sexual identities as socially constructed, queer theory aims to dissolve the naturalisation and pathologisation of minority identities. As Hedges has remarked, from a queer perspective:"characters may prove interesting precisely because they parody or disrupt received identities, or reveal the contingencies of any identity" (1997: 2). However, as Seidman notes, queer theory's rebuttal of identity may paradoxically lead to the denial of difference: "This very refusal to anchor experience in identifications ends up, ironically, denying differences by either submerging them in an undifferentiated oppositional mass or by blocking the development of individual and social differences through the disciplining compulsory imperative to remain undifferentiated" (1993: 133). As with poststructuralist and postmodern analyses, then, queer theory presents the dilemma of how to deconstruct identity categories and account positively for difference, without losing sight of the subjective experiences that constitute difference.

From a queer framework certain transgender cultures are seen to rupture existing gender and sexual identities, and have been regarded as the epitome of identity deconstruction. Trans writers such as Bornstein (1994) and Stone (1991) reflect a queer subjectivity in positioning themselves not as transsexuals, but as 'gender outlaws' (Bornstein, 1994) who "speak from outside the boundaries of gender, beyond the constructed oppositional nodes which have been predefined as the only positions from which discourse is possible" (Stone, 1991: 351). Although not explicitly aligned with queer theory, Garber's work is synonymous with this approach to transgender. Garber's wide-ranging literary and cultural analysis illustrates the paradox of Western culture's 20th-century attitude towards transvestism, which dually represents an obsession with, and a pathologisation of, transgender. The transvestite represents a 'category crisis', by "disrupting and calling attention to cultural, social, or aesthetic dissonances" (1992: 16) and thus is seen to challenge the notion of a fixed or coherent identity. For Garber, transvestism is a *"space of possibility structuring and confounding culture:* the disruptive element that intervenes, not just a category crisis of male and female, but a crisis of category itself" (1992: 17, italics in original). Transgender practices are therefore embraced as a deconstructive tool.

Queer analyses have, however, been criticised by other transgender theorists for denying the material contours of transgender, and, particularly, transsexual, lives (Felski, 1996; Rubin, 1996; MacDonald, 1998; Prosser, 1998; Namaste, 2000). Thus Namaste argues that Garber views the transvestite solely in terms of performance. In doing so, she "reduces the transvestite to a mere tropological figure, a textual and rhetorical device which points to the crisis of category and the category of crisis" (Namaste, 1996a: 189). This, Namaste believes, has "undermined the possibility of 'transvestite' as a viable identity in and of itself" (1996a: 89). Though MacDonald acknowledges that the focus on difference within deconstructive analyses is preferable to the hostility of gender and sexual diversity within much traditional feminist thinking, she too argues that this work has a tendency to ignore the specific subject positions under analysis:

> In its promotion of transgender identity as a transcendence of identity, postmodern theory assimilates transgender to its own intellectual project through presenting transgendered experiences as chimera, play, performance or strategy. It does so at the expense of investigating the actual lives, political demands, or feelings expressed by transgendered people of having an identity that is often experienced as 'authentic' or 'integral' and that it is considered to be neither 'chosen' originally nor 'performed' strategically. (MacDonald, 1998: 4)

MacDonald's critique highlights the fissure between the theoretical positioning of transgender as a subversive act of gender transgression and the subjectivities of those transgender people who articulate notions of authentic (trans)gendered identities, a tension that will be examined throughout the following chapters of this book. She argues that the celebration of difference thus needs to be accompanied by an analysis of the specific experiences of difference: "to postmodern theory, transgender argues, then, for the reality of difference, and the need to investigate the social structures which enforce sex/gender incongruity and stability at every level" (MacDonald, 1998: 10). While, for Stryker, transgender phenomena are postmodern in that they are "imagined to point beyond contemporary modernity" (2006: 8), transgender theory is inextricably postmodern in that it "takes its aims at the modernist epistemology that treats gender merely as a social, linguistic, or subjective representation of an objectively knowable material sex. [...] Transgender phenomena, in short, point the way to a different understanding of how bodies mean, how representation works and what counts as legitimate knowledge" (2006: 8–9). Materiality is central, however, to such epistemological questions: "These philosophical issues have material consequences for the quality of transgender lives" (Stryker, 2006: 9). Similarly, Whittle foregrounds materiality:

> It is all very well having no theoretical place within the current gendered world, but that is not the daily lived experience. Real life affords trans people constant stigma and oppression based on the apparently unreal concept of gender. This is one of the most significant issues that trans people have brought to feminism and queer theory. (2006: xii)

Queer theory offers valuable insights into the ways in which *some* transgender cultures radically challenge normative taxonomies of gender and sexuality, and it provides a radical vision of deconstructed genders and sexualities. However, employed in isolation, this theoretical model is limited by a lack of attention to lived experience, which often leaves non-performance-related transgender identities unaccounted for. McNay's (2000) use of Bourdieu's concept of habitus is a useful way of working through the possibilities of a queer social analysis of transgender. 'Habitus' denotes the ways in which gendered norms are both internalised and negotiated through bodily practices or styles. The body is thus a signifier of normative practices and of individual agency. McNay's intervention locates the gendered body within social structures while also allowing for change across time. Embodied experiences can thus be theorised as significant, though not determinate. The limitations of a queer approach to transgender may also be overcome through queer sociology (Seidman, 1996; Roseneil, 2000), which shares many of the characteristics of Namaste's (2000) framework for poststructuralist sociology. As I will explore further in Chapter Two, a queer sociological approach would enable recognition of difference, while also exploring lived experiences and competing narratives of difference. It would additionally develop postmodernist approaches to gender by grounding deconstructionist analyses of gender plurality within a sociological framework.

Transgender theory

Throughout the 1990s, a number of transgender writers articulated their personal gender trajectories, and engaged with the theoretical debates of feminism, postmodernism and queer theory, as well as providing an explicit critique of medical discourse. The burgeoning area of transgender studies brings different meanings to the term 'transgender' and reflects a diversity of theoretical positions. Transgender studies incorporate a body of work that is autobiographical in its style and content, and includes political commentary aligned with transgender community activism. In common with much feminist work there is no strict demarcation between these areas, leading many writers to move between the theoretical, the autobiographical and the structurally political; thus bringing subjectivity and social and political comment to theoretical engagement.

Transgender studies are interdisciplinary (including academic fields as diverse as the humanities, arts, sociology, psychology, law, social policy, literature, anthropology, history and politics) and intertextual (often mixing academic scholarship with autobiography). In her introductory chapter to the recently published *The Transgender Studies Reader* (the very publication of which is a marker of the recognition of transgender theory/studies), Stryker (2006) traces the advent of transgender studies to two publications from the early 1990s. First, in her 'The *Empire* Strikes Back: A Posttranssexual Manifesto', Sandy Stone (1991) critically responded to Raymond's thesis by calling for transsexuals to leave behind claims of authenticity and to come out as transgender men and women. Second, in a political pamphlet entitled *Transgender Liberation: A Movement Whose Time Has Come* (1992), Leslie Feinberg envisaged a united movement of all individuals who fell outside gendered social conventions and embodied norms. The speedy development of deconstructions of sex, gender and sexuality from postmodernism and queer theory focused the academic gaze on transgender during the second half of the 1990s. Alongside community activism and political organisation, transgender studies developed rapidly to become visible in all areas of academia (as a taught university subject; at seminars and conferences, in anthologies and journals, and as the focus of postgraduate dissertations and theses) (Stryker, 2006). As Stryker comments, "by the end of the last century, transgender studies could make a fair claim to being an established discipline [...]" (2006: 6). Importantly, Stryker traces a range of broader social and cultural shifts that have given rise to an increasing focus on transgender. Like Whittle (1996), she suggests that the growth of home computers gave increased access to a 'transgender community' for transgender people, which, in turn, gave a new impetus to community activism. Moreover, a changing economic and political climate, and the dawning of a new millennium lent transgender a zeitgeist flavour:

> If a frame as totalising as 'East/West' at least momentarily lost its explanatory purchase in a chaotic pre-9/11 world that seemed increasingly structured by diasporic movements and transnational flows, how likely was it at that time that the equally hegemonic construction 'woman/man' would remain uninterrogated? Transgender studies stepped into the breach of that ruptured binary to reconceptualise gender for the New World Order. [...] 'Transgender studies' emerged at this historic juncture as one practice for collectively thinking our way into the brave new world of the twenty-first century, with all its threats and promises of unimaginable transformation through new forms of biomedical and communicational technology. (Stryker, 2006: 8)

Over the last decade, then, an array of autobiographical work, political commentary and critical scholarship has emerged that can be located within the sphere of transgender studies. Of particular relevance to the remit of this book, in the US and, to a lesser extent, in the UK, a number of studies have employed a social framework to analyse transgender; the following chapters will link with such work. In the final section of this chapter, though, I wish to turn particularly to UK work that offers a distinctly sociological perspective of transgender.

A sociology of transgender

There is an important interdisciplinary body of work on transgender in the UK that examines transgender in relation to theoretical (de)constructions of gender identity (Prosser, 1998; Kaveney, 1999; Whittle, 1996, 2006; More and Whittle, 1999; Whittle and Turner, 2006); however, here I engage directly with recent UK sociological studies of transgender in order to contextualise the aims of this book in relation to this literature.

Ekins and King are British sociologists who have been working individually and collaboratively on transgender since the 1970s. Their edited volume *Blending Genders* (1996) envisaged a sociologically attuned transgender studies: "We had in mind that the book laid down the parameters for what transgender studies may look like once the emphasis was made on problematising previous conceptualisations and categories of 'transgender' knowledge from the standpoint of the social construction of knowledge" (Ekins and King, 2006: 28). Building on this work, and influenced by Plummer's (1995) work on 'sexual stories', their recent collaborative publication *The Transgender Phenomenon* (2006) draws on empirical data gathered over a period of more than 30 years to set out a sociological framework that incorporates a diversity of 'transgendering' forms and that traces the interrelations between these.

Employing a sociological imaginary that is finely attuned to the diversities among and the lines of connection between transgender trajectories, Ekins and King map out four modes of transgendering: 'migrating', permanent crossing from one side of the gender boundary to the other; 'oscillating', temporary movement from one side of the gender boundary to the other (and back again); 'negating' – 'ungendering' – whereby the story tellers refute the existence of a binary gender divide; and 'transcending', wherein story tellers speak of being 'beyond' gender. Ekins and King situate each of these modes within their specific historical context to indicate the ways in which 'ways of being' are intertwined with social and cultural systems and discursive frameworks. Thus the story of the migrate is that of the 'transsexual', while the 'oscillator' tells the tale of the 'transvestite', each brought into being by, through and in opposition to medical discourse and practice. Stories of negation are the lives lived on the outside: "Here we find neglected, misunderstood and largely untold stories. They are stories that, for the most part, do not appear in medical tales. [...] Here we find 'raw' tales of experience and desire told to achieve a voice, as well as those told in justification" (Ekins and King, 2006: 36). Stories of 'transcending' mark a sea change: "Transcending stories are stories whose time has come [...] medical authority is questioned, diversity is celebrated, and the certainty of sex and gender categories is called into question" (Ekins and King, 2006: 36). Significantly, Ekins and King's framework enables transgender practices – acts of transgendering – to be considered as social processes that emerge and develop within particular sociocultural conditions. As Ekins and King stress, modes of being do not exist in isolation; either to each other or to wider society. Modes may be chosen and then discarded; modes can be traversed and combined; modes coexist with, and live against the tide of, alternative identities and lifestyles. As I hope the later chapters of this book will indicate, there are always a number of identity practices under construction and at work at any given time: "It is within transgendering as a basic social process that transgender identities emerge, are contested, ebb and flow" (Ekins and King, 2006: 33).

As the aims of this book seek to contribute and develop Ekins and King's premise of mapping the diversity of transgender practices as they are lived out and intersect in contemporary society, my scope also has strong links with Monro's body of work on transgender. Monro (2000) writes against a radical feminist perspective on transgender yet is critical of an unhesitant move towards poststructuralist theorisations of transgender. In her work on transgender citizenship (2000, 2005) and cross-cultural practices of gender diversity (2006a), Monro recognises the importance of poststructuralist accounts of transgender: "only poststructuralist and postmodern approaches enable the inclusion and representation of the full range of gender diversity" (2005: 13). Nonetheless, she draws attention to the ways in which these models have neglected the corporal body. For Monro, the answer lies in a theory of gender pluralism, which would build on poststructuralism but take greater account of the ways in which sex and gender are a spectrum that "include male and female as well as a range of (probably) less common, but socially viable, other-gendered positions" (Monro, 2005: 19). There is much in common with Monro's concept of gender pluralism and my notion of a queer sociology of transgender, which aims to extend the notion of 'queer' to a range of non-normative subject positions (gendered, sexual and embodied), and to bring materiality and corporality to poststructuralist analyses. Here the remit of this book also links to the work of Hird (2000, 2002a, 2002b, 2006), who is both influenced by and cautious of poststructuralism in her analyses of gender diversity.

Like Ekins and King and Monro, Hird is concerned with developing a social analysis to account for gender difference. Following Butler (1990, 1993), Hird theorises sex as well as gender as socially constructed. Hird's (2000) work on intersex and transsexuality brings attention to the ways in which the 'sexed' pole of the sex/gender binary may work to disrupt the dual system. Thus intersexed and transsexed bodies bring a binary understanding of sex and gender into question. 'Sex', then, is not written on the body, but rather is a consequence of a "particular nexus of power, knowledge and truth" (Hird, 2000: 578). Returning to biology, Hird (2006) shows that though bodies are significant, sex, as well as gender, is capable of diversity, multiplicity and mutation (see also Roughgarden, 2004). Gender variance in non-human species thus highlights the partiality of the sex/gender binary. For Hird, such concerns are deeply sociological and it is to this end that she calls for a sociology of transsexualism (Hird, 2002a, 2002b). In a vein similar to Ekins and King, she maps out the different ways that transsexuality has been conceptualised: 'authenticity', whereby sex is analysed as a stable characteristic; 'performativity', whereby sex, alongside other identity markers, is theorised as constructed and subject to change; and 'transgressive', whereby trans holds the potential to bring the downfall of the sex/gender binary.

The analytical frameworks for understanding transgender that are being developed by the UK sociologists discussed here provide the impetus for as well as sketching out the wider context of this book. They variously engage with, though seek to amend, poststructuralist analyses of transgender that were discussed in previous sections of this chapter. Moreover, each seeks to stress how gender diversity is a set of social processes that are constructed in relation to dominant modes of being and seeing, and to each other. Such concerns form the backdrop of this book.

Conclusion

In reviewing key theoretical approaches to transgender, my purpose in this chapter has been to situate the theoretical approach to be developed in the subsequent chapters of this book. While recent medical understandings and practices of transgender represent a more complex insight into transgender practices than was offered by founding medical perspectives and practices, there remain significant problems with a medical approach that continues to correlate transgender practices and biological or psychological pathology. Moreover, in the main, a medical approach continues to work from a heteronormative framework, the premise being that gender is heterosexually practised so that post-surgery a transgender man will perform as a heterosexual male and a transgender woman as a heterosexual female. This approach is unable to take account of the complexities of non-heterosexual transgender sexualities. Through its continued focus upon surgical 'treatment', a medical model of transgender fails to account for the gender-diverse subjectivities of transgender people who reject medical interventions.

The chapter moved on to discuss a range of ways in which social theory has critiqued a medical approach to transgender. Ethnomethodology offers valuable early insights into how gender is socially produced and practised, and presents a significant challenge to the deviant positioning of transgender. However, ethnomethodological studies of transgender problematically assume a heteronormative analysis, which collapses the categories of gender and sexuality and is unable to account for the contemporary diversity of transgender identity positions. Next, the chapter discussed approaches to transgender from within lesbian and gay studies. Although this work moves beyond the heteronormative focus of previous approaches to transgender, its anthropological gaze is largely problematic through its translation of Western gender and sexual classificatory systems onto non-Western cultures. Moreover, its focus upon non-Western practices of gender diversity means that this body of work is limited for a study of transgender that is located within the UK.

The chapter then moved onto to address feminist approaches to transgender. Radical feminist approaches to transgender are highly problematic. Radical feminist critiques of transgender reproduce a binary model of gender that rests on a biological understanding of sex as fixed from birth. This approach refutes the self-identified genders of transgender people and offers a selective reading of transgender that states that transgender men and women reproduce gender norms. Such a perspective is thus unable to incorporate transgender into feminist theory and politics. Pluralist feminist analyses are important for the argument of this book as they offer a framework through which to theorise divergent gender expressions as unfixed to the 'sexed' body. Poststructuralist and postmodern feminisms, and queer approaches to transgender, are also relevant in their understanding of gender as distinct from sex. These approaches can be incorporated into a queer sociological approach to transgender that accounts for multiple gender expressions. However, the tendency to focus upon fluctuating and fluidly performed expressions of gender difference within these bodies of work raises problems for a queer sociological approach to transgender, which needs to be aware of (trans)gender identities that are subjectively positioned as neither fluctuating nor fluid, but, rather, as corporally experienced. An emphasis upon gender as socially relational as well as performatively constructed (MacDonald, 1998), is key to overcoming the theoretical problems within deconstructionist perspectives. Thus, it is MacDonald's injunction to both deconstruct and specify gender difference that I wish to carry forward in developing a queer sociological approach to transgender in the later chapters of this book.

Transgender studies offers a further example through which to develop a social theory of gender diversity that is able to account for a range of (trans)gendered expressions, understandings and identity positions. It is work from transgender studies and, in particular, the current work in the UK on transgender that is guided by a social framework of analysis that I hold as significant for developing my points of discussion in the following chapters. It is this body of work that this book seeks to engage with and contribute to.

TWO

Analysing care, intimacy and citizenship

This chapter relates gender diversity to existing work on the practices and meanings of care, intimacy and citizenship. What follows is a selective discussion of this body of literature; it is impossible here to address this extensive field in its entirety. For example, the chapter does not include feminist work during the 1970s that focused upon the role of women within the family, theorising the capitalist and/or patriarchal family as an agent of women's oppression (Wilson, 1977; McIntosh, 1978). Although this work relates to the arena of care in its analysis of women's role within the family, its broader premise of theorising the family from a Marxist–feminist perspective is beyond the scope of this book. Likewise, the chapter does not examine recent studies into changing family practices, which have illustrated shifting gender roles and suggested an increased fluidity of identities within contemporary family life (Irwin, 1999; Morgan, 1999; Smart and Neale, 1999). Rather, the aim here is to explore the ways in which recent work has challenged notions of gender essentialism and/or heteronormative understandings of care, intimacy and citizenship. In particular, the aim of the chapter is to consider how, by moving beyond the restrictions of a binary gender model, this book may contribute to studies that challenge a heteronormative analysis of care, intimacy and citizenship.

Care can be broadly defined as:"the [...] day-to-day activities which are so central to the sustaining of family lives and personal relationships – helping, tending, looking out for, thinking about, talking, sharing, and offering a shoulder to cry on" (Williams, 2004: 17). Moreover, I agree with Williams' understanding of the concept of 'care' as practised at both an individual and collective level. Such an understanding of 'care' goes beyond a political comprehension of care as it relates to welfare policy, to explore care as a practice of everyday support. In discussing 'intimacy' and 'intimate relationships', I refer to close, caring, personal relationships that are both sexually (partners and lovers) and non-sexually (friendships) experienced and practised.

The first part of the chapter examines how early feminist work on care challenged the idea that unpaid caring work was a 'natural' female role through which the carer demonstrated her love for, and commitment to, her family. Rather, from a feminist perspective, care came to be analysed as an integral feature of women's exploitation (Finch and Groves, 1989; Finch, 1989). Next, the chapter charts the ways in which feminist work has challenged this overarching analysis by examining the subjective meanings of care for women (Graham, 1983, 1990; Ungerson, 1987). Other work, particularly by those writing on disability, 'race' and ethnicity, and sexuality, has shown how women are also the receivers as well as the providers of care, stressing how the subjective meanings of care for women are diverse and non-universal (Begum, 1990; Carabine, 1996).

The second part of the chapter addresses work that explores non-heterosexual practices of intimacy (Weston, 1991; Weeks, 1995; Dunne, 1999; Weeks et al, 2001). This section also considers work that examines concepts of care through the themes of intimacy and friendship (Giddens, 1992; Nardi, 1992; Weeks, 1995; Jamieson, 1998; Roseneil, 2000). Although recent work has begun to explore the role of care and intimacy within same-sex relationships and lesbian and gay communities, practices of care and intimacy within transgender relationships and communities remain absent from the current framework of analysis. The final section of the chapter considers how debates around citizenship speak to transgender practices of identity, intimacy and care.

Feminist studies of care

Feminist work initiated a critique of social policy on community care in the late 1970s and early 1980s. Finch and Groves (1980), in particular, questioned the assumption within community care policy that unpaid caring work represented a 'natural' female role within the family. They argued that the normative underpinnings of community care policy, which saw unpaid care work as a 'labour of love', reinforced women's economic inequality by restricting their availability for paid work. Their work also highlighted how this 'silent work' went unrecognised by policy makers. Feminist analyses of care during the early 1980s thus focused upon gender divisions within the family, which were seen to structure and determine relationships of caring (Williams, 2000). Finch and Groves' (1980) work exemplified the feminist approach to care at this time, through which unpaid care work was seen as a key facet of women's exploitation. This perspective, however, was later challenged by feminist scholars who argued that it assumed a homogeneous experience of caring for women. In addressing care and disability, Morris and Lindow (1993), for example, locate Finch and Groves' work as belonging to a dominant feminist analysis that took as its subject young, non-disabled women and, thus, marginalised the experiences of those with different needs.

As the unified category of 'woman' came unstuck within the broader politics and theories of feminism, so challenges were brought to bear on feminist writing on care. Traditional feminist analyses were seen to neglect experiences of diversity. Graham argued that the inclusive use of the category 'woman' clouded a feminist analysis: "As a result, some relationships and experiences find a secure place within feminist research, while others are left on the margins of analysis" (1990: 127). Developments within feminist social policy led to a methodological shift as a broader range of subjective experiences of care became incorporated into research frameworks. Thus, rather than gender being viewed as an overriding structure that determined female experiences of caring, feminist work on care became localised and increasingly attentive to difference.

The recognition of diversity led to a broader analysis of the meaning of care for women. Rather than positioning care as a negative feature of women's lives, Graham (1990), for example, argued that caring may be an arena through which women gain social acceptance and a sense of belonging. Ungerson's (1987) research pointed to the divergent experiences of caring by showing that, while a feminist analysis of caring as exploitative labour resonated with some of her respondents, others located their role as carers as a source of fulfilment. Her study also addressed the experiences of male carers, fracturing the assumption that caring was an essentially female role. The experiences of male carers were also taken up by Arber and Gilbert (1993). Developments in feminist analyses of care were further reflected in studies examining the role of care in relation to 'race' and ethnicity (Bhalla and Blakemore, 1981; Gunaratnam, 1990), class (Graham, 1990) and sexuality (Carabine, 1996). Other feminist approaches to care addressed the themes of ethics and morality (Gilligan, 1982; Noddings, 1983; Tronto, 1993) and citizenship (Sevenhuijsen, 1998).

Yet, despite this increasingly diverse framework, much of the work on care has recently been found wanting in its analysis of the specificities of difference; particularly in relation to the ways in which sexuality impacts upon the practices and meanings of care: "this reflects an uncritical assumption within the literature of the universality and desirability of heterosexual-family-network systems" (Williams, 1999: 19). Carabine (1996) has questioned the heteronormative assumptions of social policy, and has illustrated how the discipline has been slow to theorise the relationship between sexuality and social policy. While sexuality has been a key policy area (for example, around HIV/AIDS, the age of consent and sex education), she points to the scarcity of theoretical analyses of sexuality within social policy: "Sexuality has, in general, failed to be awarded any analytical power within the discipline of social policy" (Carabine, 1996: 32). Carabine proposes that analyses of sexuality are important not only in ensuring that social policy examines sexuality, but also in enabling the concept of sexuality to illuminate the ways in which social policy itself constructs sexuality. Likewise, Dunne's aim in researching lesbian experiences of work and family life is to "counter a tendency in academic feminism to treat lesbian experience as 'other' or 'different'" (1997: 1). Dunne thus suggests that the significance of researching non-heterosexual social practices is that it brings a greater level of understanding of the organisation of sexuality per se. Similarly, researching social experiences of transgender enables a richer understanding of the construction of the category of gender.

Non-heterosexual practices of care and intimacy

Research into practices of care within non-heterosexual families and social networks is limited to work by a small selection of writers, many of whom are based in the US. Much of the research to explore non-heterosexual practices of care draws upon the role of care within gay male partnerships and friendship networks within the specific context of HIV/AIDS (Adam, 1992; Weeks, 1995). Weeks speaks of a 'new altruism' whereby the "immune (often well-meaning middle-class women in a passable revival of nineteenth-century philanthropic intention) have sometimes taken responsibility for caring for the 'vulnerable'" (1995: 179). More positively, Weeks recounts how an 'ethic of love' is embedded in practices of care for and by people living with HIV/AIDS. Significantly, the correlation of care and femaleness is fractured by accounts of new practices of care developed within gay communities as a response to HIV/AIDS: "Gay men organized from the beginning into groups devoted, of necessity, to an ethic of caring for one another" (Adam, 1992: 178). Thus Adam discusses a cultural shift in male intimacy in the US as large numbers of men took on an extensive range of caring duties:

> Care, organized by community-based AIDS groups, includes
> a wide range of professional services, from counselling and
> legal assistance to food banks and therapeutic support, but
> it is also of the most mundane sort: running errands, house
> sitting, cat feeding, being there, nursing and all the realm

of domestic labour. Yet it is this most unglamorous and
'un–masculine' work which meets very real needs. (Adam,
1992: 81)

The study of same–sex intimacy by Weeks et al (2001) illustrates how a
range of caring practices was developed by specific communities affected
by the HIV/AIDS epidemic. The lack of response in the early stages
of the epidemic has been well documented (Altman, 1993; Berridge
and Strong, 1993; Weeks, 1993). Insufficient government funding and
support and the lack of action by the public health service and wider
population resulted in the marginalisation of certain communities
who were affected by HIV/AIDS. Consequently "ostracised groups of
black people, women and haemophiliacs, as well as gay men, developed
distinct practices of care, which fit with the notion of community as a
site of identity and resistance" (Weeks et al, 2001: 90). Such practices
of care developed through a range of voluntary organisations, help and
information lines and self–help groups on a local and national level.
As Chapter Eight will address, transgender organisations and support
groups have also developed methods of care that are lacking outside
transgender communities. Without denying the significance and
necessity of the practices of resistance developed within communities
affected by HIV/AIDS, Weeks et al (2001) argue importantly that
practices of care within a strong voluntary sector need the backing of
the state. We can add on to this demand the need for greater government
recognition of transgender community care organisations.

   Outside the context of HIV/AIDS, studies exploring the role of
care within non–heterosexual practices of partnering and parenting
are scant. Although not explicitly concerned with care, Dunne's
(1999) UK research into lesbian experiences of work and family life
raises some relevant issues concerning the greater levels of equality
in divisions of domestic labour and child care within "families of
choice" (Weston, 1991; Weeks et al, 2001). Likewise, Weston's (1991)
research into lesbian and gay family life in the US emphasises agency
and equality within families of choice. The most comprehensive study
to speak about the role of care within non–heterosexual patterns
of partnering and parenting in the UK is provided by Weeks et al
(2001). Like Dunne (1999), the authors argue that developments in
non–heterosexual patterns of intimacy are linked to wider changes in
society, and that understanding the social organisation of families of
choice enables a greater understanding of changes within the family
and intimate relationships more broadly. Drawn from empirical research
into same–sex intimate relationships, the study shows a diversity of 'life

experiments' taking place. The findings support Dunne's assertion that same-sex intimate and parenting relationships hold greater possibilities of equality in the organisation of domestic life, employment and child care. Likewise, the potential within same-sex relationships for emotional support, honesty and agency in creating new patterns of intimacy are supported by the majority of respondents: "[...] emerging non-heterosexual ways of being can be seen as indices of something new: positive and creative responses to social and cultural change, which are genuine 'experiments in living'" (Weeks et al, 2001: 5).

It has been widely suggested that intimacy has become a site of social transformation within modern society (Beck, 1992; Giddens, 1992; Beck and Beck-Gernsheim, 1995; Weeks et al, 2001; Roseneil, 2003). Intimacy is seen to acquire new meanings and increased importance, both personally and socially. For Giddens (1992) an 'ideal of intimacy' is personified by the desire for a 'pure relationship' representing an increased level of emotional and sexual democracy, with the stress on choice and trust. An important feature of the pure relationship arises from what Giddens terms 'plastic sexuality', where sexuality attains distinct signification as it becomes liberated from reproduction. Although Giddens sees such shifts as taking place within heterosexual relationships, he suggests that lesbians and gay men have long been practitioners of the 'pure relationship'. While Jamieson (1998) warns against overstating the extent of the pure relationship, stressing how structural inequalities continue to hamper its existence, she too concedes that same-sex relationships offer the greatest potential for pure relationships. Although inequalities obviously exist within same-sex relationships and abuses of power undoubtedly occur – as, for example, Taylor and Chandler (1995) show in their examination of violence within lesbian and gay relationships – research findings on same-sex partnerships show that equality and autonomy are seen as necessary features within intimate relationships, and the notion of care is held central.

Transformations within the realm of intimacy have also been drawn upon to analyse the role of friendship within non-heterosexual practices of care. Various studies have shown that for many lesbians and gay men, friends are granted levels of importance equal to family members (Altman, 1982; Rubin, 1985, Weston, 1991; Nardi, 1992; Weeks, 1995; Weeks et al, 2001; Roseneil, 2000, 2003). One of the significant themes to emerge from studies of same-sex patterns of care is the importance of friendship networks. Drawing on gay men's experiences of AIDS, Nardi (1992) shows how the role of friendship becomes increasingly prominent in times of illness. Likewise, Weeks et al (2001) suggest that for lesbians and gay men, friendship networks are crucial providers of care.

Roseneil (2000, 2003) suggests that the desire for a pure relationship is also increasingly witnessed within hetero relations. This reflects the workings of 'queer tendencies' within postmodern society, which, in turn, are problematising the traditional hetero/homosexual binary. For Roseneil (2000), a key mover here is the increasing importance of friendship across the hetero/homosexual divide. She identifies a number of social changes that have contributed to the increased importance of friendship in contemporary society: increased geographical mobility, higher divorce rates, the decline in marriage and increasing later marriage, more births outside marriage, higher numbers of women choosing not to have children, an increase in single-person households and higher numbers of people who are living outside the heterosexual nuclear family. The empirical material that informs this book also shows that friendships are central to the lives of people undergoing gender transition.

Central to the work on non-heterosexual patterns of partnering, parenting and friendship is the emphasis placed upon emotional agency. Here active choice is central to social relationships. Writing about lesbian and gay kinship networks, Sandell (1994) points to the queering of emotional boundaries within such extended kinship patterns. She suggests that these affective relationships reflect fluidity in the demarcation of friends and lovers. This point has also been made by Weeks et al (2001) and Roseneil (2000, 2003). Additionally, the body of work on non-heterosexual relationships supports the assertion that individualisation and detraditionalisation in modern society has led to greater levels of reflexivity (Giddens, 1991; Beck, 1992; Weeks et al, 2001). Weston's (1991) research into lesbian and gay families, for example, shows how the notion of 'choice' was articulated by many of her respondents when discussing their kinship networks. The conscious process of choosing kinship networks also runs through the subject narratives in the study by Weeks et al (2001). While the degree of individual and collective agency is undeniably uneven and subject to structural constraints (Jamieson, 1998), there is considerable evidence of heightened degrees of agency within the creation of equitable and caring social networks. Moreover, unless such accounts are simply reduced to narratives of 'difference', the creative shifts in same-sex patterns of partnering, parenting and friendship can shed light upon the changing role of care and intimacy within wider society. As Weeks et al propose: "If the traditional family is indeed in crisis, then the experience of those who have often been forced to live outside its walls can tell us something important about new challenges and new possibilities" (2001: 27).

Weston's premise that gay kinship ideologies have "transformed, rather than copied, existing kinship networks" (Weston, cited in Sandell, 1994) is relevant to the arguments of this book, as is Roseneil's (2000, 2003) assertion that the hetero/homosexual binary is increasingly fragile within contemporary society. Likewise, Weeks et al (2001) point to an 'increasing flexibility' and 'moral fluency' in intimate life that stretches across the hetero/homosexual divide. Consequently, there is much to suggest that transformations of intimacy are actively at work within heterosexual patterns of partnering and parenting, and that friendship networks are also beginning to play a significant role in practices of care within heterosexual social arrangements. As Sandell argues, these developments hold significant social and political possibilities:

> By emphasising the social aspects of queer identities, there is a greater potential for gays and lesbians to make alliances with, and draw attention to, the large numbers of people living in non-traditional family groupings. This would mean building upon a sense of queer community that is not only based on sexual identities, but on social ties, thus facilitating connections with other communities. (Sandell, 1994)

Sandell's (1994) premise of adopting a queer analysis, which moves beyond identity politics in order to forge connections with other marginalised communities who are creating distinct kin and friendship networks, is important for this book both in relation to the incorporation of transgender communities into analyses of care,[1] and in terms of extending notions of 'queer' beyond lesbian, gay and bisexual (LGB) communities. A literature search reveals a dearth of research on the nature of intimacy and practices of care within transgender communities. Work previously discussed in this chapter illustrates how challenges have been brought to the heteronormativity of traditional care research by studies of practices and meanings of care within lesbian and gay communities, family and friendship networks. However, transgender lives and experiences remain absent from this analytical framework, which rests on an uninformative and naturalised binary gender model that recognises only male or female gender categories. Thus feminist analyses of care and studies of same-sex intimacy have yet to take account of the specificities of transgender.

Conceptualising citizenship

The concept of citizenship gained academic capital during the 1980s and 1990s and was articulated as a means through which to stress the importance of political activity (Phillips, 1993). Citizenship has been broadly defined as the collection of rights and responsibilities that establish political membership and enable access to benefits and resources (Turner and Hamilton, 1994). Though dominant Western notions of citizenship have traditionally followed a liberal model in which individual rights are stressed alongside minimum state intervention and market freedom (Marshall, 1950), citizenship is a contested concept that is culturally and historically specific. While neoconservatives argue that the balance between rights and duties is weighted too heavily in favour of the former, radical critics have variously pointed to how the rights of dominant social groups are protected at the expense of marginal groups (Turner and Hamilton, 1994).

Such perspectives stress the need to broaden the concept of citizenship to take greater account of the social positioning of minority groups. Work on citizenship and ethnicity (Lewis, 1998; Back and Solomos, 2000), for example, has illustrated how traditional models of citizenship have failed to acknowledge ethnicity and nationality, while feminist work on citizenship has drawn attention to the ways in which women's interests have been neglected by a traditional model of citizenship that focused upon the 'private' (paid labour) rather than the 'personal' (domestic), thus marginalising women's interests in the latter – for example, in unpaid caring work (Lister, 1997). Feminist scholars have challenged traditional assumptions of the citizen as male (Pateman, 1989; Walby, 1994; Lister, 1997; Bussmaker and Voet, 1998). Lister (1997) draws attention to the ambiguities of citizenship for feminism: on the one hand citizenship offers the possibility of universal rights, which are central to feminist goals, yet historically women have been excluded from citizenship debates, and inequalities remain. As Monro argues:

> Inequalities persist despite support for formal equality in many countries, partly because mainstream notions of citizenship continue to be based on implicit assumptions that citizenship means the same thing for women and men, masking differences in their interests. Current notions of citizenship still hide gender inequality. (Monro, 2000: 150).

Writers within sexuality studies (Evans, 1993; Cooper, 1995; Plummer, 1995; Weeks, 1995, 1998; Richardson, 1998, 2000; Bell and Binnie, 2000; Weeks et al, 2001) have also addressed how traditional models of citizenship mask difference; in this instance to marginalise the experiences and discriminate against the rights of those who variously live outside the hetero norm. Thus traditional notions of citizenship imply heterosexuality so that the domain of citizenship itself is heterosexualised (Richardson, 1998). The concept of 'sexual citizenship' has been developed to draw attention to sexuality, which has been excluded from the 'public' notion of citizenship. In the first discussion of 'sexual citizenship', Evans (1993) maps the relationship between sexuality, morality and the capitalist market. He argues that the process of 'consumer citizenship' enables capitalism to detach morality from legality. In order for the state to capitalise on the economic power held by some sexual minority groups – for example, middle-class gay men – legal rights are granted at the expense of political rights. For Evans, 'consumer citizenship' has led to the commodification of sexuality, which loses its political edge through the branding of sexual identity as 'lifestyle'. While the 'male homosexual citizen' holds economic rights, he remains an 'immoral' citizen. Moreover, sexual minorities who hold little obvious economic capital, for example, bisexuals and transvestites, are marginalised and granted neither economic nor political citizenship (Evans, 1993).

Richardson (2000) suggests that sexual citizenship articulates sexual rights, alongside wider rights and their impact on sexuality, in recognition of sexual minorities; while Weeks (1998) contextualises sexual citizenship in relation to broader social shifts. Weeks (1998) identifies the prerequisite of sexual citizenship as the respect for diversity and the consideration for the claims of minority groups. He positively suggests that these requirements are in sight; pointing to the democratisation of sexual relationships, an increased reflexivity about sexuality and the emergence of new sexual subjectivities in contemporary society. Others, however, are less optimistic. Richardson argues that the granting of lesbian and gay rights leads to the privatisation and circumscription of these sexual identities: "lesbians and gay men are granted the right to be tolerated as long as they stay within the boundaries of that tolerance [...]" (1998: 90). Since notions of citizenship are heterosexualised, such boundaries of tolerance depend upon rights-based claims (such as the right to marry), which fit with a heterosexual model of the 'good citizen'. For this reason Stychin points to the perils of articulating lesbian and gay rights through the concept of citizenship: "[...] lesbians and gays seeking rights may embrace an ideal of 'respectability', a construction that then perpetuates a division between 'good gays' and (disreputable) 'bad queers'" (1998: 200). It is the latter who are excluded from notions of citizenship. Similarly, Bell and Binnie (2000) suggest that sexual citizenship implies a set of 'rights-based' claims, for example, the right for lesbians and gay men to marry and to serve in the military, which, in turn, entails a set of duties, notably the duty to assimilate. This constructs a binary between the 'good homosexual' (the assimilator) and the 'bad homosexual' (the dissident), with the former granted citizenship: "The effect of this manoeuvre on activist strategies can be to surrender some 'rights' for the sake of others. This means that agitating under the banner of sexual citizenship is always going to involve potential compromise" (Bell and Binnie, 2000: 204). Bell and Binnie propose queering citizenship to acknowledge and celebrate the ways in which non-normative sexual practices and arrangements (for example, non-monogamy) challenge the institution of heterosexuality and traditional conceptualisations of citizenship.

A further way in which the relationship between sexuality and citizenship has been considered is through the notion of 'intimate citizenship' (Plummer, 1995; Weeks, 1998; Weeks et al, 2001), which offers a framework for discussing rights and responsibilities emerging from the diversification of intimate life. Plummer (1995) defines 'intimate citizenship' as the rights concerning people's choices about their bodies, emotions, relationships and desires, and proposes adding 'intimate citizenship' to the traditional models of political, social and civil rights. For Weeks, intimate citizenship concerns "those matters which relate to our most intimate desires, pleasures and ways of being in the world" (1998: 121).

Together, work on feminist, sexual and intimate citizenship has addressed how traditional definitions and requirements of citizenship neglected the complex features of gender and sexuality (Richardson, 2000). Broadening the notion of citizenship in this way enables the recognition of difference and problematises the public/private dichotomy. Yet this work largely assumes a gender binary that acknowledges only male and female categories. Importantly, Monro and Warren (2004) and Monro (2005) have brought to light the ways in which existing models of citizenship work within a gender binary system that presumes the citizen is either male or female. A gender binary model of citizenship has discriminated against gender-diverse people in terms of the 'public' (employment and welfare rights) and the 'private' (the rights of self-identification in gender of choice and of partnership recognition). The 2004 Gender Recognition Act (GRA) is important in enabling such processes of self-identification. In enabling transgender people to change their birth certificates and to marry, the GRA marks a dramatic shift in sociolegal attitudes that has been welcomed by transgender organisations and individuals as a marker of increased tolerance. Additionally, employment and welfare rights for transgender people increasingly occupy a place on the public agenda. Such moves represent a dramatic shift in conceptual understandings of 'gender' as distinct from 'sex' (Butler, 1994), and indicate how feminist, and to some extent queer, scholarship has entered the mainstream public and political agenda.

Before the GRA, Britain was one of four European countries that failed to recognise legally the acquired gender of transsexual people (Whittle, 2000: 44). The transgender campaigning organisation Press for Change (PfC) was instrumental in setting up the cross-party Parliamentary Forum on Transsexualism and, for a decade, worked closely with government on drafting and amending the Bill. For PfC, the GRA is highly significant: "The Gender Recognition Act is a crucial step towards ending 33 years of social exclusion for trans people in the UK" (www.pfc.org.uk homepage). Indeed, for many transgender people the GRA is momentous, as the following quotation from a letter posted on PfC's website testifies: "This morning I received an envelope containing a document, which I have been longing for over a length of time bordering forty years. To say that I am happy is the understatement of the century [...]" (www.pfc.org.uk). While I do not wish to diminish the significance of the GRA, unpacking current debates about transgender citizenship calls for caution against a perceived trajectory of progress in relation to (trans)gender transformation and social change. Normative binary understandings of gender that underpin the legislation mean that some transgender people are excluded from these new citizenship rights, while others remain unrecognised. Moreover, as Chapter Eight explores, debates around the desirability of assimilation suggest that understandings and experiences of social citizenship are complexly situated. Thus while the structural framework of the gender binary model of citizenship has flexed to concede that a person may change her/his gender, the male/female poles of the structure remain firmly intact. The effects of this bear down not only on the rights afforded to gender-different people but also on a more profound level that impacts upon self-identification. As Chapter Eight addresses, a gender binary model of citizenship continues to marginalise both the experiences and subjectivities of those who cannot or will not define as 'man' or 'woman', and, as such, is unable to account for the full spectrum of gender diversity.

Conclusion

This chapter has addressed understandings of care, intimacy and citizenship. In different ways, these bodies of work have attempted to move beyond gendered essentialism and heteronormativity. Recent work around practices of care stresses the importance of understanding care as holding divergent meanings that operate in different contexts and sites, and that involve social relations of power. Analyses of contemporary family practices and intimacy have significantly broadened understandings of the characteristics and experiences of social life by emphasising the creative affective practices of same-sex relationships and families of choice, and through focusing attention on the significance of friendship. Likewise recent work on citizenship has brought to light how traditional understandings and requirements of citizenship have been underpinned by gender and heteronormativity; thus neglecting the features of gender and sexuality.

To fully address the diversities of gender and sexuality, and to enable a greater understanding of the breadth of intimate and caring practices, however, this body of work has also to be attentive to the meanings and experiences transgender people bring to identity, intimacy, care and citizenship. To this end, subsequent chapters will move on to show how, in moving across, between or beyond the boundaries of a binary gender system and frequently the hetero/homo divide, transgender narratives articulate a range of non-normative individual and collective practices of identity, intimacy, care and citizenship.

THREE

Transgender identities and experiences

Transgender identities are cut through with multiple variables such as gender, sexuality, 'race' and ethnicity, class, age, transitional time span and geographical location. While the subsequent two chapters focus specifically on gender and sexuality in relation to the construction of transgender identities and subjectivities, this chapter explores how transgender identities are constructed and experienced in relation to a range of additional composites.

There is a wealth of autobiographical work on transgender identity formation and recently work that can be considered under the banner of 'transgender theory' offers a postmodern mix of critical analysis, political critique and autobiography to explore the experiences of gender transition. Nataf (1996) and Feinberg (1996), for example, articulate a range of female-to-male (FtM) gender and sexual identities. Although Nataf explores gender as a performative concept, he does so by drawing on a range of transgender lesbian subjective experiences of the expression and interpretation of gender. In Feinberg's work, the author is placed at the centre of the narrative as the analytical investigation of transgender histories links with Feinberg's gender trajectory. Feinberg's later work (1999) vocalises a diversity of (trans)gender and sexual identities, and calls for an inclusive trans politics that is able to dually celebrate and specify difference. Significantly Feinberg incorporates the structures of age, class and ethnicity, as well as gender and sexuality, into the discussion of transgender identities, thus paving the way for a material and social analysis of transgender.

There are a number of studies within sociology, social policy, anthropology and literature and cultural studies that adopt a micro analysis variously to explore transgender identity constructions, behaviour patterns and politics. Devor (1989), Lewins (1995), Nataf (1996) and Cromwell (1999) explore a range of FtM gender and sexual identities. Halberstam (1998) makes visible the historical and contemporary diversity of female masculinity. Kulick (1998) examines the identities and experiences of transgendered prostitutes in Brazil. Wilson (2002) looks at the formation of transgender identities in Western Australia. Monro (2005) explores collective identities and transgender politics. Ekins and King (1999) have developed a cartography of transgendering to take account of the ways in which transgender narratives are distinct. Hirschauer (1997), King (2003) and Ekins and King (2006) employ the concept of gender 'migration' to examine experiences of transition. King suggests that this concept be employed within sociological studies as it "enables sociology to get a grasp of the micro and macro social process involved in 'changing sex'" (2003: 187). Much of this body of work, however, is from the US and there is an absence of empirical work from the UK on transgender identity formation.[1] It is from this juncture that the chapter moves on substantively to explore a number of ways in which transgender experiences and identities are constructed.

First, the chapter considers understandings and experiences of gender identity prior to transition; second, it explores the formation of transgender identities. Next, the chapter draws upon recollections of 'significant moments' within the process of transgender identity formation. The chapter then addresses the notion of the 'wrong body' in relation to medical discourse and practice, and subjective understandings of embodiment. Here I consider the extent to which participants' narratives may be read as 'rehearsed narratives', which are constructed and reconstructed through repetition and retelling to particular audiences. The chapter then develops the theme of embodiment to consider the impact of bodily changes upon identity. The penultimate section considers the relevance of analysing transgender identity positions as gender performances and looks at discourses around gender authenticity. Finally, the chapter explores the ways in which transgender identities are linguistically articulated to produce distinct identity positions.

Pre-transition identities

While recollections of childhood may be read as constructed narratives, they remain "materials from which individuals mold current identities and, therefore are valid and significant" (Gagne and Tewksbury, 1997: 486). In recollections of pre-transition identities, all but one of the people interviewed spoke of transgendered feelings or experiences during childhood or puberty. For some participants these feelings manifested themselves at a very young age. David (age 26), for example, says:

> I'd always just identified as being male, I'd never thought of myself as anything else. [...] I knew there was a difference at

four years old between a boy and a girl, but I never thought of myself as a girl. I thought that one day I'd wake up and I'd be a boy and that would be the end of it. I didn't see it as a long-term thing. I remember having arguments with my parents and having tantrums as a child, saying 'I want to be a boy'. I remember on one occasion crying and my mum telling me 'you're not a boy and that's the end of it'. And I don't remember what led up to it. And so I felt there was nothing my parents could do about it so I didn't talk to them about it. I knew who I was but no one could see that.

And in my teenage years I grew a chest and it was 'where has this come from?'

Dan (age 37) also recalls discomfort with the conventions of femininity as a child:

[…] I had my hair very short. I hated wearing skirts. When I had to wear skirts for school uniform I'd make sure that I did things like wear my father's ties as a rebellious token, something that was my identity because I was different. So conforming in one direction, but not going the whole way. And I used to argue with the teachers at primary school because I wasn't allowed to do woodwork. My parents gave us no gender stereotypes at all. There were three of us and we did everything, we all did the washing up, we basically had the choices we wanted and we played with each other's toys. There wasn't a problem in that direction. My father did a lot of DIY and I was always the one who helped him and so I couldn't understand why at school I couldn't do woodwork and I had numerous arguments and all they said was 'you can't do it, you're a girl'. […] But the answer as to why I couldn't do these things was because I was girl, which didn't make any sense at all.

Both David and Dan present narratives in which their understandings of the relationships between gender identity and body parts and appearance is arrived at from a young age. While David locates tension between assumed gender identity and self-identity in the home, for Dan, this was worked out at school. In Dan's story, clothes are identified as a key signifier of gender identity and his discomfort with gender identity is linked to his hatred of wearing skirts. Moreover, in modifying his school uniform by wearing his father's ties, Dan used clothes as a means of gender rebellion.

Clothes also appear as a signifier of gender rebellion in the narratives of transgender women. A frequent theme to arise in the childhood recollections of transgender women is the wearing of female clothes as a child. Dionne (age 40), for example, says: "I know I've always had these feelings from when I was a kid. I used to dress up as a girl, all my life, but always in secret." In childhood, participants learnt that clothes are a key cultural indicator of gender. Moreover, dressing in female clothes as a boy can be seen as a form of gender resistance through which assumptions around the intrinsic relationship between biological sex and gendered appearance are challenged. Such a challenge, however, is not easy and, in articulating the secrecy of cross-dressing, participants show that they were aware of the cultural imperative to perform gender appropriately.

In addition to clothes, toys and activities are key signifiers of gender roles in childhood. Common to the narratives of both transgender men and women are childhood recollections of disassociating from perceived gender-appropriate toys or activities. Karen (age 31), for example, says:

> As I was going through my younger years I used to identify with females a lot more, I used to have a lot of female friends. I didn't have many male friends, didn't want to play their games and so on. When I got to comprehensive school I tried to be more masculine and to do sports like football and rugby, which I didn't feel very comfortable with but I did them anyway.

Participants' recollections of childhood, then, illustrate how gender rules are learnt from a young age in the home and at school. These stories indicate a developing awareness that resistance to ascribed gender identity is socially unacceptable. Consequently, gender rebellion is largely experienced and practised individually and out of sight of family, friends and teachers. Alienation from culturally determined appropriate gender behaviour is not, however, an exclusive prerogative of transgender biographies. Thus common to both feminist and lesbian life-story narratives is a childhood rejection of stereotypically gendered appearance or activities. Within transgender narratives, however, puberty can be seen to be a particularly significant time for disassociation with assigned gender. Thus many participants speak of the occurrence of transgender feelings during puberty and early adulthood. Amanda (age 45), for example, says:

> Like the old clichés, I didn't feel like the other boys. But it was when puberty came when all the wrong signals came up on the screen so to speak. And then all your hormones are racing and that was a troublesome period that started off massive depressions, clinical depressions. Everyone else was having a great time and I was in and out of the hospital with clinical depression.

Although puberty may mark a subjective turning point in relation to an increased awareness of gender discomfort, the social and cultural pressure to live within the gender binary means that many participants worked hard at conforming to their ascribed gender role. Thus Gabrielle (age 45) speaks about how she worked to maintain her ascribed masculine identity: "I was successful at being a young man as far as other people were concerned and I maintained that externally for quite a long time." Gender management is also evident across the life course. As I will explore in the next section, gender appearance may be maintained, and appropriate gender behaviour practised, for many years through adulthood.

Coming out

The formation of a transgender identity came at different life-stages for participants in this research. While a small number of participants came out as transgendered in their teens or early 20s, for many others, transition took place later in life. Gender management is frequently evident across the life course as normative gender appearance and appropriate gender behaviour are practised into adulthood. For many participants, social and cultural pressures to conform to ascribed gender identity are experienced as problematic and, for some, can bring detrimental psychological and physical consequences. Although she had cross-dressed for many years, Lynne (age 67) was in her 50s when she began the process of gender transition:

> I got into a very secret cross-dressing situation, which was really dangerous when I think about it. I mean my livelihood was with the Air Force and by this time I'd got a wife and two kids. It was a stupid thing to do really, looking back on it. You only have to think about attitudes from the military to

gay people. And so imagine what would have happened if I'd have said 'I want to be a woman.' So I just kept it to myself. Basically I became a workaholic and when that happens your family life suffers and my wife and I drifted apart.

Here career considerations and family commitments are presented as reasons for later transition. In the following quotation, Gabrielle (age 45) draws attention to the significance of transitional time span in impacting upon experiences and identities of transition:

In those times, we're going back to late 1960s, early 1970s, that was when I was at school, there was nothing positive that you could ever read or find about transsexual people or trans issues. It was all sort of drag cabaret type places, in England anyway, or dry medical text books that were basically saying trans people were crazy, or bad, and if they didn't want to be cured they were very bad.

Thus transgender identities and experiences are constructed within specific social and temporal contexts. Certainly, the medical advice given to Bernadette's parents to "[...] make a man of him [...]" (Bernadette, MtF, age 71) contrasts with the experiences of younger participants. David (age 26), for example, was in his early 20s when he transitioned and his narrative contrasts positively with those of older participants:

I made the decision that I was going to get in touch with a doctor. I was still living at home. I went to the doctor and got myself referred to a psychiatrist. I had a meeting with the psychiatrist who said 'right, we'll start you on treatment'. It was good when my voice started to break. There was no mental change. It was just the changes I had been waiting for a long time. It was just exciting.

For younger participants, social pressures may be less severe, leading to less troubled narratives of transition. In sharp contrast to older participants' recollections of childhood experiences of gender, William (age 25), who transitioned as a teenager, presents a narrative in which gender difference is viewed as a positive attribution: "I always knew something was different and I always liked being different even though maybe I wasn't sure what that was. And I don't know if that is different to some people, but that was quite nice. I've always liked being a bit different."

There are significant differences, then, in the narratives of older and younger participants. As well as benefiting from a medical system that, following pressure from transgender organisations has become more attentive to the demands of transgender people, shifts in cultural politics and social attitudes can be seen to have enabled a less hostile climate. In turn, this can enable people to transition at an earlier age. In addition to enabling greater levels of self-confidence, findings suggest that these moves have also impacted positively upon social worlds and affective communities that give shape to self-understanding. As I will explore in the next section, affective relationships and intimate networks are also positioned as important factors in the decision to begin the process of gender transition.

Significant moments

A shift in the established routine of work or family life is a significant theme in many participants' narratives of developing a transgender identity. Tony (age 39), for example, connects his decision to begin transition to the break-up of his relationship: "I had known for a long time and I think splitting up with her had a lot to do with it as well." For Dionne (age 40), the decision to begin transition came about after losing a long-standing job: "I had a big trauma in my life. I was in the motor trade and I lost my job. It was about 1988 and my life was in turmoil and I had time to think about everything and what I wanted. And it developed from then."

For these participants, ruptures to key structures brought gender issues to the fore. As well as acting as a significant factor in participants' decisions about when to transition, occupation also impacts upon life experiences through and beyond transition. Findings indicate a notable difference between the identity experiences of participants who are self-employed within cultural fields such as art and music, and those who are employed in more formal occupations. For those employed within manual trades, in particular, coming out to colleagues is often difficult. Cheryl (age 45), for example, who works in engineering, has yet to disclose her transgender identity to her work colleagues: "I sit there at work and this goes over and over in my mind, if we have a quiet day or night it just goes round and round in my head. I really don't know how some of them are going to take it." Cheryl's fears are borne out by the experiences of Amanda (age 45), who works as a security officer for a large urban police force. In the following quotation,

Amanda discusses how a work colleague disclosed her transgender identity to the national press:

> They [the tabloid press] did a real number on me. I was betrayed from someone who got into my personnel file [...] The papers were everywhere, people were sitting outside my home, camera lenses everywhere, knocking up the neighbours, going to my dad's, to where my ex-wife works, they even went to the pharmacy where I get my hormones from. They went everywhere, they knocked on every door. It was horrendous.

These narratives contrast with those of participants who work in more progressive environments. For example, Del (age 44), who is an artist, says:

> **D:** I used to think 'if I can do it then anybody can do it', but the truth is that not anybody can do it. People aren't all, you know, wired up like me. I'm pretty fearless and you can't teach somebody to be fearless. So what works for me is not necessarily going to work for somebody else.
>
> **S:** So do you feel that you have more privilege?
>
> **D:** Yeah. I do. I absolutely do. Not privilege that I was born into, but privilege that I have developed through a sporadic education and privilege that comes with having [pause]. Yeah I am privileged. I can live my life as an artist, as a poor artist but I don't have to go out and work in the same kind of ways. I feel like I've paid my dues. I've done that, but I don't have to come into contact with bigoted people in general.

Gabrielle (age 45), who is a musician, also gives a positive account of transitioning at work:

> I officially changed my name and said to the people that were employing me 'I'm ready now, so please call me she' and they were really nice and I kept working in the places that I'd been working. But to be honest I was playing music in bars so it wasn't a big deal.

Significantly, Cheryl and Amanda use the term 'transsexual' to describe their identities, whereas Del and Gabrielle use the term 'queer'. Queer subjectivities, then, may be lived out more smoothly in less constraining work environments, which, in turn, can enable less problematic experiences of transition. Taken a step further, this suggests that social class impacts upon the access to, and the articulation of, queer transgender identities. Findings here contribute to and build upon critical commentary that shows how 'queer' is classed (Hennesy, 1995; Fraser, 1999; Binnie, 2004; Taylor, 2005). Moreover, findings from this research show that participants who are anxious about the reaction of work colleagues seek to adopt normatively feminine or masculine appearances. Participants who are concerned about discrimination at work place more stress on the importance of 'passing' and are more likely to present a medically approved narrative of 'gender dysphoria' to psychiatrists in order to obtain the hormone therapy and surgical procedures required to 'pass'. In contrast, Del (age 44) made his queer identity explicit when requesting hormones from a private psychiatrist:

> I was very clear. I did go to [name of psychiatrist] and I was very clear with him that I wasn't a transsexual. And I said I wanted hormones and I would get them one way or another, but I would prefer it if he prescribed them to me.

A further significant factor within transitional narratives is intimacy, and the formation of new intimate relationships is often linked to increased self-recognition. Rebecca (age 55), for example, discusses how meeting a new partner enabled her to explore her feelings around gender:

> It wasn't really until maybe eight or ten years ago when my last partner allowed me to explore this in a way in which I never had done before that I actually started looking closer at it and believing that I could move to a gender description that was more congruent with my own feelings.

Self-validation may also come from other sources. For Greg (age 44), leaving home represented a significant moment, which led to developing self-awareness: "I went to university and that was when I first broke away from parental control which had tried to stop me being who I was. [...] I was quite excited that there was a category that I did fit into. I wasn't unique. I wasn't on my own."

In these discussions, the emergence of new milieux through breaks with the past routines of work, home life and intimate relationships, enables a shift in gender identity. In discussing emerging self-validation, participants frequently relate to the importance of naming their feelings, which in turn brings the awareness that there are others with similar gender experiences. Cultural resources may also bring collective identification. Amanda (age 45), for example, connected with a song:

> My first contact with anything transgendered was 'Lola', you know, 'The Kinks', which was around the same time. And a spike came straight out of the radio every time I heard it. I thought 'God, wow'. It was a defining moment when I heard the record for the first time.

These discussions point to the significance of cultural representations in developing self-awareness. There is a link here to the role of community in identity formation (Taylor and Whittier, 1992). However, the power of gender normativity meant that for most participants self-validation of gender difference was not enough, leading a majority to seek legitimisation from professional authorities. From their US-based study of the coming-out experiences of transgender women, Gagne and Tewksbury argue that "those whose gender identity and gender presentations fall outside of the binary are stigmatized, ostracized, and socially delegitimized to the extent that they may fail to be socially recognized" (1997: 480). One way of gaining social recognition is through the sanction of the 'expert'. Thus the construction of a transgender identity frequently relies upon medical discourse and practice and access to medical intervention. Findings from this research largely support the argument of Gagne and Tewksbury that "while new identities are emergent, they are created within the constraints of current understandings" (1997: 490). As I discussed in Chapter One, at the heart of medical understanding and practice is the notion of the 'wrong body'. The following section develops this theme to examine how trans-subjectivities are both constructed through, and practised in opposition to, medical discourse around the notion of the 'wrong body'.

Medicalisation, the 'wrong body' and rehearsed narratives

As Chapter One explored, medical and psychological studies have constructed particular ways of thinking about gender diversity that continue to inform social, cultural and legal understandings of transgender. Benjamin's *The Transsexual Phenomenon* (1966), Stoller's *Sex and Gender* (1968) and Green and Money 's *Transsexualism and Sex Reassignment* (1969) introduced the notion of 'gender' into discourses of transsexuality, and 'gender' came to be recognised independently of 'sex'.

Though later medical insights represent a more complex understanding of transgender practices than was offered within founding medical perspectives, there remain serious problems in the correlation of transgender and biological or psychological pathology, as illustrated by the 1996 report for the Parliamentary Forum on Transsexualism:

> The weight of current scientific evidence suggests a biologically based, multifactoral aetiology for transsexualism. Most recently, for example, a study identified a region in the hypothalamus of the brain which is markedly smaller in women than in men. The brains of transsexual women examined in this study show a similar brain development to that of other women. (Parliamentary Forum on Transsexualism, 1996)

The epistemological power of medical discourse has thus worked to structure specific aetiologies of transgenderism. Significantly, the concept of 'gender dysphoria' remains a key classificatory term within medical discourse and practice. The 2004 Gender Recognition Act (GRA) marks a significant shift in sociolegal understandings of 'gender' as distinct from 'sex'. Importantly, gender reassignment surgery is not a requirement of gaining gender recognition; however, the Act is shaped by a medical perspective of transgender that privileges a connective relationship between gender identity and body parts and presentation. Press for Change's advice on seeking gender recognition under the GRA states:

> If you can demonstrate reasonable evidence that you have undergone 'surgical treatment for the purpose of modifying sexual characteristics' (i.e. surgery to alter the shape and function of genitals) then this is by far the easiest way to apply [...] The alternative way in which the law allows an application to be accepted by the panel is if you can provide evidence of having being diagnosed with 'gender dysphoria'. (www.PfC.org.uk)

From its inception in the 1970s, then, the concept of 'gender dysphoria' has guided understandings of, and practices towards, transgender. Therefore, it is not surprising that the central tenet of the concept – dissonance between sex (the body) and gender identity (the mind) – figures large in many transgender narratives.

Stone (1991) engages directly with medical constructions of transgender by challenging the conceptualisation of transgender as characteristic of living within the 'wrong' body. Debates around the 'wrong body' provoke fierce debate within transgender communities and account for substantial theoretical comment within transgender studies. Indeed, the question of the 'wrong body' may be read as the theoretical lens through which meanings of transgender are presently contested. In her discussion of male-to-female autobiography, Stone shows how accounts of the 'wrong body' lie at the heart of many personal accounts of transition:

> They go from being unambiguous men, albeit unhappy men, to unambiguous women. There is no territory between. Further, each constructs a specific narrative moment when their personal sexual identification changes from male to female. This moment is the moment of neocolporraphy – that is, of gender reassignment or 'sex change surgery'. (Stone, 1991: 286)

Corresponding with medical discourse, this transition story focuses upon the idea of the 'wrong body' as a vehicle in which the essential self is trapped. Research participant Bernadette (age 71) reflected this in reply to my question 'what are the most important changes transition has brought?': "Before I transitioned, I had become terrified of mirrors. I couldn't look at myself. I was absolutely horrified looking at myself and this was completely resolved. […] These are the things which have changed, and made me feel what I am. They are the external manifestations that balance."

Surgical 'correction' is related by Bernadette as the means through which her authentic gender is released. Such an account is oppositional to poststructuralist, postmodern and queer theory's social constructionist framework, in which all gender and sexual identities are denaturalised, and notions of authenticity deconstructed. Much debate within transgender studies has thus been concerned with addressing the contradictions between a deconstructionist analysis of transgender and the representations of fixed identities articulated in many transgender autobiographies. Prosser's book *Second Skins: The*

Body Narratives of Transsexuality (1998) can be read as a deliberation on the contradictions between transgender narratives of authenticity and queer theory's destabilisation of identity as a categorising device. Prosser contends that queer theory has bypassed the importance of embodiment for transgender people and has neglected subjective transgender narratives: "queer studies has made the transgender subject, the subject who crosses gender boundaries, a key queer trope" (1998: 5). He argues that Butler, in particular, presents a selective reading of transgender by emphasising certain transgender practices at the expense of others: "The transgendered subject has typically had centre stage over the transsexual: whether s/he is transvestite, drag queen, or butch woman, queer theory's approbation has been directed towards the subject who crosses the lines of gender, not those of sex" (Prosser, 1998: 6). Thus Prosser draws a distinction between transsexuals who search for a gendered 'home' and those who live on the 'borderlands' between genders. As such, he follows Rubin (1996) and Felski (1996) in proposing a distinction between the 'transgenderist' and the 'transsexual' to avoid the "universalizing of trans" (Prosser, 1998: 201). While it is crucial to theorise the subjective differences under the umbrella of transgender, such a distinction may turn the tables of negation problematically. In viewing transsexuality as representative of the 'authentic' experience, the transgenderist is positioned as an almost frivolous postmodern player.

A key question for Prosser is how to theorise sex, gender and identity in the light of continued transsexual demand for reconstructive surgery, and it is to these ends that he draws attention to transsexual embodiment: "Transsexuality reveals the extent to which embodiment forms an essential base to subjectivity [...]" (1998: 7). He suggests that the 'wrong body' narrative reflects a genuine transsexual emotion, which he discusses as the desire for an embodied 'home':

> My contention is that transsexuals continue to deploy the image of wrong embodiment because *being trapped in the wrong body is simply what transsexuality feels like.* If the goal of transsexual transition is to align the feeling of gendered embodiment with material body, body image – which we might be tempted to align with the imaginary – clearly already has a material force for transsexuals. The image of being trapped in the wrong body conveys this force. It suggests how body image is radically split off from the material body in the first place, how body image can feel sufficiently substantial as to persuade the transsexual to

alter his or her body to conform to it. The image of wrong embodiment describes most effectively the experience of pre-transition (dis)embodiment: the feeling of a sexed body dysphoria profoundly and subjectively experienced. (Prosser, 1998: 69, my italics)

As Halberstam (1998) and Heyes (2000) point out, however, it is not only transsexuals who express disharmony between the imagined and the material body. Thus Prosser does not account for why such dissonances occur, and his analysis fails to address the historical and political contexts in which such experiences appear (Heyes, 2000). Stone's work can be drawn upon to provide some explanations to these questions. Stone contextualises autobiographical narratives of essentialism within medical discourse. She shows how early gender identity clinics used Benjamin's *The Transsexual Phenomenon* (1966) as a rulebook for assessing who was eligible for surgery. Moreover, transsexual clients were using the same piece of literature as a rulebook to gain authorisation for surgery:

It took a surprisingly long time – several years – for researchers to realize that the reason the candidate's behaviour profiles matched Benjamin's so well was that the candidates, too, had been reading Benjamin's book, which was passed from hand to hand within the transsexual community, and they were only too happy to provide the behaviour that led to acceptance for surgery. (Stone, 1991: 291)

Central to Benjamin's diagnosis of gender dysphoria was the experience of living in the 'wrong body'. Thus it has been widely acknowledged that, in order to gain access to hormone therapy or surgical procedures, transgender people frequently reproduce the officially sanctioned aetiology of transsexualism: that of gender dysphoria (Green, 1978; Stone, 1991; Hausman, 1995; Bolin, 1998; Cromwell, 1999). Indeed, in the 1970s, Stoller acknowledged this process, remarking: "Those of us faced with the task of diagnosing transsexualism have an additional burden these days, for most patients requesting 'sex change' are in complete command of the literature and know the answers before the questions are asked" (1975: 248). As Stone remarks: "This raises several sticky questions, the chief two being: Who is telling the story for whom, and how do the storytellers differentiate between the story they tell and the story they hear?" (1991: 291). Subsequently, medical professionals have suggested that transgender people may "distort their autobiographies (and) tend to be less than honest about their personal histories" (Lothstein, quoted in Cromwell, 1999: 124). In the following quotation from our interview, research participant Gabrielle (age 45) illustrates how this process may work:

> **G:** If you see a doctor for an hour once every three months and they go 'how are you?' and you go 'I'm fine'. And they go 'any issues?' you go 'no'. 'Cos you want what they've got to give you and so you quickly learn the script, as people call it, for what you should say and not say. And I think people buy into that, people do say these things that the doctors need to hear to tick off on the form to make you eligible.
>
> **S:** And what are those things?
>
> **G:** 'I'm a woman trapped in a man's body' or 'a man trapped in a woman's body'. 'I've known always', you know, those sorts of things, the things that people say.

Gabrielle's narrative connects with Shapiro's argument that "One cannot take at face value transsexuals' own accounts of a fixed and unchanging (albeit sex-crossed) gender identity, given the immense pressure on them to produce the kinds of life histories that will get them what they want from the medical-psychiatric establishment" (quoted in Nataf, 1996: 19). The extent to which trans people continue to research diagnostic guidelines is illustrated in the Harry Benjamin 'Standards of Care', which formulate the "professional consensus about the psychiatric, psychological, medical, and surgical management of gender identity disorders" (Harry Benjamin International Gender Dysphoria Association, 2001) The document details the means by which trans people may find 'new gender adaptations', stating that "both genders may learn about 'transgender phenomena' from studying these Standards of Care, relevant lay and professional literatures about legal rights pertaining to work, relationships, and public cross-dressing" (Harry Benjamin International Gender Dysphoria Association, 2001).

The 'wrong body' narrative may consequently be seen to be medically constructed and internalised as a means to an end: "The idea has been imposed upon transpeople by those who control access to medical technologies and have controlled discourses about transpeople. Some individuals may believe or come to believe that they are in the wrong body or at least use language that imparts the same meaning [...]" (Cromwell, 1999: 104). Stone proceeds to argue that this narrative has led to the invisibility of transsexualism: "The highest purpose of the transsexual is to erase him/her, to fade into the 'normal' as soon as possible [...] What is gained is acceptability in society. What is lost is the ability to authentically represent the complexities and ambiguities of lived experience [...]" (1991: 295). She proposes that analyses of transgender move away from the 'wrong body' paradigm in order to negotiate "the troubling and productive multiple permeabilities of boundary and subject positions that intertextuality implies" (Stone, 1991: 297). Additionally, Cromwell (1999) suggests that the medical and psychological focus upon the 'wrong body' has led many transgender people to believe that genital surgery is a necessity. Such critiques accordingly represent a direct challenge to medical models of transgender.

Questions around the impact of a medical model on transgender subjectivities bring to mind Foucault's writing on the body. For Foucault, the body is constructed through systems of power: "The body is directly involved in a political field; power relations have an immediate hold upon it; they invest it, mark it, train it, torture it, force it to carry out tasks, to perform ceremonies, to emit signs" (1977: 25). Thus subjects are produced *through* discourses of the body. Complicity with a medical model of transgender both supports and paradoxically challenges Foucault's notion of the 'docile body', which is a direct locus of control produced by external power. Thus while the 'wrong body' hypothesis can be seen as a discourse that produces its subject, the self-conscious repetition of the 'wrong body' narrative can be read as an agency-driven process whereby trans people employ knowledge as power. Foucault's later work is more relevant to this interplay between structure and agency. In discussing "techniques of the self" (1986), Foucault creates a space for agency by examining the relationship between external power and subjectivity. From this point, the notion of the 'wrong body' can be conceptualised as a rehearsed narrative that is consciously repeated as a means to an end. Yet rehearsed narratives are not only characteristic of transsexual stories, as Shapiro acknowledges:

> To take the problem one step further, the project of autobiographical reconstruction in which transsexuals are engaged, although more focused and motivated from the one that all of us peruse, is not entirely different in kind.

> We must all repress information that creates problems for
> culturally canonical narratives of identity and the self, and
> consistency in gender attribution is very much a part of
> this. (Shapiro, quoted in Nataf, 1996: 19)

For many participants in this research, the 'wrong body' narrative was
deeply unsatisfactory, and transgender identification was discussed as
a more complex and nuanced process. I asked Rebecca (age 55) how
she felt about the 'wrong body' metaphor: "It's [Transition's] been a
progression. It's never been fixed from the outset and I've never had
those overwhelming feelings of being in the wrong body. There's always
been fluidity in my feelings."

In the following quotation Amanda (age 45) presents an explicit
critique of the 'wrong body' and, like Rebecca, suggests that gender
transition is more complex than this metaphor indicates:

> The way in which some people talk about being born
> in the wrong body is such a cliché and to come back to
> components, we all have a male and a female component.
> [...] So 'wrong body', that's a plumbing job. That's nothing to
> do with the core person I am, what makes me a person.

For these participants, gender identity formation is a nuanced process
that does not necessarily signify movement across a gender binary. Del
(age 44) attempts to work through these complexities:

> [...] the wrong body stuff does bother me. I think a lot of
> it is that our culture is wrong, and if our culture was more
> accepting of gender diversity, would we need to? You know,
> if men could wear make up and dresses, and for women if
> there was no glass ceiling, would it be necessary? [...]

While the narrative of the 'wrong body' within discourses of 'gender
dysphoria' is repeated to gain surgical reconstruction, the demand
for surgery may be seen to be an outcome of the social and cultural
investment in a gender binary system. This is particularly significant
since the medical model of transgender, which influences access to the
new framework of rights, remains tied to a gender binary model.

Halberstam provides a further critique of the 'wrong body' diagnosis
by asking "who, we might ask, can afford to dream of a right body?
Who believes that such a body exists?" (1998: 154). In contrast to
Prosser's suggestion that transsexual identities constitute an authentic

transgender experience, Halberstam shifts the focus away from debates about who constitutes the 'real' transgender subject:

> Many bodies are gender strange to some degree or another, and it is time to complicate on the one hand the transsexual models that assign gender deviance only to transsexual bodies and gender normativity to all other bodies, and on the other hand the hetero-normative models that see transsexuality as the solution to gender deviance and homosexuality as a pathological perversion. (Halberstam, 1998: 154–5)

She argues that Prosser's analysis of transsexualism depends upon a strict demarcation of gender: "it relies on a belief in the two territories of male and female, divided by a flesh border and crossed between surgery and endocrinology" (Halberstam, 1998: 164). Prosser's focus upon transsexual narratives of the 'wrong body' may consequently be criticised for implying that all transsexual narratives are alike and, moreover, for denying instances of gender dysphoria within other subject positions (trans and non-trans). His emphasis may work against the interests of transsexuals by further pathologising their 'condition' through reinstating the dual categories of 'wrong' (trans) and 'right' (non-trans) bodies. Halberstam draws upon postcolonial work to critique Prosser's location of transgender/transsexual identities as either at 'home' or on the 'borders'. Rather, "some bodies are never at home, some bodies cannot simply cross from A to B, some bodies recognize and live with the inherent instability of identity" (Halberstam, 1998: 164). Postcolonial work on migration has frequently discussed the notion of 'home' in terms of the exclusion of others. In this respect, Halberstam states that "the journey home for the transsexual may come at the expense of a recognition that others are permanently dislocated" (1998: 171). In contrast to analyses of transgender as migration, Halberstam argues for a politics of transgender mobility that is specific in its analysis and takes account of a number of variables:

> Who, in other words, can afford transition, whether that transition be a move from female to male, a journey across the border and back, a holiday in the sun, a trip to the moon, a passage to a new body, a one way ticket to white manhood? Who, on the other hand, can afford to stay at home, who can afford to make a new home, build a new

> home, move homes, have no home, leave home? Who can
> afford metaphors? (Halberstam, 1998: 164)

While Prosser's (1998) emphasis upon wrong embodiment reinforces Descartes' mind/body split, Merleau-Ponty's (1962) work offers an alternative framework through which to explore issues of transgender embodiment. In challenging the duality of mind/body, Merleau-Ponty theorises the intersections between the material body and the phenomenological realm to explore how the body is consciously experienced. The 'corporeal schema' indicates how the embodied agent is positioned between the subjective and the social world. For Merleau-Ponty, embodiment is not necessarily a conscious state, but may be experienced as an 'inner sense' that influences our bodily actions and responses. The intersections of the subjective, material and social were apparent in this research when participants discussed surgery as a way of reconciling self-identity and social identity. David (age 26), for example, spoke of the fissure between his gender identity and self-bodily image prior to transition:

> Surgery was very important. Because even without
> hormones, the way I presented myself and the way I dressed,
> people would see me as male. But because of my chest I had
> to bind myself up every day and, apart from the discomfort,
> I just felt they shouldn't be there [...]

In articulating the complex relationship between embodiment and gender identification, these narratives resonate with Freud's (1923) notion of 'bodily ego', whereby our sense of 'self' develops through our sense of the body. Grosz (1994) conceptualises this as a 'psychical map', through which our formation of 'self' involves a psychical image of our body. Yet while the understandings and experiences of surgery of several participants in this research suggest that the material body 'matters', as Nataf argues: "the achieved anatomy is a way of relieving the confusion and anxiety, and the body is a point of reference, not a nature" (1996: 45). Although the significance placed upon a congruent relationship between gender identity and bodily appearance is reflected by some participants, the desire for surgery is rarely a straightforward manifestation of 'gender dysphoria'. The only participant to articulate the 'wrong body' experience straightforwardly was Cheryl (age 45), who, in answer to my question 'how do you describe your gender identity?' replied "female trapped in a male body". Significantly, Cheryl had sought medical advice from her GP only four months before

---

our interview and was still waiting for her first appointment with a psychiatrist. Epstein's (1995) application of a Foucauldian analysis is useful for understanding the influence of a medical model upon trans-subjectivities. Through medical surveillance the 'patient' is viewed as a special type of person and individual experience is lost as the person emerges as a "medical type" (Epstein, 1995: 26). Thus personal accounts are written into medical discourse that converts "unclear subjectivity into an interpretable text, which takes precedence over the fragments of human experience" (Epstein, 1995: 29). Power is transferred from the "'speaking subject' to the 'expert'" (Sharpe, 2002: 25) to sustain a 'regime of truth' (Foucault, 1980). In this way, medical case studies do not simply 'record', but work to 'produce' knowledge. As well as constructing trans-subjectivities, this process regulates claims to citizenship. Nevertheless, in critiquing the medical construction of the 'wrong body', it is important to be mindful of the significance of the material body within transgender narratives. In the following section, bodily narratives are explored in relation to the corporeality of transgender experiences.

Bodily transformations

Many participants have spoken of the fissure between their gender identity and self-bodily image prior to transition. Dan (age 37), for example, speaks of bodily discomfort prior to transition:

> I just spent my whole life in front of the mirror thinking 'where's my stubble?' and it was always good for me that my figure was very up and down and I was small on top. But I was always very concerned that I looked as boyish as possible. That's what was important to me. And when I looked in the mirror it was always 'how masculine do I look?'

Like Dan, Philip (age 42) makes explicit the relationship between embodiment and gender identity when discussing pre-transition identity:

> **P:** I'd be really angry if anyone treated me as a woman. So despite my female stockbroker appearance, for want of a better description, if someone came up to me and said or did something; opened the door for me, or ushered me into a seat, or indeed going in a restaurant with a male friend and having him addressed and not me, I would be ready to

punch someone. And this sort of thing would be happening a lot and so frequently I'd be getting really angry and I didn't twig what it was really. I think what was happening was that it felt so totally wrong. It felt emasculating, so I would get really angry. And of course no one would understand it because I looked like I was a female.

S: But did you not connect that anger to your feminist politics? Did you not make sense of these feelings through your feminism?

P: I suppose I did, yeah, 'why should women be treated like that?' But I wasn't a woman, so that's the difference. Because that's not me and it was wrong in that context, you know, 'I'm not a woman and can't you see?' I didn't have anything outside of myself; it all came from within inside me. And it became an absolutely overwhelming need to do something about it.

It is the intensity of embodied dissonance, which can override the feminist concerns of participants such as Philip, that lead the majority of participants to modify their bodies through the use of hormones and/or surgical procedures. For Philip, taking hormones has reinforced his masculine identity: "Well I've felt a lot more solid. I've put on a stone in weight. Yeah, I feel more male physically."

Here bodily transformations can be seen to reconcile self-identity and social identity (Goffman, 1979). Bodily modifications may also bring increased levels of safety and emotional ease as bodily appearance and gender identity meet to confer with normative assumptions around the gendered body; as illustrated by Del (age 44): "It made my life easier; it made my passage through the city and the world smoother and less dangerous."

Body modification through the use of hormones and/or surgery, then, can bring security within a culture that is hostile to gender ambiguity. As Nataf states "very few people can cross-live, get employment successfully and be safe in the streets without hormones and some surgery" (Nataf, 1996: 43). Other participants, however, discuss how the initial exhilaration of taking hormones can give way to more perplexing experiences. The 'real-life experience'[2] demands that while on hormones people present as their desired gender for a significant period before being eligible for surgery. Hormones do not bring immediate physical changes, however, and, in the following quotation, Greg (age 44) details the problems this may bring:

> It was a very frightening time. So psychologically it was hard to say what was down to the hormones. I did go through some depression, part hormonal, part psychological. And you've got the downside of taking hormones, the acne, your whole self esteem, your sense of being an attractive person. And half the people who see you think you're a boy and half [pause]. You're travelling round London on your rail card and half are challenging whether that's your card or not. It's stressful and there's no way you can feel particularly good about yourself at that stage.

The significance placed upon a congruent relationship between gender identity and bodily appearance is reflected in some participants' discussions of the importance of surgical reconstruction. In the following quotation, Lynne (age 67) illustrates how surgical procedures are experienced in relation to physical comfort and wellbeing, and physical and emotional confidence:

> Since I've been post-op I have no problems standing in front of a mirror when I've had a bath or something with nothing on and I'd never have done that as a male. I feel much happier within my body. And I used to suffer from migraines, bad ones, and psoriasis, all gone. I don't get headaches and I've no psoriasis. It was all stress.

Subjective understandings and experiences of surgery articulated here, then, suggest that the material body matters. Yet as Nataf, argues, "The achieved anatomy is a way of relieving the confusion and anxiety, and the body is a point of reference, not a nature" (1996: 45). In thinking about surgical reconstruction as a 'cosmetic' procedure, Halberstam offers a useful way of disengaging the desire for surgery from medical discourses of the 'wrong body' and can be seen to call for a post-identity politics of transsexual surgery:

> The reason that I say its cosmetic surgery is because people are always changing their bodies, especially in America. I suppose that if we considered what we're now calling transsexual surgery as cosmetic, maybe we would take the stigma away. Maybe we wouldn't see it as the

complete, pathological rearrangement of identity, even if it's experienced as such. Maybe we'd begin to see it as a way of organising your body to suit your image of yourself. And then we wouldn't have to have this whole therapeutic intervention, where people are saying, 'Why do you want to become a man? What's wrong with you?' You could say 'Because I prefer the way a penis looks on my body to the way a vagina looks on my body.' (Halberstam, quoted in Nataf, 1996: 56)

Nataf (1996) and Califia (1997) have made similar points in their discussion of gender reassignment surgery as body modification practices, while Boyd develops these arguments to rethink transgender surgeries as forms of 'transmogrification' in order to "acknowledge important similarities, overlaps, resonances, and intersections between a range of modified bodies" (2006: 561).

While chest surgery is a relatively simple and available procedure, the construction of a penis through phalloplasty surgery is a complex and expensive practice. Significantly only one of the male participants in this research had had phalloplasty. For most of the men, phalloplasty was seen to be a risky and unsatisfactory procedure. Greg (age 44), for example, says:

> Phalloplasty is still far from perfect, and at the moment I don't want it. Not because I don't want to have a penis, but I feel it's still not a penis, it doesn't do anything. I mean some do look quite good but there's no surgeon yet who will create a fully functioning sensual, so you can have sexual pleasure, penis through which you can pee and which is erectile. It's just not possible so I just feel it's a massive risk to take 'cos it's a massive procedure.

Other men, such as Dan (age 37), question the relationship between masculinity and male body parts: "I cannot see that having a phalloplasty will then make me say 'right that's it, I'm a man'. [...] I am a man. I'm the man that I want to be."

Like Dan, Amanda (age 45) questions the assumption that surgical reconstruction authenticates gender identity:

> This thing about being complete when you have the op [...] I don't go with that. I think I'm as complete now as I ever will be. I don't really have any other changes that

need to be done that the world needs to know about. My social changes – the side that the world will see – that has now been established and I am supremely comfortable with that.

Far from being uniformly accepted, then, surgery was viewed as problematic by a significant number of participants. In the following quotation, Rebecca (age 55) suggests that there is insufficient discussion within transgender communities about the complexities surgical reconstruction may bring:

> One has to worry that there may be people who have gone down the transsexual route and were reassigned and are having difficulties with that reassignment, who may well have benefited from a more liberal view. I mean, I have come across one or two transsexuals who are desperately unhappy in their new gender role and it's too late. And that's really sad. And the other problem is that so much of our futures are in the hands of medical professionals and I suspect that many lay people take as read that doctors know best and so therefore 'transsexual' is in many ways a medical term, 'that's what the doctor says I am'. And I wouldn't want to say that people follow it like sheep but there is a degree of thoughtlessness about possibilities and they fall into that rut, and they don't question it or ask themselves 'is this what I really want?' It's just a solution to what they see as a problem and it's the only one they're offered, so take it or leave it, it's Hobson's choice.

Rather than being straightforwardly experienced, the desirability of surgery reflects a key area of contention within transgender communities. In this way, some participants spoke of a hierarchy in which surgically reconstructed transgender people renounce the self-identified gender of transgender people who do not wish to go down the surgical route. Gabrielle (age 45) draws attention to a hierarchical politics of identity that is based upon surgical procedures: "There's a horrible pecking order amongst trans people, stereotypes, you know, a pyramid of validity against heterosexual cross-dressers with their suitcase in the garage and the box in the loft, and all those horrible ideas, a sort of elite."

These debates illustrate how definitions of authenticity, which are largely constructed in the light of societal discriminatory discourses and practices, may lend themselves to essentialist identity claims that refute the non-normative identities of others. The discussions here lend support to the findings of Mason-Schrock (1996), which showed how community support groups can construct particular transgendered identities.

While drawing attention to the existence of a hierarchy based upon the ability to 'pass' as non-transgendered, Whittle (1996) has pointed out that transgendered women can never be entirely secure that their former status will not be brought to light. In contrast, Whittle believes that transgendered men do not face the same issues around 'passing': "any transsexual man can take testosterone, grow a beard, have his voice break, and pass anywhere, anytime, with great success" (1996: 63). In the following quotation, Del (age 44) presents a direct challenge to a politics of identity that is based upon notions of authenticity:

> I feel kinship with transsexual communities, because I have a lot of transsexual friends but in some ways there's a political division between how I think and how they think. I'm critical of a hierarchy in transgendered circles based on what surgery you should have. And I think that sometimes transsexual communities promote those concepts. I found myself being very sceptical. I'm not across the board anti-surgery, but I think that if gender wasn't so polarised, if there wasn't such a cultural imperative to be either male or female, that surgery would be less necessary.

Like Del, Rebecca (age 55) is doubtful of the benefits of genital surgical reconstruction. For Rebecca, rejecting the surgical route of transition has enabled increased gender fluidity. She says:

> I suppose my story has changed and matured as time has gone, and my view of my gender has appeared differently to me at different times. In terms of my place in society now in many ways I feel that I have the best of both worlds. I have an inner peace because I'm more congruent in terms of my external description and internal beliefs and I can move in society comfortably in that female role on the whole. It has been a struggle and there have been problems along the way, but also by not losing the male side of my being I can call on that and I can become very male at times [laugh], which is quite confusing for people who may be threatening me because they really don't know how to handle me and

that is a bonus. I see that as a benefit because I don't live in fear of being acknowledged as a male, or having male characteristics, should I say.

Narratives of gender fluidity such as Del and Rebecca's provide the springboard for the theorisation of transgender as the paragon of queer whereby transgender is signposted as a signifier of gender performance within queer analyses of identity.

Gender performance and hierarchies of authenticity

For some participants, transition is a process that enables gender play. Gabrielle (age 45), for example, says:

> The interesting thing was by the time of being a year post-op and being much more secure in myself and having been to San Francisco, I dragged up as a guy. I did drag king for the night. And that was very liberating for me, because to have reached that confidence to be able to do it was amazing.

Svar (age 41) links his initial use of testosterone to experimental gender performance:

> I decided to experiment. I'm an artist, I have an alternative lifestyle and I've always been experimental, and in a way my own transition reflects my work. I actually went to a friend of mine who was a good old female-to-male transsexual in his 50s and I scrounged some hormones from him and went up to a drugs, needles, place and got the right syringe, the right needle, and I had my first shot, which was an illegal one, unprescribed, let's say. And then I decided to go for it. I had no nasty side effects and I didn't turn into the incredible hulk, I just felt good, so I decided to do it some more. At that time as well we started a club in 'Madame Jo Jo's' called 'Club Naïve' and it was all about, it was a drag club, so it was for women to drag up as men, drag kings, and, you know, women who didn't want to drag up, so you had femmes. It was really playing with the butch and femme thing, playing with gender.

In discussing his current understanding of identity, however, Svar goes on to address how gender subjectivity may shift through the stages of transition:

> […] when I talk to you I tell you that I'm a female-to-male transsexual. I used to just refer to that medically but as the years have gone by in actual fact that is who I am. I was transgendered for years and years and I can still use that and it's good fun and there is that good fun in it and that has to be acknowledged. Whereas the transsexual thing, I mean, not that I'm not enjoying my transition, but it's got much deeper implications, with family, in society, sports, swimming, going to the beach, surgery. It's a whole different ball game.

Similarly Philip (age 42) suggests that his experiences of gender performance have altered through the stages of transition:

> I think I'm a bit bored with it, with dressing up and playing a role. But I think also that the more I've transitioned the less I think it's me, to be honest. I mean, if I get dressed up and go down to the 'Way Out Club' [cross-dressing club] I just feel like a total trannie, you know, if I put a mini-skirt and high heels on. And I wouldn't particularly expect anybody to see me as anything else.

Rebecca (age 55) provides a further distinction between her gender expression and what she perceives as transvestite:

> And you see people down Canal Street [gay street in Manchester, UK] in their beehive wigs and their mini-skirts and all of that. And they look a million dollars and I wish them the best of luck, but that is not me. I have developed a style of my own and this is my life. For many of those people it is an activity which they will only do at a certain time; they are what I would consider to be transvestites and that is fine. But for me this is my life and I've never wanted to dress like that anyway, it would never enter my head to wear those clothes.

While Rebecca presents an impartial distinction between her gender expression and the gender performances of transvestism, other participants are more aggressive in differentiating between the identities of transsexual and transvestite. Amelia (age 47), for example, says:

> I just think those groups [transsexuals and transvestites] have got nothing in common. What have I got in common with a heterosexual guy who gets off on wearing a dress? Not a lot really. I've got no objection to him doing that if that turns him on, but please don't expect me to call you 'Gloria' and 'She' because you're not. Please don't ask me to treat everyone as my brothers and sisters.

Stryker (2006) shows that there has been a strong history of mixed membership within support groups in the UK. In contrast to groups that developed during the 1970s in the US, British support groups were made up of "[...] not only part-time crossers, but also pre-operative transsexuals, and various others who occupied diverse niches within the gender system" (Stryker, 2006: 5). Yet, 30 years on, such diversity can be seen to have waned. Gendered appearance, and particularly clothing, is positioned as important in distinguishing between transsexual and transvestite identities. As well as drawing on the importance of clothes, Karen (age 31) uses temporality and permanence, and depth of desire to differentiate between transvestite practices and transsexualism:

> Transsexuals wear the clothes that they feel comfortable in and they don't really want to be outlandish or whatever. Transvestites wear the clothes to get out of their usual lives once or twice a month and I can understand that but they don't really want to change anything, they're quite happy with their gender. [...] But there is some continuum. [...] There are transvestites who are thinking about being transsexual. I think there's a continuum on all sorts of things and gender is no exception.

Roen (2001b) has discussed tensions in the transgender community around a duality of 'either/or' (which supports a gender binary and emphasises the need to 'pass') and 'neither/nor' (which criticises the gender binary and values subversion). Roen's empirical work on transgender identities in New Zealand shows that such dual thinking "fails[s] to take into account the diversity of contexts and experience of transpeople" (2001b: 521). These discussions highlight the fissure between the theoretical positioning of transgender as a subversive act of gender transgression and the subjectivities of those transgender people who articulate notions of authentic (trans)gendered identities. There are similarities here with debates around assimilation among lesbian and gay communities. In Karen's narrative, transvestite practices are positioned as transsexualism's frivolous 'other'; however, unlike Amelia, Karen suggests a possible continuum between these different identity categories. Echoing Karen, Gabrielle (age 45) stresses the need to move beyond hierarchical claims of gender authenticity:

> Because I know what it feels like to be excluded from things I can't understand why people who have an experience of being excluded then become exclusive themselves. I can't relate to that. I don't want to become an oppressor and I certainly don't approve of the idea of a sort of strata of acceptability and realness, and success and inadequacy and adequacy in anything.

These comments question the finding of Gagne and Tewksbury that "to 'blend in' to society as a woman was something that most transgenderists, especially transsexuals, saw as an ultimate goal" (1997: 502). While these sentiments were reflected by a small number of participants in my research, assimilating into a gender binary model was not a universal concern. Indeed, assimilation was often a contentious political issue, as the following comments by Amanda (age 45) illustrate:

> The one thing that disgusts me about our community is that some trans women – I don't know that many trans men – but some trans women, do disappear into the woodwork and don't want to be identified as trans anymore. I understand why they do that but it annoys me, it really annoys me. I will never ever do that. I promise that I will never opt out of the trans community. Hand on heart, I will not do that because I'm very comfortable with trans people and will always want trans people around me because they're my home. They are what I am and I don't want to lose my home [...].

Similarly, Jamieson Green (2006) forsakes his ability to 'pass' and talks of the importance of being visible as a transgender man. While Gagne and Tewksbury found that "among most transsexuals and cross-dressers, there was an overwhelming desire to pass as women, for it was through such interactions that femininity and treatment as a woman were achieved" (1997: 501), this research found that concerns around assimilating among transgender women often diminished through the stages of transition. Karen (age 31) speaks of her lessening concerns around assimilation, and articulates shifting ideas around gendered appearance and behaviour through transition:

> I think I've probably learnt that I'm not really that different from before. I can still be quite aggressive. I still have a competitive side. Initially I went way over to the feminine side and became really girlie, which isn't me. But now I've got a bit of male and a bit of female in me which has been interesting for me and I've settled down to where I am.

These narratives suggest that while identity is experienced through gendered presentation, rather than being rigid, the relationship between gender identity and presentation shifts and evolves through transition. Research findings support Nataf's comment that "the form gender identity and role finally take can be more or less fixed or fluid, depending upon the individual" (1996: 20). Transgender diversity can be further explored by analysing the ways in which transgender identities are linguistically articulated.

Articulating gender diversity

Sociological accounts of 'identity work' (Snow and Anderson, 1987) explore the ways in which language is used to construct an image of the self (Dunn, 2001). Applying this model to transgender practices indicates the ways in which a diversity of gender identity practices are discursively constructed. A range of trans-subjectivities and identity positions are brought into being through the various ways in which participants describe their gender identities. In answer to my question 'how do you describe your gender identity?' only three out of the 30 people interviewed described themselves solely as 'female' or 'male', or use the nouns 'woman' or 'man'. Among these are Amelia (age 47), who answers "I'm me and I'm female" and Tony (age 39), who states "I'm a man. I'm about as male as you probably get. There is no ambiguity at all as far as I'm concerned." Although Philip (age 42) answers "I'd say I was male," he also states that "I don't like labels and I'm getting more and more interested in stepping to the side of that."

Many participants describe their gender identity as 'FtM' or 'MtF', or as 'trans' men or women, to articulate their transgender subjectivities. Dan (age 37), for example, says he is "male but I'd describe myself as being FtM rather than straight male", while Lynne (age 67) describes herself as a 'transfemale'. Only one participant, Amanda (age 45), straightforwardly uses the term 'transsexual', saying that she described herself as "a pre-operative transsexual"; however, she also says: "I think male and female components exist in all of us." Thus when the term 'transsexual' is employed, it is rarely used as a single signifier. Rather, the term 'transsexual' is qualified in a variety of ways. Svar (age 41), for example, says, "well, simply I would describe myself as male. But I would also describe myself as female-to-male transsexual, but mostly as male", while Paul (age 34) says: "Well, I guess officially I'm transsexual, but I don't give it a lot of thought on a day-to-day basis. Sometimes I forget. I just consider myself an ordinary guy really, but, yes, transsexual, female-to-male-transsexual."

Although Paul relates to the impact of an 'official' model of transgender upon self-identity, rather than unreservedly accepting the medicalisation of transgender, most participants contest medical terminology. While narratives indicate how identity is constructed through dominant discourse, they also indicate that self-identity may be reflexively defined in opposition to that which is discursively imposed. Karen (age 31) discusses how she uses the term 'transsexual' in order to offer a simple explanation of her identity:

> I use that term [transsexual] for other people who like to categorise but I see myself as female now or whatever. I don't think we should be categorised into transsexuals. [...] Transsexualism is something that has been coined to explain what I'm going through so I never want to be termed as transsexual really.

Here Karen presents a critique of the term 'transsexual' by locating it as a constructed concept developed through medical discourse. These narratives suggest that identity is a relational process, understood and practised within social contexts. As Butler states: "the act of self-reporting and the act of self-observation take place in relation to a certain audience, with a certain audience as the imagined recipient, before a certain audience for whom a verbal and visual picture of selfhood is produced" (2001: 629). Accordingly, when I asked 'how do you define your gender identity?' several participants replied that their answer would depend upon who was asking the question. William (age 25), for example, says: "It depends who's asking. I would say male and then I would say trans man if the person was on the scene. Yeah the term trans man comes very close to the end, behind the male, but definitely male." Whereas Bernadette (age 71) says: "It depends who

I'm talking to, whether it's technically knowledgeable people or people who are less sophisticated and have some idea of their own about what the terminology is."

While William's description of his gender identity is contingent upon subcultural understandings, Bernadette's understanding of her identity as arising from a medical condition leads her to contextualise her self-identity in relation to degrees of medical knowledge. For both William and Bernadette, identity descriptions are dependent upon the 'insider' knowledge of their audience, although the subject of authority is divergently located in each instance. Moreover, the social contextualisation of identity may be problematic for transgender people due to ways in which their self-identities are often refuted by others. Gabrielle (age 45), for example, says: "I mean, words are really tricky. I'd say I'm a trans lesbian, but I don't know because it's like 'Who controls the boundaries of what is anything?'"

In discussing the variety of terms he has used to describe his gender identity, Del (age 44) also locates identity as a relational concept:

> **S:** Can you tell me something about how you describe your gender identity?
>
> **D:** I think in a way it depends on who I'm talking to and what they understand. 'Cos there are lots of different levels so there's not just one way in which I describe my identity. I've called myself a gender terrorist, I've called myself intersex by design, an intentional mutation, FtM, but not transsexual, and FtM is more about how people perceive me. I call myself a hermaphrodyke sometimes. I've been a lesbian or a dyke; I've been a queer dyke. Queer is probably the term I feel best describes me. I could call myself a queer trannie boy. Everything is qualified in one way or another [laugh].

Del's narrative indicates the ways in which some trans embodied identities are consciously constructed on the borderlands of gender. Bornstein (1994) also blows apart any categorisation of sex as defined by biological genitalia and articulates a diversity of gendered bodies that are peripherally located against the comfort of a gendered home:

> Most folks would define a man by the presence of a penis or some form of penis. Some would define a woman by the presence of a vagina or some form of vagina. It's not

that simple though. I know several women in San Francisco who have penises. Many wonderful men in my life have vaginas. And there are quite a few people whose genitals fall somewhere between penises and vaginas. What are *they?* (Bornstein, 1994: 56–7, italics in original)

Bornstein employs queer theory's deconstruction of identity categories: "I know I'm not a man–about that much I'm very clear, and I've come to the conclusion that I'm probably not a woman either, at least not according to a lot of people's rules on this sort of thing" (1994: 8), and reflects poststructuralist and postmodern notions of agency-driven gender fluidity: "When I get too tired of not having an identity I take one on" (1994: 39). Bornstein thus articulates herself not in the 'wrong body', nor as belonging to a 'third sex', but as a 'gender outlaw'.

Stryker (2006) discusses the development of such varied language forms in relation to a range of social and cultural shifts that took place in the 1990s:

> The emergence of transgender studies in the 1990s was one such moment of change, when socio-political activism, coupled with brad and seemingly unrelated shifts in material conditions, worked in concert to create the possibility of new performative utterances, unprecedented things to say, unexpected language games, and a heteroglossic outpouring of gender positions from which to speak. Previously people who occupied transgender positions were compelled to be the referents in the language games of other senders and addressees [...]. (Stryker, 2006: 11)

The linguistical queering of gender is evident in a range of autobiographical, political and cultural commentary by transgender writers throughout the 1990s (Stone, 1991; Feinberg, 1992; Bornstein, 1994; Califia, 1997; Wilchins, 1997), who articulated new and creative models of living beyond the gender binary. Ekins and King (2006) compare their own empirical findings with those of American anthropologist Bolin (1994, 1998). Bolin's work (1998) identified three categories of identification for transgender people: the transsexual, the heterosexual transvestite or the TV (transvestite)/TS (transsexual) dichotomy. The latter category was made up of people who were overtly concerned with their positioning within this dichotomy. In her later work Bolin found that there had been a shift from this dichotomy to transgender diversity (Ekins and King, 2006). Assessing their own empirical research, Ekins and King (2006) connect with Bolin's findings, stating similar differences in their work between 1975 and 1985 and that between 1993 and 1995. The research on which this book draws can be seen to show further cultural shifts away from the identity of transsexual and in terms of a move towards transgender diversity.

While many participants in this research offer a range of linguistic possibilities to articulate gender diversity, others still express frustration at the limitations of existing classifying systems that rest upon a male/female gender binary. Rebecca (age 55) said:

> The thing that defeats me is language at the end of the day. There isn't a term which I'm absolutely content and happy with. I usually describe myself as transgendered and now I feel reasonably content with that description. In terms of my gender bias I suppose I feel much closer to the female end of the spectrum, but I do not consider myself to be a woman, neither can I believe that I am a man. And that is not an issue of sitting on the fence and not making my mind up because I do believe that this whole gender issue is a spectrum but there isn't a word which describes that.

Within these narratives, identity formation can be seen to be complexly situated and experienced. Thus these research findings challenge those of Gagne and Tewksbury, who comment that "given the limited range of identities available to them, it is interesting, but not surprising, that the overwhelming majority of transgendered individuals adhere to traditional conceptualizations of sex and gender" (1997: 504). Further, these findings contrast with those of Lewins, who, from his study into the experiences of transgender women, argues that "[…] all [transsexuals] revealed a deep structural similarity in the necessity for the body and one's gender to correspond. Such correspondence is to a conventional image of feminine women [...]" (1995: 144). Moreover, when talking about articulating self-identities, many participants in this research differ from those in Wilson's study who "did not want to be 'marked by' their difference and did not understand their gender in terms of a new gender category" (Wilson, 2002: 427). To the contrary, this research suggests that many transgender people articulate gender identities that fall beyond a traditional binary framework. Yet (trans)gender identity is experienced through the corporeal body. In this respect, I concur with Halberstam that:

The end of identity in this gender fiction does not mean
a limitless and boundless shifting of positions and forms;
rather it indicates the futility of stretching terms like lesbian
or gay or straight or male or female across vast fields of
experience, behavior and self-understanding. It further hints
at the inevitable exclusivity of any claim to identity and
refuses the respectability of being named, identified, known.
(Halberstam, quoted in Nataf, 1996: 57)

Conclusion

Halberstam's comments can be read as a caution against an analysis of
transgender that positions transgender identities as infinitely fluid. This
is significant when considering the divergent identity positions and
varied subjectivities that fall under the broad umbrella of 'transgender'.
Transgender identities are cut through with difference, while the
concept of 'difference' itself is contingent upon social, cultural and
temporal factors. Halberstam's cautionary note is borne out by this
research, which indicates a tension between the conceptualisation
of identity as fluid and the subjective investment in identity. Thus
discussions of transgender identity formation in this chapter show the
tensions between rejecting and holding on to identity.

While some participants clearly speak of the pleasures of gender
transition, and articulate identities that are fluidly situated and
practised, others relate constancy of gender identification and gendered
embodiment. Rather than signifying universal transgression or dominant
gender conformity, this research suggests that transgender identity
positions and subjectivities are contingent to divergent (trans)gendered
experiences. The corporeal body is central to transgender sensibilities,
and the body is experienced, managed and modified through subjective
and social understandings of gender. Likewise, transgender identities
can be seen to be constructed and negotiated both through and in
opposition to medical discourse and practice, affective relations, and
social, cultural and political understandings and networks. The emphasis
upon embodied understandings and experiences before, during
and following transition supports Prosser's (1998) critique of queer
theoretical approaches to transgender, which have often neglected the
material and embodied contours of transgender lives. However, the
narratives considered in this chapter also point to the importance of
developing an analysis of transgender that moves beyond a framework of
gendered authenticity to transgress the deviant/transgressive binary.

Though the similarities and differences in some of these identities may overlap, convergence is structured through social, cultural and individual time and place. Moreover, some identities may be diametrically opposed to prevent social or political convergence. A central theme emerging from narratives of transgender experiences and identity thus relates to the importance of developing a queer sociological approach to transgender, whereby an emphasis upon identity transgression is accompanied by attentiveness to the lived experiences within multiple subject positions.

FOUR

Gender identities and feminism

As was explored in the previous chapter, participants in the research on which this book draws used a variety of terms to describe their gender identity. While some participants identified as 'man' or 'woman', most used the prefix of 'trans' before gender nouns, or employed the terms FtM or MtF to articulate the ways in which their gender identities were distinct. This chapter further develops previous discussions of gendered understanding by exploring participants' discussions of the relationship between transgender and feminism in order to consider the ways in which transgender and feminism are theoretically correlated and connected through lived experiences. In this way, feminism is utilised as a lens through which to analyse both subjective (trans)gender identities and the divergent links between feminism and trans masculinity and trans femininity. Feminism and lesbian, gay and bisexual movements are significant here as social movements that challenge the meanings of gender. Meanings of feminism are explored in this chapter and movements around sexuality in the next.

Research data is initially analysed to address the ways in which transgender male participants articulate their experiences of second-wave feminism. To posit the argument that there are important connections between feminist concerns and transgender practices and experiences, the latter part of this section moves on to draw out some of the ways in which these participants relate to contemporary feminism by looking at how they situate themselves in relation to feminist concerns. The next section examines these issues in relation to the narratives of transgender women. The separation of the narratives of transgender men and women is purposefully employed with the aim of distinguishing between (trans)gendered identity positions and subjectivities. While there are common themes within feminist thinking on transgender masculinity and transgender femininity, and similarities between the experiences and understandings of feminism for transgender men and women, I believe that these gendered narratives merit individual consideration. As discussed in the previous chapter, transgender identities and subjectivities are cut through with multiple variables. In examining transgender men and women's narratives independently of each other, my aim here is to pay heed to (trans)gendered difference. In doing this I also hope to go some way towards remedying the tendency within analyses of transgender to focus on the experiences of trans women (Ekins and King, 1997), and thus to marginalise the experiences of trans masculinity.

While the relationship between transgender people and feminism is a contentious issue, this research suggests connections between feminist concerns and the 'things that matter' to many of the transgender men and women interviewed. Many transgender male participants, for example, articulate an involvement in feminist and/or lesbian communities, and particularly within queer subcultures, before and/or during transition. However, they largely convey the decades of second-wave feminism as socially and politically problematic. Yet many of these participants express a continued involvement within feminist politics and queer communities, and locate contemporary feminism as a less hostile personal and political space. Findings further show that many transgender women have a heightened awareness of the feminist critiques of transgender femininity, discussed in Chapter One, and consciously attempt to construct gendered expressions that are in contrast to stereotypical models of femininity. The concluding section of the chapter proposes that findings from this research trouble feminist critiques of transgender practices. Thus I argue for a comprehensive incorporation of transgender experiences into future analyses of gender.

Living through the sex wars: narratives of trans men

As feminist attention during the 1980s focused on sexuality, feminist politics became dominated by fierce debates around the meanings of lesbianism and lesbian sexual practices, the key protagonists being radical feminists and lesbians associated with a range of sexual subcultures. Findings from this research resonate in showing how these debates cut through many contemporary transgender male narratives.

While not suggesting that trans men as a homogeneous group have a pre-transition identity as either feminists or lesbians, this research identifies a recognisable pattern of trans male involvement in feminist and lesbian communities. This research speaks of divisions between a politics of sexuality that was highly influenced by a radical feminist perspective and a range of subcultural feminist and/or lesbian communities that were more in tune with burgeoning queer theory. Yet subcultural sexual communities were not always consistent in their queer politics when it came to gender diversity. Many participants talk about their involvement in feminism, although they are precise in pointing out that they were not 'radical feminists'. Likewise participants have related their former experiences within lesbian communities, although they have qualified this by saying they identified as 'dyke' or 'queer', rather than as 'lesbian'. Svar (age 41), for example, says:

> I think the first time I fell in love it was with a woman. That was when I was 15, so I was a baby lesbian for a while and then when I came up to London to go to art school, when I was 18, then I just started hitting the gay scene and I have quite an extensive dyke history, you might say, in the London scene. I'd say more dyke than lesbian. I was never really one of these, you know, goody-goody sort of wholesome shoes, sort of lesbian as such, I always considered myself more as a dyke. I was never a lesbian separatist, sort of like man hater, angry, even though I was at Greenham Common [women's peace camp, UK] all those years ago [laugh].

Dissociation with radical feminism can be analysed as an effect of Raymond's (1980) work that, as I addressed in Chapter One, instigated a feminist politics of hostility towards transgender people. Participants' experiences of this time also resound with the political and cultural debates within second-wave feminism around stylistic expressions and gendered images. In talking about his involvement during the 1980s within subcultural feminist and lesbian communities, Philip (age 42), for example, remembers arguments over appropriate fashion:

> I used to wear lots of different costumes and I always used to play around with image and one of my images was mini-skirt, high heels and fishnets and that was at a time when lesbian feminists were saying women shouldn't wear make-up, so therefore I went and did all that to annoy them. Some of what I was doing was a reaction to that attitude, 'cos I was in the gay scene. So I was part of the people who wanted to wind the radical feminists up, basically.

While still living as a woman, Philip was aware of the constraints of radical feminist thought. Part of this awareness concerned how transgender people were understood in the stand-offs between radical feminist and pro-sex feminist and lesbian communities. Philip continues:

That's reminded me of something that happened in the '80s. There was the Fallen Angel, one of the first gay pubs that existed, in Islington, and on Tuesday night or something it was women only and 'SM Dykes' decided to go down there and all these women knew we were coming and we had a transsexual with us, 'cos we happily included trans women, and we walked in and it was full of women and they were all silent and there were only about six of us. And this woman stood up and said something like 'will all women who object to the presence of these women now leave' and they all stood up one by one and filed out, it took about 10 minutes. And that was also directed at the presence of this transsexual as well.

As I discussed in Chapter One, Rubin's (1989) discussion of a sexual hierarchy illustrates how certain sexual practices are privileged above others. Although Rubin's schema does not take account of transgender identities beyond those of the transsexual and transvestite – and it somewhat conflates transgender practices with sexuality – her discussion of a Western system of sexual stratification importantly draws attention to the ways in which feminist thought has failed to address levels of discrimination. Indeed, as Philip's account shows, feminist and/or lesbian communities frequently employed their own systems of sexual and gender stratification. Exclusion based on a social ordering of sexual and gendered practices appears as a frequent theme in transgender men's stories. Paul (age 34) discussed the reactions of feminist and lesbian friends after his transition: "I kind of had mixed reactions from the lesbian community. They almost kind of laughed in my face. I remember one girl who just couldn't deal with any of it and that's when I'd already been on hormones six months, so, you know, I thought 'well, bye, bye'."

In the following section of our interview, Svar (age 41) explicitly addresses the feminist critique of transgender masculinity as an unethical process through which women are able to access male power and privilege, thus contextualising the political debates couched in Paul's account:

Sv: There was actually from the dyke, feminist scene, there was quite a lot of opposition to female-to-male transsexuality. I mean, one friend did actually say to me 'oh I see, so you're abandoning the female race then?'

S: So did you experience problems around acceptance from within the lesbian community?

Sv: With some, but then I'd just say 'I'm not doing this to myself to create a master race or something'. But yeah, there was some accusations, you know, 'you're trying to have power, get power'. And it was kind of quite shocking really, when you say 'Look, I've made this decision because I'm trying to deal with something in myself and I can do without all that, I can do without that attitude, what I could do with is your support here, you know, how can you say these things?'

The experiences of Del (age 44) illustrate how feminist critiques, such as those discussed by Svar, collapse divergent transgender masculinities and heteronormative white male identities:

I've had experiences fairly recently where close friends who're dykes, I realised after five years that they were having a problem with my gender identity and that they really didn't understand where I was coming from and they were presuming that I was like this kind of straight white man. And a magazine that I have contributed towards since its beginning didn't want my work any more and I was really shocked. That group of people who had the magazine, I go way, way back with them and I was shocked, absolutely shocked that they would do this. And there are clubs that friends of mine are going to and I want to go to and I can't and this is something that's a real hold over from lesbian separatism in the 1970s and 1980s in this country. It's ridiculous. And it's funny because people who probably weren't even born then are forcing these boundaries. I see it as lesbians still feel very much under threat, so instead of building bridges they're erecting barricades.

Del directly engages with the debates around sex that fuelled feminist and lesbian politics during the 1980s and 1990s. While radical feminists and political lesbians characterised lesbianism as a political position (Rich, 1979; Leeds Revolutionary Feminists, 1981), other lesbians argued against de-sexualisation by emphasising the dynamics of erotic agency within lesbian practices (Califia, 1981; Rubin, 1989). As radical feminism infused cultural battles around sexuality, debates around sexual imagery and practice dominated second-wave feminist and lesbian concerns. Significantly, transgender men and women often became the focus of contestations around exclusion and community belonging. Transgender practices trouble the authenticity of biological 'sex' and raise key questions about the construction and ownership of gender identities. A radical feminist response to these complexities has been to reinforce a gender and sexual binary model in order to regulate gendered belonging. In questioning a unified concept of gender, transgender practices pose central questions to feminist theories and politics of identity. As Feinberg states: "The development of the trans movement has raised a vital question that's being discussed in women's communities all over the country. How is woman defined? The answer we give may determine the course of women's liberation for decades to come" (1996: 109).

Although exclusion from feminist and lesbian communities is a recurring theme, some of the same participants concurrently express an ongoing professional and personal involvement within lesbian and particularly queer communities. Del (age 44), for example, says:

> I feel that there's a filmmaking community, a queer filmmaking community that I feel part of. I'm still on the lesbian photography show touring around. I'm on the lesbian artist news group that I've always been on. That's part of my history and that's part of who I've been and I've produced a lot of work within those communities, I don't see any reason to leave them.

The importance of belonging to established networks is further reflected when Del contrasts his experiences of exclusion from British lesbian cultures with continued acceptance while working for lesbian magazines in the US:

> I'd been in America working for lesbian magazines and taking pictures for them and it was great 'cos in California I didn't feel any separation. I was working for *On Our Backs* [lesbian sex magazine] and I did a porno shoot with these four young dykes, one of whom is transgendered butch, or might become transsexual I don't know, but it was kind of like a butch/femme photo shoot and they were getting down to it and I had no sense that there was any [...] They were absolutely not uncomfortable with me. I was still a role model for them and my gender seemed not to matter.

> I seemed to get a lot of respect from the youngsters, like
> from teenage to 30 years old. They weren't having any
> problems with me.

As some feminist, queer and transgender communities were developing
fierce critiques of an essentialist approach and developing varied
gendered and sexual identities and practices, some academic feminists
proposed a politics of sexual diversity in which gender and sexuality
were theorised as distinct though overlapping categories. Indeed it is
no coincidence that feminist calls for caution around the ownership
of gendered and sexual identities were frequently raised in the late
1980s and throughout the 1990s. Here the divisive rhetoric of radical
feminism can be seen to give way to a more considered enquiry into
the questions that transgender raises for the non-trans who 'came of
age' during this politically highly charged era. On the ground, non-
normative gender and sexual identities such as S/M, butch dyke, lesbian
boy, drag butch and drag king, initiated by lesbian subcultures, were
influential in the unfolding of feminist perspectives that attempted to
move away from the positioning of transgender as suspect. Themes
here resound with Halberstam's (1998) discussion of the frequent
connections between non-normative gender identities and sexual
subcultures. I do not, however, wish to suggest an overall liberalism
towards transgender within feminist and lesbian politics. Rather, it
is important to recall that during the 1980s and early 1990s, radical
feminist theory held widespread popular appeal within feminist and
lesbian politics. Thus this research indicates that *despite* transphobic
rhetoric, some transgender men were able to find a home and, indeed,
were often key players within certain feminist and lesbian communities
before, during and, in some cases, following, transition.

Writing about the invisibility of transgender men within feminist
theory, Cromwell argues that:

> Female-to-male transpeople constitute a prime subject for
> feminist thought and methods, if for no reason than being
> born biologically female or assigned at birth as female.
> Feminists should be concerned that male-dominated
> discourses have made female-to-male transpeople virtually
> invisible. (Cromwell, 1999: 9)

Wilchins, likewise, draws parallels between feminism and transgender:
"gender-queerness would seem to be a natural avenue for feminism to
contest Woman's equation with nurturance, femininity, reproduction:

in short to trouble the project of Man" (2002: 57). Echoing Butler, she states that it is because transgender questions the concept of woman that feminism has not taken this line of reasoning: "[...] queering Woman threatens the very category on which feminism depends" (Wilchins, 2002: 57). Similarly, Monro and Warren state: "Transgender poses a serious threat to feminism. Feminisms, particularly radical feminism, are based on the notion of an unequal gender-binaried system. Transgender scrambles gender binaries and opens up the space beyond or between simple male–female categorization" (2004: 354).

This research suggests that transgender masculinity is significant for feminism because some transgender men continue to identify as feminists. Del (age 44), for example, says: "Women feel betrayed, or that I've left them, or that I think there's something wrong with being a woman, which I absolutely don't think that there is. I mean what my work is about is female empowerment. I will always be a feminist."

Halberstam (1998) points out that historically FtM transition represented social and economic mobility, and gender and sexual conservatism. Halberstam rightly cautions against the supposition that FtM transition per se is an indicator of gender and sexual radicalism. Nevertheless, in talking about identity, politics, values and relationships, many of the men I spoke with articulate masculinities that are distinct from traditional notions of male power or privilege. As Del (age 44) notes, the interaction of a feminist transgender masculinity with a more traditional masculinity can be troubling:

> And then of course there's the way in which men don't guard what they say when they're with someone they think is a man. Even my hairdresser who knows, my barber, he's told me about rape, rapes that he's committed when he was a kid, you know getting the girls drunk.

Del's points connect with Hale's consideration that "for some FtMs one of the more disconcerting aspects of social and medical transition is the extent to which we become privy to displays of non-transsexual men's sexism as our gender presentations and embodiments come to elicit attributions as men, fellows of our fellows" (1998: 118). A comparable theme arises when participants employ a feminist perspective to discuss the precarious aspects of gender roles in relation to their intimate relationships with women, as illustrated in the following section of my interview with Del (age 44):

D: It's hard. I'm in a relationship now that I feel like the man, I'm getting things that men get and it makes me wonder would I get these if I hadn't taken testosterone?

S: What sort of things?

D: Would I be in this kind of relationship? Would someone be doing my laundry? I've never had anyone doing my laundry before. And now, is it just a coincidence or [pause]?

S: Is that problematic for you?

D: It is problematic, yeah, as a feminist it's problematic.

Similarly, Svar (age 41) says of his relationship with his partner:

She treated me sometimes a bit too like a guy and since then we've actually talked about this and I've had to say, you know, 'I am not one of "these" men, I am not like that, I am not a man's man. You seem to forget that I actually was a female human being for longer than you have been a female human being, so don't treat me like that.'

These stories disturb the claims of renunciation that are central to feminist critiques of FtM transition. Thus, as Monro and Warren argue, transgender: "[…] highlights the flaws in some types of feminist theory, for example, the simplistic equation of masculinity with oppression" (2004: 355). Moreover, underlying a feminist critique of transgender is the knowledge that some transgender men have been actively involved in feminist and lesbian cultures. The argument thus goes that transgender men are negating their feminist politics for male privileges (Raymond, 1980, 1994; Jeffreys, 1997). Rather than reflecting hegemonic assimilation, however, findings from this research show that some transgender men actively explore the distinct meanings of transgender masculinity. Del (age 44), for example, clearly distinguishes his masculinity from normative masculine models:

You have to understand that someone like me is never going to be able to access real male privilege, I found that out when, even though I was wearing a suit and a tie, when I was travelling back from LA to London and I wanted to get an upgrade, well, I'm not alpha male. You have a six-foot man come next to me, stand next to me, and we are another species. And I can't even really impersonate that kind of man. So, I will always be beta male or epsilon male or whatever.

Findings challenge the other mainstay of feminist critiques of transgender practices, that transgender men and women seek to ape traditional gender roles (Raymond, 1980, 1994; Hausman, 1995; Jeffreys, 1997). Rather than reflecting an imitative agenda, however, participants have frequently reflected on the distinguishing characteristics of transgender masculinity, as shown in the following section of my interview with Dan (age 37):

> **D:** I would describe myself as FtM as opposed to straight male: Because of my background and my upbringing it gives me more depth than just being bio male and I think that that's an important distinction. So while I want to be perceived and understood and taken totally as male, I will never be 100% male because of my background.

> **S:** Can you tell me more about that distinction?

> **D:** I suppose there's a lot greater awareness. It's to do with female conditioning, being brought up in a gentler society, a more caring environment, being more aware of people, what they're doing, how they're feeling, if something's wrong, a greater intuition, which I can also observe with other FtMs that I can't see with bio men.

While Dan's distinction between transgender and non-trans masculinities rests on his perception of how non-trans masculinity is 'acted-out', William's (age 25) differentiation relates to degrees of gendered reflexivity. In the following quotation, William positions reflexive gendered understandings among transgender people against a lack of gendered awareness in non-trans people: "The trans thing, there's a lot more of a blurring of these boundaries of what men and women are. A lot of people in the world don't think about their own identity enough and outside of the trans community there's a lot of people who don't think about gender."

Work that deconstructs a singular model of masculinity is significant to my points here, as are empirical studies of non-normative masculine trajectories (Connell, 1995; Halberstam, 1998; Maltz, 1998). The place of men within feminism has long been disputed; fuelled by the insistence that "one must inhabit a female body to have the experiences that makes one a feminist" (Bart et al, cited in Adu-Pou, 2001: 163). Yet, as I explored in Chapter One, the past decade has witnessed significant theoretical opposition to the conflation of 'sex' and 'gender'. Theorists of masculinity (Schacht and Ewing, 1998; Adu-Pou, 2001) and pro-feminist men (Hearn, 1989; Seidler, 1989) have problematised the exclusion of men from feminism by exploring how male involvement in feminism requires personal and political transformations that, in themselves, can be seen to disturb the concept of a unitary male sensibility. Similarly, a central theme expressed by the majority of transgender male participants has been the wish to stand aside from hegemonic masculinity, or, in other words, not to behave or be seen as 'typical' men. While it is important to live and be seen as male, then, a key area of concern raised is to be understood as different men.

Riding the waves: narratives of trans women

As I explored in the previous section, the impact of a radical feminist attack on transgender practices was both personally and politically problematic for transgender men. Similarly, feminist and/or lesbian transgender women frequently found themselves excluded from feminist and lesbian communities. At the core of feminist discussions around transgender femininity lay debates about the concept of 'woman'. In exploring the marginalised histories, experiences and social and political demands of women, second-wave feminism applied 'woman' as a fixed category to differentiate against the particulars of 'man'. As Butler remarks: "For the most part, feminist theory has assumed that there is some existing identity, understood through the category of women, who not only initiates feminist interests and goals within discourse, but constitutes the subject for whom political representation is pursued" (1990: 1).

Accordingly, the definition of 'woman' became inextricably tied to biological 'sex'. For Raymond, this meant a denial of self-gender identifications that differed from that as defined at birth. Raymond's biological essentialism fractures, however, through her frequent recourse to gender role socialisation. While arguing that transsexual women cannot be 'authentic' women because of their chromosomal balance, she additionally states that they cannot be acknowledged as women due their lack of female socialisation: "We know that we are women who are born with female chromosomes and anatomy, and that whether or not we are socialised to be so-called normal women, patriarchy has treated and will treat us like women. Transsexuals have not had this same history" (Raymond, 1980: 114). Her fiercest criticisms are directed at transsexual women who identify as feminist and/ or as lesbian: "The transsexually constructed lesbian–feminist may have renounced femininity but not masculinity and masculinist behaviour (despite deceptive appearances). It is significant that transsexually constructed lesbian–feminists have inserted themselves into positions of importance and/or performance in the feminist community" (Raymond, 1980: 10).

Such an analysis presents a restrictive model of gender that negates expressions of masculinity within lesbian and/or feminist identity positions. It also overlooks the contributions that transgender people have made to the early gay liberation movement (see Feinberg, 2006). Raymond's antipathy towards transsexualism is made clear towards the end of her book: "I contend that the problem of transsexualism would be best served by morally mandating it out of existence" (1980: 178).

Raymond's book was widely read and affected the dominant feminist perspective on transsexuality throughout the 1980s in both the US and Britain. Riddell (1996) documents how transsexual feminists and/or lesbians were frequently excluded from feminist and lesbian communities, and argues that Raymond's work had personally and politically damaging consequences: "My living space is threatened by this book. Although I have had to challenge its attacks on transsexual women, its dogmatic approach and its denial that female experience is our basic starting point are a danger signal of trends emerging in the whole women's movement" (Riddell, cited in Ekins and King, 1996: 189) Many transgender women in this research also speak of rejection from feminist and lesbian communities; as illustrated by Rebecca (age 55):

> I have come up against opposition. I'm a clubbing animal and there used to be a club in Liverpool that was very gay friendly that I used to go to. And a lot of gay women went to it and I was, how can I put it? They didn't want to engage. I know that has been the experience of a lot of people.

Questions about the place of transgender women within feminism cut to the heart of discussions around the constitution of 'woman'. While some feminist theorists and activists welcomed the destabilisation of identity politics that was characterised by a universal narrative of women's experience, others took a more defensive attitude to these ruptures. Anna's (age 28) narrative explicitly illustrates how a female identity has been fiercely defended:

> Lesbians tend to steer clear 'cos they don't know what they're dealing with. When you stake a claim on a lifestyle, if someone threatens that, you rebel against them and they see that I make a mockery out of it. And people who you'd expect to be the most understanding 'cos they've had a difficult ride as well, turn out to be the least accepting sometimes.

Contrary to the claims that transgender women exemplify problematic masculine behaviour (Raymond, 1980, 1994), many of those interviewed employ feminist critiques to reject what they view as 'unacceptable' attitudes in other transgender women. In this way, Gabrielle (age 45) describes the dynamics within a gender identity clinic:

> There were some trans women who were very sexist behaving and had a mindset of very sexist men and we really took them to task, a few of us, and said 'Listen, you'd better go and sort yourselves out because from where I'm sitting you're really an outrage and I'm insulted by what you say and your attitudes towards women. [...] Trans people often over-compensate at certain times such as through excessively exteriorly feminine behaviour among trans women. But I think a lot of trans people become a lot more balanced as they go through transition and become people who are mature in their trans experience after having transitioned and then it becomes a lot more balanced.

Overcompensation is exacerbated by the fact that psychiatric practices frequently demand that transgender women model an outmoded feminine style before being accepted for hormone therapy or surgery. Several women discussed this in their interviews. Rebecca (age 55) says: "I find it highly insulting that someone, usually a man, will tell someone how to be a woman. And anyway, in contemporary Britain, what is a woman? It has changed greatly and thank goodness. You know, what is femininity? What is feminine dress?" Likewise, Amelia (age 47) challenges the restrictive dress codes within gender identity clinics:

> I suppose because I'd come up through the feminist era [pause]. I am me, and black leather looks good on a man

or a woman. I used to live in black leather. Clothes were not the issue, they never were the issue. These idiots in the gender identity clinics say 'you can't be a woman if you don't wear a skirt'. Who dares say that? How dare they say what makes a woman and what makes a man? And to me, if I took this dress off and put on my husband's suit, I'd still be me.

The following comments from Dionne (age 40) provide a strong critique of expectations of feminine presentation, and illustrate her developing agency as she rejected the correlation of femininity and female identity:

If a butch dyke wants to present as masculine she's still mostly seen as a woman. But if I'd have gone in butch, or even in a pair of jeans, they wouldn't have treated me. I had to go in as feminine. And initially I had to present as heterosexual. I wouldn't have said I liked women. And why do women have to dress in a certain way? It's wrong and I've started to realise that and now I hardly ever wear a skirt. I've realised that you don't have to be feminine to be a woman, you can have short hair. But if I'd gone in at the start and said 'I want to be a butch woman, a butch dyke', they wouldn't have treated me. I felt I had to be very feminine. And that's all to do with how society perceives women, which is something women have fought for a long time and I'm just finding it all out.

Here we can see transgender women employing feminist critiques of the 'beauty myth' (Woolf, 1991) to confront conventional forms of gender presentation. Thus the basis of 'real life' within the 'real-life experience' is radically questioned. Experiences of sexism during transition, then, can be seen to bring about a feminist identity for transgender women. These points concur with Hale's (1998) discussion of how the themes of bodily autonomy and freedom of choice run through both feminist and transgender politics. Subsequently, a feminist framework can be used to theorise divergent gendered identities and expressions that are unfixed to the 'sexed' body. This approach allows for the frictions between self-gender identity and bodily appearance, as exemplified by those who identify as gender queer and who reject surgery or by people who do not have access to the surgery and/or hormone therapy they desire.

Paralleling the narratives of transgender male participants, transgender women have frequently identified contemporary feminism as a more welcoming space than second-wave feminist communities. Emma (age 54), for example, says: "There has certainly been an element of transphobia within feminist and lesbian communities. Although recently I've got on very well with sections of that community and have been pretty well accepted as me." Similarly, Gabrielle (age 45) reflects:

> Having been to Pride for maybe 10 years in a row and always feeling out of it 'cos we weren't included and then we were included and it was magical. And, yeah, I do feel included now. And I remember going to Pride and going in the women's tent and it was fantastic, scary but fantastic, really exciting.

Gabrielle suggests a positive shift in feminist attitudes towards transgender, and credits her friends for the support they gave her during early stages of transition. She continues:

> And I've been lucky to know such wonderful people, 'cos over the years I've said stupid things, just in my naivety, because I'd been conditioned the way I was, I would say things in a blasé way, which now I look back on and cringe, and they were very understanding and didn't pick me up on it, or beat me up, so one learns. You just recondition yourself, well, I hope you do. I always considered that it was a really great privilege to do something in society which a lot of people would never do, which is to re-evaluate everything that you've been taught and that you accept and that you've been conditioned, and to keep that which you consider to be worthwhile and to chuck out and replace a whole load of stuff that you don't.

Moreover, Gabrielle links the previously explored relationship between transgender men and feminist and lesbian communities to broader changes in attitudes towards transgender:

> I think it's a really interesting thing, 'cos obviously you've got a lot of trans men who came through a lesbian community and were affiliated to very much a sense of community through that 'cos there is a strong sense of community and having come through that they keep their friends with them, they may be rejected by some, but they

keep quite a lot of those friends. And quite a lot of those women work through their issues with the trans thing and quite a lot resolve it and come out OK, which is really good. So there are quite a lot of lesbian women who are supportive and I've felt really supported.

Despite experiencing alienation from some feminist communities, then, Gabrielle largely speaks positively about her relationship with current feminist and lesbian communities, corresponding with other narratives of transgender men and women.

However, while celebrating an increased feminist engagement with transgender, it is important not to portray a linear account of a theoretical or cultural trajectory from radical feminism to queer. Rather, the complexities within these narratives show that the arguments of radical feminism continue to inform feminist theory and cultural politics. Yet while the impact of radical feminism may live alongside queer movements, I suggest that the influence of poststructuralist theory and queer politics has encouraged contemporary feminism to pay greater attention to gender variance.

Conclusion

This chapter has explored participants' understandings and experiences of feminism. First, the research shows that the gender of transition impacts upon participant's understandings of feminism. As social groups, transgender men and women have different experiences and understandings of feminism prior to transition. Second, gender has considerable bearing on the divergent experiences within feminist communities for transgender men and women during and after transition. Transgender men and women encounter distinct feminist challenges, which, in turn, impact upon the different levels of acceptance they experience within feminist and/or lesbian and queer communities. There are, however, many common themes between the narratives of transgender men and women. In particular, both draw on experiences of exclusion from second-wave feminism. The stories told here resonate with autobiographical and activist work by trans writers (Riddell, 1980; Stone, 1991; Feinberg, 1992; Bornstein, 1994; Califia, 1997; Wilchins, 1997) who speak of rejection from feminist communities. Yet the narratives here also speak more positively about trans people's relationships with contemporary feminism.

In attempting to forge stronger links between feminism and transgender, I do not want to fall into what Henry Rubin terms an "ideal feminist identity paradigm" (1996: 308), in which feminist identity is based upon biology. This dynamic locates trans men as the 'good guys' who, because of female socialisation and experience, possess a degree of understanding about what it is to be a woman and, as such, may be perceived as feminists. Although this liberal hypothesis differs from biologically centred theory, which reduces gender to sex, it continues to employ biology as a reflector of 'true' identity and negates the self-identities of transgender men. In turn, if we transfer this paradigm to transgender women, they must inhabit a male sensibility and are not feminists. In contrast to an identity paradigm, Rubin proposes an 'action paradigm' in which feminist identity arises out of political commitment rather than female biology. He argues that "'Womanhood' is no longer a necessary, nor sufficient qualification for feminist identity. A feminist is one who acts in concert with feminist ideals" (Rubin, 1996: 308). Thus political practice, rather than biology, lies at the heart of feminist identity. Subsequently, analyses of embodiment may be developed without essentialist connotations. Rubin illustrates how embodiment may be employed dialectically to enable a feminist approach that can take account of "differently located bodies which appear similar in form" (1996: 308). This may allow "a way of knowing that can provide me(n) with a feminist viewpoint, and that is not generated out of a woman's experience of her body. Instead, it is generated out of subjectively located struggle" (Rubin, 1996: 308). We can add on to this that a feminist viewpoint need not depend upon female socialisation in order to enable the feminist voices of transgender women to be heard.

Koyama's (2003) discussion of transfeminism, which expresses the feminist concerns of transgender women, shows how transgender politics may enable contemporary feminism to move beyond the confines of second-wave feminism. Koyama (2000) writes: "[Transfeminism] is not merely about merging trans politics with feminism, but it is a critique of the second wave feminism from third wave perspectives." In conclusion, I suggest that, if attentive to gender diversity, contemporary feminism may provide a collective arena in which difference acts to produce a more extensive feminist knowledge.

FIVE

Sexual identities

As I sketched out in Chapter One, transgender practices have been the subject of much debate within feminism, lesbian and gay scholarship and queer theory. Moreover, trans sexualities have been subject to intense medical gaze. As Schrock and Reid comment: "Most people [however] do not have their sexual biographies evaluated by mental health professionals who determine whether they can inhabit the bodies they desire" (2006: 84–5). Moreover, these studies have largely neglected the subjective meanings and lived experiences of sexuality for transgender people. The dominance of a medical model of transgender has frequently positioned transgender people, and transsexuals in particular, as asexual. As Cromwell states: "Medico-psychological practitioners insisted that 'true transsexuals' had low libidos, were asexual or autoerotic. They were also said to feel disgust and abhorrence for their sex organs" (1999: 124).

This chapter addresses the relationship between gender transition and sexual desire, identity and practice. The first section of the chapter explores the negotiation of sexual desire and identity through transition. Initially, it considers how sexuality is located as a fluid process within participants' narratives. It then moves on to look at the ways in which sexual desire, identity and practice may be understood as stable factors within other participants' narratives of transition. Here I examine the links between sexuality and gendered experiences of embodiment. The second section considers the links between transgender identities and non-heterosexual practices by examining subjective understandings of similarity and difference. The third section builds upon this theme in relation to understandings of commonalties and divisions between transgender and lesbian and gay politics.

Negotiating sexual identity and desire through transition

Fluidity of sexual identity, desire and practice

In discussing theoretical approaches to transgender in Chapter One, I examined how lesbian and gay theorists and radical feminist writers in the 1970s and 1980s critiqued transgender practices by arguing that transgender people assumed conservative gender and sexual roles, which left dominant relations of power intact (Ekins and King, 1997). Yet, in this research, 16 of the sample group identified as non-heterosexual. Del (age 44), for example, explicitly articulates a queer sexuality, as shown in the following section of our interview:

> **S:** How do you define your sexuality?

> **D:** Queer, pansexual. I would not say bisexual because semiotically that reinforces the binaries. I would say that men are more sex objects for me, and women, I'm more happy to have a relationship with a woman, an emotional and a romantic and a sexual relationship with a woman, whereas I have emotional or sexual relationships with men, but rarely, not never, but rarely do I have emotional *and* sexual relationships with men. I like sex with men, but it's just never happened that I've had, you know, that I've had a boyfriend as such.

Del's critique of the semantics of the term 'bisexual' demonstrates an informed understanding of theoretical discussions around sexual categories, which supports a poststructuralist critique of binary oppositions. In discussing his sexuality, Del reflexively situates his sexual desires and relationships as fluidly practised. In articulating a fluidity of sexual desire, William (age 25), who has had sexual relationships with men and women since transition, also distances himself from the term 'bisexual':

> What I enjoy is kind of flitting in and out of communities. In terms of my identity I never identified sexually. I don't really know. I can't really articulate it. If you say bisexual, I don't agree with that. There are lots of attractive trans people and if they identify as male then I would say 'OK' and start this relationship with them. There are lots of people who come in between, but bisexual, it's such a strange word and sometimes I say it, but normally I'd just go 'well I don't care, I don't mind'.

Significantly, several participants found it hard to describe their sexual identity and related to the failings of existing classificatory systems in accounting for transgender identities and desires. Rebecca (age 55), for example, says: "[…] there's a lack of language to describe my sexuality". On this level, findings resonate with Hale's comment that "categories and terms always assume a nontransgendered paradigm – nontransgendered people's subjectivities and embodiment are always the reference points for these categories" (Hale, cited in Cromwell, 1999: 130).

Medical and psychiatric practitioners have found the issue of transgender sexualities hard to comprehend. Transgender clients were believed to have highly problematic relationships with their bodies and sexual identities: "disgusted by their genitals, transsexuals masturbate rarely and indulge less in sexual relationships with others" (Stoller, cited in Cromwell, 1999: 131). Medical thinking generally assumed that a heterosexual identity would automatically follow surgery. People whose sexual identities fell outside a heteronormative framework were generally denied access to surgical procedures (Cromwell, 1999). Later studies have, however, begun to address non-heterosexual transgender sexualities – Clare (1984), for example, coined the term 'transhomosexuality' to take account of non-heterosexual transgender people. British psychologist Tully (1992) has examined same-sex intimacy among transsexuals before gender transition. Nonetheless, he too suggests that, post-transition, most transgender people will assume heterosexual identities. Though the work of clinicians Bockting and Coleman (1992) represents a shift from the traditional heteronormativity of medical and psychoanalytic perspectives in highlighting the experiences of gay trans men, most medical and psychoanalytic perspectives continue to presume that gender transition will reinforce a heterosexual identity (Cromwell, 1999).

Bailey's study of transsexuality is, according to Bockting, the "latest challenge to what already was a fragile relationship between the scientific and the transgender communities" (Bockting, 2005: 1). Bailey reduces MtF transition to two 'types', distinguished by their sexuality. The first is the homosexual transsexual who transitions to attract men sexually: "Those who love men become women to attract them" (Bailey, 2003: xii). The second is the autogynephilic male who desires himself as a female: "Those who love women become the women they love" (Bailey, 2003: xii). Bailey's thesis is based upon a biological link between gender and sexuality: "[…] homosexual male-to-female transsexuals are extremely feminine men" (Bailey, 2003: 146). The concept of gender dysphoria and its connection with the advancement of reconstructive surgery is theoretically problematic in its perpetuation of a binary model of gender and sexuality, which is unable to account for practices and experiences of gender and sexual diversity. Though later medical insights represent a more complex understanding of transgender practices than were offered within founding medical perspectives, there remain serious problems in the correlation of transgender and biological or psychological pathology. While psychoanalytic perspectives largely view relationships with women as inherently troubling for trans men (Pauly, 1969), findings show that sexual relationships with women do not stand opposed to a trans male identity. Moreover, as Svar (age 41) suggests, relationships with women may serve to reinforce masculine identity:

> When I met my partner it was very interesting for me, having had relationships, lesbian relationships, or with women who identified as lesbians. It was really refreshing; it was just when I was six months or a year into my transition, to start this relationship with a woman who was used to having relationships with men. Because she treats me like a guy, she calls me 'he'.

Philip (age 42) is also reluctant to define sexuality through conventional taxonomies. Philip defines himself as a single man who has sex with men although, as the following section of our interview shows, his sexuality cannot be easily characterised as that of a gay man:

> **P:** At this time I've got a couple of male partners that I have sex with and I would say they are men who have sex with men, rather than gay men on the gay scene. 'Cos they're not on the gay scene, but they have sex with men. Again, it's labels. I don't really like the labels.
>
> **S:** Do you identify as a gay man?
>
> **P:** Sort of because that's where people would put me. And if anyone said 'who do you have sex with?' I'd say 'men' so they think you're a gay man.
>
> **S:** So who is a gay man?
>
> **P:** Well, for me, a gay man is to do with a certain lifestyle, going to gay places and I don't do that. And I think if I had to pigeonhole myself I'd say I was a gay man. But I do like women and I can get turned on by women so I dunno.

Philip's narrative illustrates how sexual identity is a relational process whereby subjective understandings are developed within social contexts. For him, then, sexual identity is as much tied up with lifestyle choice and sexual cultures as it is with sexual practice. In talking about her relationships, Gabrielle (age 45), who defines herself as a trans lesbian, also relates to the ways in which intimate interactions impact upon self-identity:

> I was with someone briefly before and she was quite a butch-presenting lesbian woman and I became quite a butch-presenting lesbian woman too when I was with her [...] When I got together with my current partner, I don't know, I just got more secure in myself and we went to San Francisco and that was really [...] You know, I went out there wishing I had smaller feet and I came back and bought a huge pair of stack-heel Buffalo boots. I really came back quite queered up by San Francisco.

Gabrielle suggests that gender transition has brought divergent possibilities of sexual identification. Other participants support this when reflecting upon the impact of transition upon sexuality. William (age 25), for example, discusses how interaction with other transgender people has led to an increased reflexivity, which, in turn, has opened up new ways of thinking about sexual attraction and desire:

> There's all these people around me, trans people around me, who are just very open about their relationships and all that [...] Yeah. I think it definitely enables you to be, well, just more honest. And if you see a lot of people round you who are being honest, it just makes you think, how do I fit into all of this? And do I fit into all of this? You know, is there something more to me? Which is what a lot of people that I know in the trans community have done [...] You've already got to be honest with yourself, come to terms with, you know, saying this is who I am. So I think people think there's no point in me, you know, hiding something else. Or maybe also, if you're open, if you're used to being open about lots of things you can just easily be open with your sexuality, you know.

For William, openness about his gender identity has led to greater sexual freedom and increased self-knowledge. Dionne (age 40) also links her experience of transition to an understanding of sexual desire as detached from gendered object of choice, articulating an increasingly fluid trajectory in which gender transition enables a more yielding sexuality:

> I could never have gone with a man as a man but occasionally when I was dressed up I fantasised about being with a man as a woman. But now I'm starting to fancy men, which I never did before. I'm very open sexually, it doesn't matter what sex someone is if they like me and I like them. I mean as a bloke if I had said that I liked men I would've got hassle, which I didn't want because I didn't consider myself as a gay man. But a bisexual woman, I'm quite happy to say that to everybody.

Bernadette (age 71), who lives with the woman she has been married to for 40 years, identifies as a heterosexual woman. She says:

> I always have been attracted to men, but I deliberately controlled this because, at one juncture, it would have been an assumption of homosexuality, and that was totally foreign to me, and so I never allowed it to be manifest because if I had, it would have been totally misunderstood. It would have given an entirely wrong impression to everybody, and for that reason, I suppressed it totally and entirely. Before, it was an aspect that I had to keep under control, as I said, because I didn't wish to be identified as something that I certainly wasn't. There was no suggestion that I was gay, or anything of the kind. Deliberately I suppressed it.

Such sentiments could be read as instances of internalised homophobia, whereby gender transition is subjectively granted greater levels of acceptability than same-sex, and, particularly, male-to-male, sexual practice. In exploring FtM sexualities, Devor (1989) suggests that societal homophobia impacts upon sexuality so that transgender people often avoid sexual relationships until after transition in order to avoid being perceived as homosexual. While the social and cultural processes of homophobia are also apparent in this research, and can be seen to have structured participants' understandings and impacted upon their experiences of sexuality, I would suggest that a straightforward reading of internalised homophobia represents a reductive analysis that neglects the role of embodiment within sexual desire, fantasy and practice. In discussing her sexual fantasies of having sex with a man when she cross-dressed, Dionne clearly locates her fantasy role as that of a woman having sex with a man, rather than as a man having sex with a man; while Bernadette makes explicit what she 'certainly wasn't'. For Dionne and Bernadette, then, sexual desire for men is coupled with the desire to express their identities as women. Moreover, since neither Dionne nor Bernadette ever considered themselves to be male, the identification of a gay man would have been incongruent to their self-gender identities as women. Thus Dionne's decision over the past year to take hormones and have reassignment surgery can be seen to have enabled the redefinition of her sexuality as a bisexual woman, while Bernadette's transition 15 years ago complemented her sexual identity as a heterosexual woman.

From their empirical research in the US, Schrock and Reid (2006) note that: "For male-to-female transsexuals with histories of male–female sex, this gendered discourse on sexuality threatens the construction of the self as real woman. More specifically, interviewees who, as men, had sexual relationships with women needed to tell sexual stories that reframed such experiences as signifying their 'true' womanhood" (2006: 80). Such sexual stories, Schrock and Reid suggest, are instances where heterosexuality is queered: "The task at hand was to 'queer' heterosexuality, by which we mean they narratively subverted the cultural assumption that sex between male- and female-bodied individuals equals heterosexuality" (2006: 80). Yet, in proposing that their interviewees assumed that "recalled subjective experience and some cultural discourses were more important than the material body in determining sexual orientation" (Schrock and Reid, 2006: 81), Schrock and Reid neglect the role of the 'corporeal schema' (Merleau-Ponty, 1962), whereby the embodied subject is located between the subjective and the social world. Thus, like embodiment, sexual orientation might not be a conscious state, but may be experienced as an 'inner sense' that influences our bodily actions and responses. This research indicates a complex interplay between (trans)gender and sexuality. Moreover, sexual experiences are layered through corporality, subjectivity and cultural discourses. These matters indicate the significance of an embodied approach that accounts for how bodily processes are socially and culturally constructed, while being appreciative of "fleshly physicality" (Shilling and Mellor, 1997: 65). Thus the body is both culturally and materially situated. While the issues here suggest that sexual desire may be inherently gendered (Jackson, 1999), transgendered identifications also clearly trouble the constitutional qualities of gender itself.

Whereas a medical perspective lies firmly within a heteronormative framework, lesbian and gay studies have often assumed homo relationality. Both these theoretical frameworks have neglected the distinct experiences and subjectivities of transgender men and women. Moreover, sociological studies have at times been reductive in their approach to transgender sexualities by positioning transgender heterosexual men as homosexual or assuming a binary homo/hetero model (Lewins, 1995). Rather than representing either a dominant hetero or homosexuality, this research indicates that sexual desire, identity and practice are experienced *through* (trans)gendered experiences. In the following quotation from our interview, Paul (age 34) explores how sexuality and (trans)gender are experienced as overlapping yet distinguishable factors across his life course:

> **P:** Well, the big thing for me was my sexual identity before the gender identity issues really came to the fore, when I started having relations with women, not men. So suddenly the issue flared up, 'was I a lesbian?' Having a big crisis over that. So that all came first.
>
> **S:** So did you ever identify as a lesbian?
>
> **P:** Not really, but that introduced me to women, so that felt right with women, so I talked to various people about that and I saw a social worker for a while and I think I went to the doctor about it, she was very unhelpful, as I remember rightly. But once that had all settled down, and I'd come to terms with that, and then it became obvious that there was more to it than that. That was just the starting point on a long road. I was heading much further than that.

Paul's narrative here resonates with Schrock and Reid's point that "People thus do not only use sexuality to interpret their biographies in line with current or desired identities, but they often use their agency to fit their lives into the culturally defined boundaries of the sexual identities they aim to inhabit (2006: 84). Such boundaries may shift, however. Thus while the interplay between transgender and lesbian, gay or queer identities is a significant theme within many participants' narratives, as Paul's narrative suggests, to interpret these sexual stories exclusively as personifications of same-sex desire would be to negate the distinguishing characteristics of gender, and, particularly, the role of gendered embodiment within transgender trajectories. In the following section of our interview, Philip (age 42) discusses his sexuality in relation to his work as a sex worker. In talking about sex work through transition, Philip relates variously to the complexities of sexuality and the gendered body:

> I have a very complex, multiple-layered professional life in sex work, which is that I have a few clients who I've had for more than five or 10 years, who don't know that I've transitioned. They come in and they're now used to seeing me with a man's voice who used to have a woman's voice, with a male haircut who used to have woman's hair, who no longer wears make-up, with incredible muscular and hairy legs and the strength in my legs, not to mention bum, wearing a skirt and that's about the only female signifier. And evidently they haven't noticed. [...] Then I advertised for a while as female-to-male TV [transvestite] during hormones and I picked up a few clients who I think really saw me as female, liked the idea of me as a butch female. And one or two still come and know about the hormones and transition, and are quite interested in it. Then my most recent reincarnation has been as a male-to-female post-op [...]

> But the thing is, the first two have gone, 'cos I advertised as female and now I can't do it. And some TV (transvestite) ads are still out. I had an ad out as male–female, no, female-to-male TS (transsexual) and some people who thought it was the other way round came to see me assuming that I was male-to-female post-op and they were quite happy. And so I realised that if they liked it other people would. So I put an ad out pretending to be a male–female post-op and I've been getting clients from it.

Philip's discussion of sex work through transitioning relates directly the nuanced and plural contexts of sexuality, and supports Butler's (1990) point that gender play is key to a variety of sexual practices that undermine the naturalness of gender. Philip's experiences indicate how transgender sexualities may bring fluidity to the interplay of gender and sexuality so that notions of gender expression and sexual identity are far from straightforwardly performed. Moreover, Philip's discussion of his multifaceted identities as a sex worker illustrates explicitly the potential for varied and contingent sexual identities and practices through transition. Yet, as the next section suggests, the relationship between (trans)gender and sexuality may be less ambiguously experienced.

Object

While many participants articulate a fluidity of sexual identity, several participants discuss how before, during and following transition, their sexual desires have been consistently gendered. Rebecca (age 55), for example says: "The objects of my desire are women. I don't know whether that makes me a male heterosexual or a female lesbian, I'm not quite sure [laugh]. I don't think it's either of those. I remain attracted to women. I have never had any attraction towards men."

Although Rebecca speaks pragmatically about the complexities of gender and sexual identification, the relationship between the two may be problematically experienced, particularly through childhood and adolescence. Tony (age 39), for example, who is single and identifies as heterosexual, discusses the confusion brought about by his sexual desire for women prior to transition:

> I began to realise that I actually fancied women more than I fancied men but I knew I wasn't gay and I got very confused then, and then for a long long time. And I went out with women but I was always absolutely convinced that I was straight but couldn't work this out at all.

The intricacies of transgender sensibilities and sexual expression may also be apparent after the process of self-identification as transgender and prior to surgery or hormone therapy. David (age 26), who identifies as heterosexual and is in a long-term relationship with his female partner, discusses how a past relationship with a woman prior to his surgery and hormone treatment failed due to their conflicting understandings of sexual identity categories: "I had a relationship with a female and I told her straight away that I was transsexual, but she thought of me as being a lesbian, so the relationship didn't work because that's not what I was."

Tensions around the relationship between transgender and sexual identification can also lead to self-reflections about sexual orientation for the partners of transgender people.[1] In this way, Greg (age 44) talks about how, during a past relationship with a woman before transition, his partner began to question her own sexuality:

When I met someone else later on we did end up having a relationship. And she's heterosexual and she was really uncomfortable with herself 'cos she couldn't understand it […] She's never had a relationship with another woman before or since and she couldn't understand how she could feel like this. She felt really uncomfortable but she worked it out, partly because I was able to explain to her where I was coming from and so she was able to make sense of it.

As gender has been variously theorised as an active ongoing process, which is achieved through interaction with others (Connell, 1987; West and Zimmerman, 1987; Fenstermaker et al, 1991), so sexuality can be seen to be a relational process whereby subjective understandings of desire and identity are continually negotiated within an intimate context with others. For participants who remain in sexual relationships with existing partners, the social perception of their relationship can be perplexing, as Karen (age 31), who remains married to her female partner, shows:

An interesting thing is the way that my work colleagues look at mine and Sam's relationship and that's not seen as being in a lesbian relationship, it's seen as being heterosexual. And I say 'well you do know, don't you?' But they never see it that way because they came to the wedding and everything. It's very strange […]. You can't easily hold hands and kiss in public without thinking about it, having to think about it rather than just doing it. I've got wedding rings on and I keep them on because I consider myself as married to Sam. And people ask about my husband. It's very difficult.

Here Karen illustrates that it is difficult to remain outside conventional structures and categories. In discussing her current understandings of the ways in which desire between women is frequently subject to self-regulation and cultural disapproval, Karen alludes to her identification with lesbian and gay politics. There are also connections here with the developing feminist consciousnesses of transgender women, which were explored in the previous chapter. Moreover, the narratives considered in this section indicate that gender and sexuality are complexly related. Thus the intersections between (trans)gender and sexuality reinforce Butler's challenge of whether the "historical and analytic distinction between gender and sexuality is finally tenable" (1994: 13). This question can be explored further in relation to the connections between transgender and non–heterosexual identification.

Transgender identities and lesbian, gay, bisexual and queer practices

Queer transgender practices

Sedgwick (1990) positions sexuality as a site of possibility for the destabilisation and reconstruction of normative values. The majority of non-heterosexual identifying participants identified as bisexual, suggesting that the category 'bisexual' may enable a stronger articulation of the fluidity of sexual desire and allow greater space for the nuances between gender and sexual identities than the categories of 'lesbian' or 'gay'. This lends support to Storr's (2003) hypothesis that bisexuality is a phenomenon of postmodernity. Here, Storr is not suggesting that bisexual practices themselves are the exclusive properties of postmodernity, but rather that "the existence of a self-conscious bisexual identity, and the recognizable forms of bisexual community organization and politics, are very clearly rooted in the early postmodernity, from the mid-1970s onwards" (2003: 159). Likewise, self-identified Western transgender identities are a contemporary phenomenon. Yet there are problems within a binary model for transgender sexual identities. As Cromwell states: "because transsituated identities and bodies are different, sexual desires likewise defy the binary of heterosexual and homosexual and play havoc with the concept of bisexual" (1999: 130). Subsequently, while some participants are hesitant to define their sexual identity, others find that the term 'queer' enables a more appropriate description than 'bisexual'. In the discussions of queer approaches to transgender in previous chapters, I discussed how, through the development of queer theory and theories of gender performativity, transgender became viewed as the epitome of queer. Moreover, trans theorists such as Bornstein (1994) and Stone (1996) reflect a queer subjectivity in positioning themselves not as transsexuals but as 'gender outlaws' (Bornstein, 1994) who "speak from outside the boundaries of gender, beyond the constructed oppositional nodes which have been predefined as the only positions from which discourse is possible" (Stone, 1996: 351). This research also finds that queer subjectivities are apparent within narratives of transgender sexual identities and practices. Thus, Rebecca (age 55) illustrates that transgender sexual identities are divergently practised and located on the borders of an inside/outside binary (Fuss, 1991):

For some trans people their sexuality will follow their sex
so they may start out as a male with female partners and
end up with a female with male partners. There are others
that start out as a male with male partners and end up as a
female with male partners. And then there are people like
me [laugh] who just muddy the water.

Rebecca's comments resonate with Valentine's (1993) discussion of
how a sex/gender binary that underscores notions of heterosexual,
homosexual and bisexual identities erases the specificities of desires and
sexual practices that fall between or outside these identity categories.
In the following section of our interview, Philip (age 42) considers his
pre-transition experiences during the late 1970s and 1980s. He speaks
of an erotic without a name, indicating a queer sensibility prior to a
theoretical queer discourse or the development of a queer culture:

P: When I came to London in 1979 I went into the gay
scene, into the mixed gay men's scene in as much as I went
into the mixed gay men's scene in the bit where women
went if that makes any sense [laugh]. I tried a couple of
lesbian places and I never ever felt comfortable in lesbian
situations and I could never have told you why then, but
I can tell you why now – because I didn't identify as a
woman with women. And I never understood that whole
mentally of women together 'cos I didn't feel part of it. So
I got involved with the gay press in the 1980s and I was
on the collective of a magazine and I was in a band and
we used to perform in gay venues and it was me and a guy.
But my gay world was always mixed, with more men in it
than women and I think I always identified with gay men
to a large extent. And I know you've asked me if I'm gay
and I said 'no not really', but this is then.

S: So did you identify as a lesbian then?

P: Yeah. I would have said 'I'm a lesbian', but it never felt
quite right really. And certainly women-only places I just
used to hate.

In discussing sexual identity and practice, the experiences of several
participants correspond with queer deconstructions of identity
categories, and link with a queer analysis of gender and sexual identities

as non-affirmative. Yet rather than being invariably unconstrained – as framed through queer theory – queer subjectivities and sexual practices are often ambiguously experienced within the relational context of gender and sexual cultures. For example, while Svar (age 41) links his transition to greater sexual agency, he also shows how sexual expression through gender transition may raise a range of composite factors:

> I think what it [transition] does is if you are a pre-op transsexual, within the […] I'm not going to say queer ghetto, 'cos that's not a word I like to use, but within the queer world, then I would say that in a way I do have another freedom. But I have to be really careful as well the way I look at […] Because I cruise everybody [laugh] I can't help it, you know, if people are cute. That doesn't just mean being gay, but especially in that environment there's going to be a lot more people who I think are attractive than walking down Oxford Street. But sometimes I do get these looks from dykes, you know, 'what are you looking at?' and it's like 'oh God, I must be more subtle'. […] I'm lucky to be in a great relationship, but if for example […] I think then it would be an issue forming new relationships. Even if I went cottaging on Hampstead Heath or something, it would be like, you know, there would have to first be some explanation and then it's like, you know, like a lot of gay men […] Gay men love cock, and so, you know, that puts me sort of a bit down the scale anyway. And at the same time, you know, lesbians or dykes, they like women, so that puts me a bit at a disadvantage as well. So there is that sort of vulnerability, being how I am and I think that is quite important in terms of sexuality.

Svar's comments indicate the importance of a grounded analysis of transgender that avoids indiscriminate projections of autonomy by recognising that identities are contingently situated. As Stryker comments: "transgender phenomena invite queer studies, and gay and lesbian communities, to take another look at the many ways bodies, identities and desires can be interwoven" (2006: 8). Similarly, Boyd (2006) has shown how transgendered bodies have troubled lesbian politics and, more specifically, the notion of 'lesbian nations' in the US in the 1990s.

The points discussed here relate back to the importance of gendered embodiment within transgender-situated identities; showing that the experiences of inhabiting a non-normative gender that troubles predictable understandings of gender identity as distinctive of a particular sexed body can bring complexities to sexual interactions. This issue is also apparent within experiences of participants who reject gender reconstruction or who are waiting for surgery or hormone therapy. Reflecting on his feelings around sexuality before meeting his current partner, Dan (age 37) says:

> I didn't have a relationship for four years or so for several reasons, one of which was because the situation didn't present itself. Secondly I didn't know what sort of relationship I wanted and thirdly I was so shy of my body. I'd had chest surgery quite early on but it's just a real fear about if someone will accept your body. I suppose you could say that if it's a gay relationship with a man you haven't got what they want, if it's a heterosexual relationship with a woman, I hadn't got what they want.

Discussions about embodiment and sexuality thus link to the contingency of identity to speak of the tensions between transgender and lesbian and gay identity politics.

Situating transgender identities within lesbian and gay identity politics

Medical practitioners and associated professionals largely assume that once an individual's biological 'sex' has been reconstructed, their sexuality will heterosexually befit their acquired gender – the MtF will assume a female heterosexual identity, and the FtM will function as a heterosexual male. On the other hand, as I addressed in Chapter One, much anthropological writing has neglected the distinct experiences of gender-diverse men and women by assimilating gender diversity into a lesbian and gay narrative. Recent work on non-Western practices of gender diversity, however, has moved beyond this tendency. Kulick's research into the *travesti* in Brazil (1998), for example, offers a specifically localised analysis of the complex ways in which the *travesti* understand gender and sexuality; while Elliot and Roen's (1998) study of transgender practices in New Zealand looks at how trans people situate their own experiences of gender in relation to psycho-medical discourses. Importantly, Towle and Morgan (2002) have more recently criticised the use of the term 'third gender' in American anthropological writing; stating that: "we join an increasing number of anthropologists who caution against using caricatures of other cultures […] the 'third' gender concept encourages Westerners to make poorly informed assumptions about the meaning and significance of gender dynamics in non-Western societies" (2002: 490).

While lesbian and gay history and anthropology has often engaged with gender diversity, the links between lesbian, gay and transgender politics and activism has an awkward history. Throughout the 1970s, a small number of transvestite and transsexual organisations developed in Britain, America and Australia. Simultaneously, the collective organisation of lesbians and gay men heralded by the emergence of the Gay Liberation Front (GLF) initiated a political critique of the individualisation of transgender. Lesbian and gay organisations argued that the individual experiences of transgender were politically significant, and transvestite and transsexual groups were criticised for their political apathy. As Ekins and King recollect:

> These organisations were attacked for their failure to engage openly in sexual politics; for their low-profile 'closed closet' form; for their support for conventional norms and structures such as marriage and the family as well as traditional sexual stereotypes exemplified in the image of women portrayed by members and in their publications; and for their attempts to normalise transvestism by excluding from or denying the presence within their membership of, for example, transsexuals, homosexuals or fetishists. (Ekins and King, 1997)

In response to these critiques, Brake located transgender people as "revolutionaries who publicly challenge the notion of ascribed gender" (1976: 188). Rather than targeting individual transgender people, he argued that criticism should be levelled at the medical profession's pathologisation of transsexuality. In reply to the assertion that transvestites and transsexuals reinforce stereotypical images of women through their dress and behaviour, he further apportioned blame to the medical profession: "the transsexual is coerced into passing as a programmed woman, with the dignity befitting a lady" (Brake, 1976: 191). His intervention symbolised an early call for the inclusion of transgender people within lesbian and gay politics. Likewise, Rubin (1992) appeals for a greater tolerance of transgender people within lesbian and gay communities, and suggests a common history, though not identity, between lesbians, gay men and transgender people. Feinberg (1996) also argues for a coalition politics in support of transgender civil rights. Rubin and Feinberg stress the specificities of transgender experience, while arguing for alliances between lesbians, gay men and a diversity of gender-diverse people.

Despite such calls, several participants in this research discussed experiences of rejection from lesbian and gay communities. Anna (age 28), for example, says: "Gay people have been the hardest group of people to talk to about me being transsexual, they've always got a problem. Lesbians tend to steer clear 'cos they don't know what they're dealing with. Gay men just have a problem. They can get, well they can get aggressive." In a similar vein Cheryl (age 45) believes that lesbians and gay men: "[…] hate us and I don't know why that is but they hate us. I used to think that because we were both minority groups we could get on. I mean we're all different, but I thought we'd be close groups but that's not the case." Gabrielle (age 45) also discusses hostility:

> There are quite a lot of unfriendly lesbians out there and gay men, and you find that wherever you are. I thought that when we were on holiday in Lesbos that people would be relaxed but actually there were still quite a lot of frosty, hostile lesbian women there. It's a terrible thing to say, but you got the same blank expression that you would have got in the pub in Stoke Newington [area of London with large lesbian and gay population] if you smiled at someone. It dismays me. Like letters you get in the *Pink Paper* [lesbian and gay London-based paper] saying 'with those freaks we're never going to get anywhere'.

Gabrielle's comments reverberate with queer theory's challenge to traditional lesbian and gay theory and politics, which have been exclusive in their attitudes towards those whose identities fall outside what is deemed to be acceptable. Conversely, the hostility towards transgender people within some lesbian and gay communities mirrors the resistance to gender diversity from some sections of feminism as discussed in Chapters One and Three. William's (age 25) experience of being challenged in a lesbian and gay club echoes these themes:

> […] the last time I was there I took my girlfriend […] And then there were about six of us left on the dance floor 'cos it was just about to close, and I was kind of getting off with her and somebody came up to us who I kind of knew, who worked there, and said, like really rudely, she said 'you either stop that or get out' and then she left. And it's interesting

> 'cos they're trans friendly and would I be allowed to do that
> if I told them about me?

William's narrative raises a number of interesting questions concerning the intersections of sexual and gender identity. As a transgender man whose masculine presentation goes unchallenged, William felt previously welcome in the club with his male friends or lovers due to the presumption that he was gay. With his female partner, however, his demonstrations of sexual intimacy were viewed as an unacceptable sign of heterosexuality. William's transgender status and his understanding of the club as 'trans friendly' raise epistemological questions about gender and (homo)sexuality in that 'trans friendly' policies within lesbian and gay communities frequently rest on an assumption that equates transgender people and same-sex desire. Anna (age 28) also discusses how transgender identity positions may challenge the binary categories of gender and sexuality to trouble their assumed correlation:

> I used to think it was because they [gay men] thought that I
> was just afraid to be gay so I was just dressing up as a woman,
> but that's just ignorance on their part. And I think it's more
> complex than that anyway. Having had to live closeted for
> so long I know what that does, so you do stake a claim on
> a lifestyle and I pose a threat to that and can be seen to
> make a mockery of it. Maybe it's to do with attraction and
> confusion and that whole coming-out process. You accept
> that you're attracted to other women and then there's this
> amorphous thing that is both and neither, so it's 'how should
> I feel towards that person?'. And the people you expect to
> be the most accepting, 'cos they've had a difficult life as well
> turn out to be the least accepting, it's very strange.

Devor and Matte (2006) detail the role of transgendered people in lesbian and gay politics, yet, as they state, their involvement has been marginalised historically: "People who are today known as transgendered and transsexual have always been present in homosexual rights movements. Their presence and contributions, however, have not always been fully acknowledged or appreciated" (2006: 387).

A number of issues are raised here about how transgender people are situated within identity politics. While identity-based feminist politics developed around the uniform concept of 'woman', lesbian and gay identity politics spoke of the shared experiences of lesbians and gay men. As the narratives discussed in this section show, transgender identities are often perceived as a challenge to notions of shared experience based upon sexual identity. As Devor and Matte argue:

> As in many other social reform movements, collective activism in gay and lesbian social movements is based on a shared collective identity. Homosexual collective identity, especially in the days before queer politics, was largely framed as inborn, like ethnicity, and based primarily on sexual desires for persons of the same sex and gender. However, such definitions make sense only when founded on clearly delineated distinctions between sexes and genders. It becomes considerably harder to delineate who is gay and who is lesbian when its not clear who is male or a man and who is female or a woman. Like bisexual people, transgendered and transsexual people destabilize the otherwise easy divisions of men and women into categories of straight and gay because they are both and/or neither. Thus there is a long standing tension over the political terrain of queer politics between gays and lesbians, on the one hand, and transgendered and transsexual people, on the other. (Devor and Matte, 2006: 387–8)

Through transition, Philip (age 42) realised that his transgender identity was distinct from some gender-identity practices within gay cultures:

> There's a certain thing among gay men of aping what they see as femininity and I'm just not very comfortable with that. You know, the thing of calling each other Sheila and all that that feels really alien to me, I can't relate to it. If I'm a gay man, I'm a straight gay man, not a camp gay man or something. I just can't relate to that kind of critical bitchy thing that does seem to be a part of some gay male culture that I can't relate to. It's the inappropriateness of pretending you're female when I'm female-to-male. I'm not female. And I'm so not female that I've done this [transition].

Chapters One and Three explored how the concept of 'woman' within feminism in the 1980s was ruptured by the articulation of distinct and contesting experiences, and by plural and poststructuralist feminist critiques. Likewise, queer politics and sexual subcultures question the notion of identity as based upon sexual preference. This is illustrated by Del's (age 44) reference to lesbian S/M culture, which, in contrast to a lesbian separatist ideology, presents a more fluid approach to identity: "SM dykes have a policy of something like if you're FtM you have a place in the dyke community and you're welcome." Despite her reservations, Gabrielle (age 45) also suggests developing connections between transgender people and some lesbian and gay communities:

> Between gay and lesbian people there are big misunderstandings and there is still a lot of misogyny and sexism in certain parts of the gay community. But having said that, I think people are being more inclusive and people are realising that there are a lot of similar political areas. I hope they are.

Queer theory and political activism may have effected a departure from sexual identity politics that are informed by rigid notions of entitlement to community membership, marking a departure from what Devor and Matte have described as "a dark corner in the struggle for gay and lesbian rights" (2006: 402). Yet, although a more magnanimous politics of sexuality may be at work within contemporary lesbian and gay cultures, not all participants support Gabrielle's wish for coalition when considering the question of political alliances between transgender groups and lesbian and gay organisations.

Lesbian, gay, bisexual and transsexual (LGBT): coalition politics?

While some transgender people argue for the inclusion of transgender within a lesbian, gay and bisexual movement, others believe that transgender issues are qualitatively distinct from those related to same-sex sexuality or bisexuality. Reflecting this perspective, Amelia (age 47) says:

> [...] I would support to the death for LGB groups to fight for basic human rights, but I think that basically the issues are somewhat different; they are not the same. An LGB person doesn't need to change their birth certificate before they can marry their boyfriend or girlfriend. I don't see that linking up to a group [pause]. I'm heterosexual. I've got nothing in common with those groups. There are some people who are lesbian and gay and that's fine, and I can see that the cause is common. [...] I think there is a small majority of people in my situation who are heterosexual and it is not the issue that we are fighting.

For Amelia there is no direct link between the goals of lesbian and gay organisations and issues pertinent to transgender. While Amelia recognises that coalition politics may be relevant to lesbian and gay transgender people, she articulates her concerns as a heterosexual transgender woman as separate from theirs. Rebecca (age 55), who acts as an independent adviser on equality to a large metropolitan police force, reflects similar concerns:

> Sexuality plays a part, obviously, in all of our existences but my belief is that the gay community have had a particular history and experience, which, although we share some of the common themes, is very different to our own. [...] I just feel it doesn't serve either community particularly because it dilutes their particular issues. And I think that the other danger and I know this from the work that I'm doing with the police, is that the gay and lesbian community have an extremely strong lobby, and I think that the trans community is so small, and the gay community in comparison is so large, that their needs will just get lost and do get lost within that.

Both Amelia and Rebecca suggest that the issues of concern within transgender politics are specific to discriminatory discourses around gender and not necessarily sexuality. A significant theme within anti-coalition arguments relates back to the common-sense perception that transgender sensibilities reflect same-sex desire. Others, however, suggest that this misinterpretation need not prevent a coalition between transgender groups and lesbian and gay organisations. Dan (age 37), for example, says:

> A lot of it is bound up in the way that the law works at the moment and as far as the law is concerned my partner and I are a same-sex couple, which automatically puts us into the same pigeonhole as gay and lesbians although we're blatantly heterosexual. We went to Pride last year and I obviously went as an FtM and my partner and I found that really strange because to everyone we were being perceived as being a hetero couple and I almost wanted an arrow saying 'we are different, we are meant to be here, we are a hetero couple but we're a trans couple'. And because I've transitioned so well it's not at all obvious that we fit into this group. But I almost wanted a big arrow. I wore my

'Transsexual Menace' T-shirt, but sometimes in a situation
like that you still want something saying 'we belong here,
we're not a straight couple', or you know, 'we're not a
conventional straight couple'. If I had been there just as
an FtM walking with all the other FtMs I probably would
have felt differently because I'd be perceived as being part
of the FtM contingency. But there were several of us who
were there with our partners as well and I just felt that
although we were part of the FtM contingent. It's really
difficult to describe.

Dan's comments indicate how legal discrimination around partnership
recognition and marriage may impact upon transgender and lesbian
and gay people in similar ways. Dan's narrative also relates back to
the tensions within identity-based politics, which have a tendency to
overlook the nuances and complexities of sexual and gender identity
categories. Accordingly, the ways in which non–same-sex affective
relationships have the potential to challenge normative values often
go unacknowledged. Del (age 44) relates to Dan's sentiments when
he reflects: "And I see a lot of transsexuals, you know, guys that pass so
seamlessly as heterosexual men, they get lost, they get queer envy, they
want to be seen, they want to out themselves and say 'OK, I'm queer
too'." For Del, transgender concerns are clearly linked to a broader
politics of equality: "I'm trying to show people that oppression is
linked. And that's why I think lesbian and gay politics […]. Let's work
towards a human right, equal rights for all people, regardless of their
gender, or their sexuality."

Greg (age 44) also suggests that the specificities of transgender need
not prevent a political presence within a queer coalition:

I think we should certainly collaborate. And in terms of
marriages the gay and lesbian community wants to have
their own choices unlimited by other people. They want
the flexibility and they don't want other people dictating
to them what they can and can't do in the same way that
they don't want to dictate to a heterosexual couple what
they can and can't do.

Here Greg makes clear the connections between issues of concern for
transgender people and lesbians and gay men. Moreover, in discussing
the importance of untying issues of sexuality from those of (trans)gender,

Greg makes a strong argument for a political framework that is guided by specificity as well as commonality.

Conclusion

Participants' experiences of sexual desire and practice, and their subjective understandings of sexual identity, add weight to Butler's contention that "identifications are multiple and contestatory" (1993: 99). Findings indicate that transgender sexualities are often fluidly and contingently situated; experiences of gender transition may enable an increased freedom of sexual expression and offer a greater diversity of sexual identification. Conversely, gender transition may facilitate a more contented sexual presence. Moreover, the significance of gender within embodied experiences illustrates the eclectic processes at work within the interplay of (trans)gender identification and sexuality. Findings show how trans sexualities highlight the limitations of existing classificatory systems of sexuality, and indicate that there are both distinctions and connections between transgender and non-heterosexual identities and practices. The resistance of lesbian and gay identity politics to gender diversity can be seen to have traditionally effected hostility towards transgender people, although there are indications that queer theory and activism has encouraged a more pluralistic outlook within some contemporary lesbian and gay cultures. Discussions about the merits of linking transgender politics with a lesbian and gay lobby suggest that there are deeply divided views within the transgender community around a politics of coalition.

I propose that the shifting gender and sexual subjectivities and identity practices at work here signify the relevance of a queer sociology (Namaste, 1996b; Seidman, 1996; Stein and Plummer, 1996; Roseneil, 2000) that would "bring queer theory's interrogation of identity categories into dialogue with a sociological concern to theorize and historicize social change" (Roseneil, 2000: 1). A queer sociological perspective enables an understanding of gender and sexuality as both distinct and conjoint. Such a framework facilitates movement "beyond the text" (Stein and Plummer, 1996: 137), therefore bringing to mind subjective investments *in* identity. Namaste (1996b) suggests that sociological queer theory is useful for understanding those practices that fall outside the binary of male/female. I add that queer sociology is helpful in accounting for identities that transgress the binary of hetero/homo. This is not to discount that some transgender people identify firmly as male or female, or as heterosexual or homosexual. Rather, queer sociology enables the recognition of identities that move (and settle) within, between and beyond these gender and sexual categories. MacDonald's (1998) injunction to both deconstruct and specify 'difference' can thus be attained through a queer sociological approach to transgender. In conclusion, I suggest that through a queer sociological gaze, an understanding of the distinctions and intersections of contemporary gender and sexual diversity is attainable.

SIX

Partnering and parenting relationships

As Chapter Two discussed, there has been an expansion of research into shifting familial and partnering structures within sociology and social policy. Intimacy is seen as a site of social transformation within contemporary society (Giddens, 1992; Beck and Beck-Gernsheim, 1995). Lesbian and gay partnering and parenting relationships are positioned at the forefront of changing affective structures (Weston, 1991; Giddens, 1992; Sandell, 1994; Stacey, 1996; Roseneil, 2000; Weeks et al, 2001; Roseneil and Budgeon, 2004). For Stacey, lesbian and gay families are the "pioneer outpost of the postmodern family condition, confronting most directly its features of improvisation, ambiguity, diversity, contradiction, self-reflection and flux" (1996: 142). This research suggests that transgender intimate practices further illustrate how family life is subject to ongoing contest, negotiation and innovation.

Studies of same-sex families and intimate relationships pose a challenge to a sociology of 'the family', which theorises intimacy through an all-exclusive focus upon the nuclear, heterosexual, monogamous, reproductive family. However, as Roseneil and Budgeon argue, non-normative patterns of intimacy tend to be relegated to "subfields of the sociologies of family and gender" (2004: 136). Further: "these practices, relationships and networks largely fail to be registered in a sociological literature which retains an imaginary which, without ever explicitly acknowledging it, sees the heterosexual couple as the heart of social formation, as that which pumps the life-blood of social reproduction" (Roseneil and Budgeon, 2004: 136).

Moreover, the partnering and parenting relationships of transgender people are ignored not only within sociologies of the family, but also within gender research. Thus sociologies of the family, studies of same-sex intimacy and analyses of gender relations have yet to take account of the specificities of transgender. While the impact of transition upon relationships with partners, lovers and children will differ in individual circumstances, the process of transition will always take place to some extent within a social framework of intimacy. It is from this juncture that I move on to explore changing experiences of intimacy through transgender practices of partnering and parenting.

In the first section of the chapter, patterns of intimacy are explored in relation to the reconfiguration of existing partnerships. The chapter moves on to consider the narratives of participants whose transition is linked to partnership separation. It then addresses the formation of new intimate relationships following transition. Finally the chapter explores how participants negotiate gender transition as parents.

Practices of partnering

Reconfigured partnerships

Recurring themes in the narratives of research participants who transition later in life are long-standing professional and relationship commitments. Bernadette (age 71) had a high-profile career as a government broadcasting adviser and a marriage of 40 years before transition. She says:

> I had a wife and children to support and I became chairman of various investigative boards and had a busy time for 11 years. Throughout all this time, I suppose, professional and academic success enabled me to keep the gender problem at bay but it never went away. I suppose it was a matter of subjugating my feelings to professional success and it worked. And I accepted that I was playing a fairly crucial role in government service at that time and it would have been irresponsible to vast numbers of people and organisations if I'd have said 'oh to hell with you, I'm going to go off and do what I've always wanted to do'.

Similarly, Christine (age 60) had a successful career as a partner in an international accountancy firm and was married for over 30 years before she began the process of gender transition. In the following quotation, she discusses how work and family obligations structured her earlier life:

> In the 1960s and 1970s the scenario was very different from how it is now. You left school and did your duty. You didn't query anything. You got your career and marriage and had children. You didn't have time to think about what you were and that was the environment that I was in.

As Christine's career developed, so did her identification as a woman; however, she negotiated her transition alongside professional considerations and decided to postpone the process of transition until she had retired:

> Over a period of time I knew what was going on and I became more aware of my feelings. But what is important here is that my career was progressing very well and I was operating at a fairly high level in a large professional firm. So the best thing seemed to be to wait until I had retired, which I did. I took early retirement and a whole new lifestyle arose. I no longer had to pretend and I no longer had the defence mechanism of having a respectable job, so those things went, and, literally within three weeks of retirement, I came out.

In these narratives, professional and relationship commitments are articulated as coping mechanisms for complex feelings around gender identity and as an explanation for late transition. Bernadette and Christine's transitions were thus reflexively negotiated and performed within the context of work and family life. These narratives also show Bernadette and Christine acting as 'energetic moral agents' in "weighing up the pros and cons of the consequences of their actions, considering others' perspectives and needs and reflecting on the decisions they make" (Williams, 2004: 42).

When Bernadette (age 71) was in her 30s, her best friend of many years died. A few years after the death of her friend, Bernadette married the best friend's wife. Although it would be 30 years before she took the decision to transition, Bernadette was open with her partner about her feelings around gender identity. As Bernadette articulates in the following quotation, her partner was to become a central source of emotional support: "I had a very helpful wife who supported me. […] She has supported me in every aspect and she supports me still." Christine (age 60) also discusses the support she has received from her wife throughout their marriage: "There's no support round here, there isn't a gender counsellor or anything like that, and so what I had in place of that for support was from my wife."

Bernadette and her wife moved to the village where they currently live four years before Bernadette's transition, and Bernadette became well known in the village. She was an active member of the village church and was elected chairperson of the local council. As the population of the village has fluctuated, Bernadette believes that her transition has become less of a public issue and that she and her partner are rarely perceived as a previously heterosexual couple. Rather, Bernadette (age 71) believes that: "everybody thinks of us as sisters. A lot of people think we are sisters." Correspondingly, Christine (age 60) says "If we have to describe ourselves we say that we are sisters-in-law." These relationships are located beyond a sexual framework and are repositioned within the context of kinship bonds. Bernadette was unconcerned that some people in her local community may view the relationship as a lesbian one, and focused upon the subjective shifting meanings of intimacy throughout the relationship's lifespan; as shown in the following section of the interview:

> **S:** Do you think some people see your relationship as a lesbian relationship?
>
> **B:** Oh, some people might, but that is their concept of it. I have a relationship with my wife, which is very intimate and loving and has been for the past umpteen years – 40 years – and it isn't any different now than it has ever been and it's very good. [...] I suppose, in the case of physical aspects of sexuality, I always seemed myself to be more of an observer, than a participant and in that respect that's the problem I had throughout all my married life, but that was OK with her.

Bernadette suggests that the continued emotional bond between herself and her partner has been possible due to the lack of emphasis placed upon sex within the relationship before transition. Christine (age 60) also suggests that sex was peripheral within her marriage: "I've never really had much interest in the physical meanings of sex. What mattered to me was tenderness. It was the larger picture that mattered, the caring aspects."

These relationships can be seen to be characteristic of a common-sense perception of long-term partnerships, and, particularly, heterosexual partnerships, whereby emotional closeness is seen as more significant than sexual desire. In de-centring sex within their relationships, Bernadette and Christine challenge the notion that sex is central to partnering and emphasise the role of emotional care. These relationships cannot be smoothly characterised as either sexual relationships or as friendships. Rather, the meanings of intimacy transgress either framework to illustrate how intimate practices may be revitalised across time and situation.

There are connections here with Roseneil and Budgeon's (2004) work on friendship and non-conventional partnerships, which suggests that contemporary practices of intimacy represent a blurring of the demarcation between lovers and friends. Weeks et al suggest that the role of friendship in the lives of lesbians and gay men is intrinsically connected to the significance placed on the role of intimate relationships:"[...] the prevalence of the friendship ethic provides some of the necessary conditions for greater intimacy" (2001: 120). In this way, friendship is held to be as important as sexual attraction or desire within a successful partnership. Further, in the research of Weeks et al (2001), the continuum of friendship and sexual desire within a long-term partnership was seen to be fluid and interchanging across time and circumstance. The blurring of sexual and friendship bonds are also apparent in Karen's (age 31) narrative. In the following quotation, Karen discusses how her relationship with her current partner developed out of a close friendship:

> We met on a course we did together and were friends for a year or so. Most people either see the physical side or see you as a friend, but it wasn't like that. We ended up getting married after we'd been together for a couple of years, and we're still together now. Although it's not a traditional marriage relationship we're glad we did it and we *are* married. She's had to be strong, and we've had to be strong together. I think the trust has grown.

Within the context of these long-standing partnerships, the meanings and lived experiences of intimacy can be seen to be fluid and adaptable to transformations of gender identity. Moreover, practices of emotional care and the values of honesty and trust are emphasised. These narratives correspond with Giddens' (1992) notion of 'pure relationships', whereby equality is foregrounded. Shifting experiences of intimacy within the changing context of gender transition are also apparent in narratives of relationship separation.

Relationship separation

Many participants spoke of how gender transition may initiate irreconcilable shifts in partnering roles, which can lead to relationship break-up. Nonetheless, intimacy remains a fluid rather than constant process that is frequently able to transgress the boundaries of sexual relationships and friendship.

Prior to her transition, Rebecca (age 55) separated from her wife, who is the mother of her son. In the following quotation, Rebecca talks about the difficulties of this break-up:

> It has been a very, very rocky road for me and my ex-wife. She was deeply in love with me and she admits herself that it took her many years, and I mean many years, to get over it. It's only in the last two to three years that she's started to become more civil. [...] She's always wanted to be friends but couldn't be. But recently she has calmed down. She was very ill a couple of years ago and she chose me to support her, which I was very happy to do. We were together for 17 years, so she's a big part of my life and if there is anything I can do for her I'll do it. I'm there for her.

Rebecca's discussion connects with broader shifts in contemporary relationships where ex-partners become important parts of support networks (Williams, 2004). Rebecca's narrative shows that intimacy can be re-formed across time to enable supportive and caring relationships to be reconfigured. The narratives of Tony (age 39) and Cheryl (age 45) also show how sexual relationships can be transformed into close friendships. Tony's partner provided emotional and, as the following quotation indicates, practical support during his early stages of his transition: "It was a decision we made to try and do it together whatever happens. Quite often if she and I would go out for a meal, if I chose to put a suit on, she would do the talking so that we just passed as a heterosexual couple." As Tony became more resolute about his male identity, his partner found the changing gender roles problematic and their relationship broke up. Yet, as the following quotation shows, the relationship between Tony and his ex-partner has shifted from a sexual relationship to a close friendship: "We still see each other and we're still very close. Her family were absolutely brilliant, and basically I've become a member of their family."

Cheryl also discusses how her partner's initial acceptance of gender transition was unrealisable. Cheryl cross-dressed for many years before beginning the process of transition. She has been married twice and both relationships ended. Cheryl was open with her partners about her feelings around gender identity, saying that she "[...] told them both, probably within a month, so that when we got married they were fully aware that I would cross-dress." Cheryl said that her first marriage ended because she and her wife 'drifted apart', although she also stated that "she [her first wife] couldn't really handle the situation very well". By the time she met her second wife, she had made friends with other transgender people and often spent weekends away at transgender social events where, initially, her wife would accompany her. Cheryl says:

> My second wife and I got on very well. She could handle it all and she came away with me for a couple of our weekends and she said they were some of the best weekends she's had. Everybody was so friendly. We used to get really close when I was dressed.

Yet the marriage broke up when her wife found that she could no longer manage the shift in gender roles. Cheryl says:

> And then basically last November things were getting more and more intense. And my wife said I should see a doctor and she said 'if you are TS [transsexual] I can't live with you any more because I married a man and you don't fulfil that role any more.' It was hard for both of us.

Like Tony, Cheryl has been able to build a friendship with her ex-partner: "My wife has said that she'll support me as much as she can and we are good friends."

Within these narratives, a range of affective possibilities are illustrated and the boundaries between sexual relationships and friendship are seen to oscillate. Issues around sexual desire and practice, however, are of key importance to experiences of forming relationships after transition.

Forming relationships

The formation of new relationships was significant within many participants' narratives of intimacy. Rebecca (age 55) is now single and, in the following quotation, discusses how transition may bring complexities to the formation of new relationships:

> I went through a really, really bad few years to begin with, where I had to come to terms with the fact that in the gender description that I have chosen, and all the complexities and ambiguities that that throws up, that the chances of coming across a woman who can accept me [pause]. I have had a couple of relatively brief relationships

with women but they have not been tenable, unfortunately, because of their confused feelings.

Dionne (age 40) has also been single since she transitioned. Like Rebecca, Dionne says that she would like to meet a partner, although she articulates a further issue in the formation of relationships after transition:

> And I'll never be able to have kids. I'll never be able to have kids as a man and I'll never be able to have kids as a woman either, and that's something I'd love to do, but it's something that I've sacrificed. So if you meet a partner it's got to be someone who doesn't want to have kids and that's hard as well, so that's another thing that I worry about, that someone won't want to be with you, because you can't have kids.

The experiences of other participants, however, show the potential for the formation of new sexual and/or partnering relationships after transition. Until he met his partner five years ago, David (age 26) had similar apprehensions to Dionne's about the prospect of parenting issues hindering a new relationship. David says:

> I wasn't looking for a relationship. I thought there were too many problems. For me to tell them I was a transsexual, that we'd not be able to get married or have children. I didn't want the hassle of a relationship. But with her it just happened. It was a sacrifice I was prepared to make, not having a relationship, if it meant I could be myself. But it's been great, and she's my main support. And now we think about maybe having a child in the future, we've talked about it. We've talked about adoption and IVF.

While David's narrative indicates that concerns around parenting need not prevent the formation of new partnerships, the experiences of other participants show more broadly how new relationships are often developed post-transition. Here Amelia (age 47) talks about meeting her current partner: "We met totally by chance and his reaction was 'so what? I've only ever known you as you, that other person is nothing to me, I never knew that other person.' Which I think is quite a wonderful reaction." Like Amelia, William (age 25) found that his current partner was unperturbed when told of his transition: "She just got it straight away, and was fine about it all. And in terms of accepting my body,

I've come a long way, and she absolutely does accept my body. And it's really important that she doesn't have any problems with my body, it validates me."

Bodily acceptance is also central to Dan's (age 37) narrative. After several years of being single, Dan felt that he wanted to begin a relationship, although he was fearful of being rejected by prospective partners once he told them about his transition. He says: "[…] I was so shy of my body. I'd had chest surgery quite early on but it's just a real fear about if someone will accept your body." Dan met his current partner through an internet dating site and they communicated for a few weeks by email and phone before meeting. It was important for Dan to discuss his transition with this woman once he knew that he wanted the relationship to progress:

> I'd decided before we met that if I really liked her and we clicked I was going to tell her that night. And so I told her, and I just rabbitted and rabbitted and she was quiet for about five minutes, didn't say a word, and I just thought 'oh no, I've blown it, I've blown it' and then she just said, 'well, it doesn't make any difference'.

Despite these reassurances, Dan worried that his new partner's feelings towards him would change once the relationship became sexual:

> You know, she was saying everything was fine, but how was it going to be when things started getting physical? I was also really worried about, you know, would I know what to do? So I was really worried and I was worried that she wouldn't like my body, that she wouldn't like it because I didn't have a willy. But I did know what to do [laugh] and for her [pause]. She wanted [pause]. She did want to be with a man but what she didn't like was, you know, the penis side of sex. So she was happy, I was happy.

The interplay between (trans)gender and sexuality is complex, and Dan's narrative reflects back to the significance of gendered embodiment within trans-subjectivities. Although these narratives question normative understandings of gender and sexuality as experienced and practised through biological 'sex', there is, however, an investment in a discourse of romance; whereby non-normatively gendered bodies 'make no difference'. Such a discourse is different from a discourse of realism, whereby non-normative bodily status would be acknowledged and negotiated. Moreover, a transgender romance discourse contrasts with a queer discourse, in which non-normative bodies would be a site of celebration and pleasure in their own right.

Cheryl (age 45) met her current partner shortly after her marriage broke up following her decision to transition. In discussing her new relationship, Cheryl positions emotional support as central: "It's a very close relationship and she's been so supportive. She's there for me when times are hard. She's been a rock, she really has. We are having a relationship, but it's also about our friendship." Cheryl's broader story articulates the fluidity and complexities of gender and sexuality as theoretical categories and as lived experiences. Within her life history, Cheryl's gender and partnering identities have shifted from a married man in a heterosexual relationship, to a female lover of a lesbian-identifying woman. Thus the binaries of male/female and hetero/homo are complicated, and a diversity of intimate subject positions reflected.

Narratives of transgender practices of intimacy raise a number of themes in relation to changing practices of partnering. The experiences of participants such as Bernadette and Cheryl lend support to suggestions of an increasing fluidity between the boundaries of friends and lovers (Sandell, 1994; Roseneil and Budgeon, 2004). Second, they resonate with findings of research into same-sex partnerships (Weeks et al, 2001) to suggest that understandings and experiences of intimacy are fluidly situated, and a range of affective processes constructed within non-normative intimate practices. Such practices support the assertion that intimate relationships within contemporary society reflect an increased presence of reflexivity and negotiation (Giddens, 1992; Weeks et al, 2001). However, narratives vary in the degree to which they speak of individuality or relations, and some narratives, such as Dan's, fit more with a conventional partnership discourse that is based around a notion of romance. Nevertheless, within narratives of partnering relationships, a strong emphasis is placed upon the value of emotional honesty, which, as the following section of the chapter moves on to explore, is also a key theme within narratives of parenting through gender transition.

Practices of parenting

Although many transgender people are parents, there is an absence of sociological research on the experiences of transitioning parents. Outside sociology, Green's (1978a, 1998) clinical studies on the impact of gender transition upon the children of transsexual people remain the only UK studies in this area. Moreover, though lesbian and gay parenting sparks much debate within contemporary society, there is a cultural reticence to speak about transgender people as parents, which leaves the practices of transgender parenting largely invisible

Telling children

Decisions around when and how to tell children about their forthcoming gender transition were central to the narratives of transgender parents. While the issues of disclosure here relate to gender and not to sexuality, there are links with the experiences of 'coming out' to children within the context of lesbian and gay parenting. Gabb comments that "heterosexual parents do not need to make 'proud' declarations of their hetero-sexuality. The image of such parents routinely 'coming out' to their children as heterosexual is almost beyond our imagination" (2001: 347). Similarly, the 'inside/out' (Fuss, 1991) gender binary naturalises non-transgender identity as something that does not have to be articulated, while transgender identity, as the outsider to the silent norm, is forced to speak its name.

Dan (age 37) was in his 30s and the lone parent of a nine-year-old son when he decided to transition. Dan felt dissonance with his gender identity as a young child. In his 20s Dan married and had a child. In the following quotation, Dan's decision to become a parent is articulated as an attempt to manage his conflicting feelings around gender:

> I didn't start dealing with it, well, talking about it, until I was in my in 30s, but I went through lots and lots of denial in that time and I got married because I thought it would make it go away. One of the reasons for having a child was that it would make it go away, it would make me whole. You destroy all this stuff that was doing my head in, but it didn't.

Dan's marriage broke up when their child was a baby and parenting commitments moderated his decision to transition during this time. Dan says:

> I had my son when I was in a can of worms. That was the hardest bit while I was sorting my head out; it was 'I need to do this for me, but what impact is this going to have on him? Will I lose him? Will he hate me? Will I have to face a custody battle?'

As his son grew up, Dan began to change the way he viewed the link between transitioning and parenting:

> My point of view then was that I was becoming so screwed up in my head that I was starting to fail my son as a parent and if I didn't sort my head out and live as me, as how I felt, then I would totally fail him because I didn't have it in me to love him and provide for him and, you know, I'd end up on tranquillisers and god knows what. So he would have ended up without a parent 'cos he wouldn't have had a parent to support him.

Thus, rather than seeing transitioning as problematising his relationship with his son, Dan began to see it as a process that would enable them to have a more successful relationship. Initially Dan's son found the situation hard to understand, as Dan describes:

> He was very distressed when I told him; he was nine, just nine. His first reaction was that it'd messed his life up. But after two weeks he came back and said 'OK, if it's got to be, it's got to be'. I think to start off he was worried that he'd go to school on Monday morning with me as his mum and I'd pick him up on the night as his dad. And I explained to him that you started off very slow and he realised it was going to be slowly.

Dan's openness about the procedures involved in gender reassignment can be seen to have enabled his son to understand the changing situation more fully. The importance of open dialogue is also stressed in terms of enabling children to adapt to the changes initiated by gender transition.

Open dialogue

As Dan (age 37) began hormone therapy, open dialogue with his son enabled a close relationship through the first stages of transition. He says:

> And he'd known that something was troubling me, but he didn't know what it was. So I'd hidden a lot from him during that time and once I'd opened up and was honest I told him everything that had happened since that time

and he actually started asking some really, really pertinent questions. But he was brilliant, especially at the beginning; if I needed to go to the loo he'd insist on going into the loo first so that he could find out where the cubicle was for me. So he was very protective of me, which was brilliant. It was nice to know he cared that much. We've always been in a close relationship and it's been tested along the way, and we talk and we've always talked.

Dan's narrative suggests that open dialogue can enable a climate of emotional care in which support is generated, not only from parent to child, but also from child to parent. Reciprocal caring between parent and child, however, may mean that the child cares for the parent by not revealing the full extent of what is happening in his/her emotional life. Children may feel more internally conflicted, or face more external conflict, than they feel willing or able to reveal to their parents.[1]

Support between parent and child is also articulated within Bernadette's (age 71) narrative. When Bernadette married she became step-parent to two teenagers. In the following quotation, she discusses her relationship with her stepchildren and talks about the support she received from them when she decided to transition: "My stepdaughter is one of my best friends, she's in her 50s now, she's a super person. Unfortunately, my stepson died, but he again was someone who was totally supportive of me. I was always entirely honest with them and it's been very good." Here we can see fluidity between parenting and friendship, which supports Pahl and Spencer's (2004) thesis of a fusion between friends and family within people's 'personal communities'. Moreover, as in discussions of significant values within partnering relationships, emotional support and honesty are emphasised.

Although at the time of our interview Cheryl's (age 45) children did not know that she was about to begin the process of transition, she too related to the importance of openly discussing the process of gender reassignment. As Cheryl's wife is the main carer of the children, Cheryl's situation with her children is more complex than that of Dan. Although Cheryl's wife supports Cheryl's decision to transition and they remain friends, she is unhappy about telling the children. Cheryl says:

She [Cheryl's wife] doesn't want to tell them yet. I'd love to live my life as I do when I'm seeing them but I respect her wishes on that. In time, when I start taking hormones and my body starts to change obviously things will change. To start with it won't be a problem, 'cos it is such a slow process so we're probably talking a minimum of 18 months and they'll be seven and nine. I want to talk to them about it, but for now the important thing is that I keep seeing them.

Although Cheryl is pragmatic here about not discussing her transition with her children at present, she indicates later in the interview that she experiences the situation as problematic. She continues:

> I live at home as Cheryl and I see myself now as a cross-dresser from female to male because I cross-dress to go to work and to see the kids. Before *her* clothes were in a suitcase in the loft, now *his* clothes are tucked away and I have to get them out to go to work. And it's the same with family and I think with kids honesty matters and is important but I'm not able to be honest. I feel resentful about that sometimes but it is going away because things are happening and the goal is getting nearer.

Here open dialogue with children not only signifies an emphasis upon honesty within parenting relationships, but is also linked to the affirmation of Cheryl's identity as a woman.

A significant component affecting relationships between transgender parents and their children relates back to partnering relationships to show that the relationship between a child's parents significantly affects how the child accepts gender transformation. Partnership breakdown can thus make parenting relationships difficult for transgender people, especially if the child lives with the other parent. Similarly, Green's (1998) clinically based study reported that children of transsexual parents said that they were affected more by the breakdown of their relationship with their transitioning parent following parental divorce than with the issue of gender transition itself. Melanie (age 41) discusses how the relationship between ex-partners significantly affects parenting relationships:

> For trans parents who go through the divorce there is the trauma of divorce that affects everyone who divorces. But if you are also trying to deal with the changes of transition, that is another aspect. And then if you put children in the frame, it is a very dynamic situation, a boiling pot. And for separations which are not amicable, the other parent may use the children as a weapon and courts are very unsympathetic

to trans people. Although some trans people do get custody in some cases and many do get access, it can be very hard. And while some children will accept, others won't and under the Children Act, if that child is over the age of 12 years old and they say they don't want contact with the parent then the law says you don't have to see them. And so the dynamic with the other parent is very important and if they are trying to undermine the trans person's relationship with their child it can be very serious. And if you have transphobic or homophobic social workers they can aid and abet this and courts are not really places to go for trans parents.

Amicability between ex-partners who are parents can thus be seen to affect a child's emotional wellbeing significantly. Moreover, the parents interviewed in this research were aware of the importance of maintaining an amicable relationship with their child's other parent. The maintenance of positive relationships between separated parents can consequently be identified as a key objective within transgender practices of care in relation to parenting. This corresponds with the work of Smart and Neale, which finds that parents frequently sustained their relationships following separation: "practical ethics which are important in these situations are based on attentiveness to others' needs, adaptability to new identities, and a spirit of reparation" (cited in Williams, 2004: 45). Balancing self-identity with emotional care for children can be complex (Lawler, 2000), however, and the process of negotiation between the two is a key theme in the narratives of transgender parents.

Negotiating transition with children

A significant issue discussed in relation to helping children come to terms with gender transition concerns the linguistic shifts that accompany changes in gender identity. Rather than reversing the parenting nouns of 'mum' or 'dad', each of the parents I spoke with had suggested that their child call them by their new first name or a nickname, which was often a variation of their pre-transition name. Dan (age 37), for example, says:

> He doesn't call me dad, he calls me 'Danny' and I think that made things a hell of a lot easier for him. And at the school he was at the headmaster talked to all the staff and

they were instructed that from that moment they were to call me 'Danny', nothing else, you know, never to say to my son 'when's your mum coming?' or 'when's your dad coming?' just 'when's Danny coming?'. That really helped things as well. And it helped with the pronouns, but for a couple of months I heard the most convoluted conversations, you know, 'ask Danny whether Danny wants a cup of tea' and it was quite interesting [laugh]. But I think that really helped him. I think one of the main issues children have problems with is changing that. A few people in the group [FtM Network], when they've been talking about problems with children, I've said 'don't try and get them to go from "mummy" to "daddy", try a nickname, even if it's not something you want to be known by, some androgynous nickname'.

Similarly, Bernadette's stepchildren called her 'Bernie', while Christine's children were able to continue to use the name 'Chris'. Considerations about how children would address their transitioning parent are thus reflexively situated in relation to enabling children to adapt to the changing gender status of parents.

A further theme within discussions of negotiating the process of transition with children concerns how children experience changes in their parent's appearance once the parent begins to take hormones and/or have surgical procedures. Some participants discussed how their transformed physical appearance proved problematic for their children. Rebecca's (age 55) son was a teenager at university when she began the process of gender transition. Although he initially appeared to accept the situation, as the process of change developed, he became unhappy. Rebecca says:

At first he was fine, of sorts. He would have been about 16 or 17 then and then the tragic point came for us about a year later when I changed my name and I had a party. I invited him to come and he declined. It was too much for him.

Christine's (age 60) and Lynne's (age 67) narratives suggest that reactions to the shifts of transition may differ between siblings. Christine says: "My son was very supportive but my daughter couldn't cope with it", while Lynne says: "My eldest daughter, she's great, and my granddaughter, she's great. My youngest daughter doesn't talk to me, no Christmas card, nothing."

For some participants, however, difficulties in relationships with children were transitory and intimacy was rebuilt. Christine (age 60), for example, says "but now we're [herself and her daughter] back together and it's resolved itself". Likewise, Rebecca (age 55) was able to rebuild a close relationship with her son after a period of distance. She says:

> We [herself and her son] had a period of about 18 months when we were out of contact and he was very angry so I left him to it. I made sure he knew that I still loved him and that I understood his feelings. [...] And now we've come back together and we're building a new and somewhat different relationship. So he's OK and he comes and stays here and I go and see him. So I'm very pleased and very proud of him.

Rebecca discusses the ways in which the passage of time can significantly change problematic relationships between a parent and child. This research indicates, then, that the parenting relationships of transgender people and their children are often able to withstand periods of instability, and are negotiable within complex gender practices.

Moreover, the research suggests that children of parents who transition from female-to-male, rather than male-to-female, may find the process easier to adapt to as the parent was more able to present androgynously before transition than were male-to-female parents. Dan (age 37), for example, says:

> I always wore a shirt and a tie to work before, anyway. That's what everybody else wore and that's what I wore, and I've still got clothes now that I was wearing seven or eight years ago and that shows how male, stroke androgynous, they were. So my clothes hadn't changed. So it wasn't like one day I was taking him to school in make-up and the next day I was in a shirt and tie.

Greater cultural acceptance of female androgyny compared to male femininity can thus be seen to impact upon the experiences of children to benefit the children of transgender men. Yet children's experiences of their parents' transition are not only affected by the ways in which their parents negotiate the process with them. In the following quotation, Dan discusses how the understanding of the head teacher at his son's school smoothed the process:

Obviously his peer group were going to be an issue at some point, but again the school dealt with that. It got to the point where some people, some of the boys, were starting to question why I was looking more masculine and the headmaster rang me up and said 'I'm telling the boys tonight'. We'd agreed it would happen at some point, and we don't know what he told them but they sent my son off on an errand and told the boys [...] All I know is that some of the parents rang me up the next day and said 'my son has come home and told me what's happening and you've got our total support'. We don't know what the headmaster said but he said something that really bound them together in a protective network and as far as I know my son has never had any difficulty.

Here Dan articulates the significance of the head teacher's role as a mediating agent. For parents of young children, the school environment and particularly the reaction of teachers, parents and other children are raised as important factors that impact upon a child's adaptation to parental gender transition.

Corresponding with the narratives of partnering relationships, a central theme to arise from narratives of transgender parenting relationships is the reflexive negotiation of the process of gender transition within the context of relationships with children. Thus, rather than representing an individualised process, decisions around the timing, disclosure and management of gender transition are considered and realised in relation to parenting concerns and responsibilities. Key values in negotiating the process of gender transition with children can be identified as trust, honesty and care.

Sandell's point in the early 1990s that "[...] men and women have, for years, formed committed same-sex relationships, and had children, but what is relatively new is for men and women to self-identify as being part of a gay or lesbian family, and to have children with that identity" (1994: 2) is pertinent to the current state of play in relation to transgender parenting. Thus historically, while many cross-dressing and cross-gender-identifying men and women would have been parents, self-identifying as a transgender parent is a recent social development. Further, as social and legislative debates around lesbian and gay parenting have contributed to the growing public profile of lesbian and gay families (Sandell, 1994: 2), the 2004 Gender Recognition Act has drawn public attention to the existence of transgender families.

Shifts in gendered parenting roles problematise normative assumptions of the link between biology and parenting identity that firmly situates motherhood with female biology and fatherhood with male. Castells argues that technological developments, such as surrogacy, sperm banks and in vitro fertilisation, have led to increased reproductive possibilities and choices, representing "growing control over child bearing and, over the reproduction of the human species" (1997: 241). Developments in reproduction technology additionally present increased parenting possibilities for surgically reassigned transgender people. Moreover, developments in reconstructive surgery and endocrinology further sever gender identity from biology. Castells' premise that technological transformations have affected a "whole new area of social experimentation" (1997: 241) can subsequently be expanded to take account of transgender practices of parenting in order to address the issues that these practices raise for theories of social change. In this way, De Sutter (2006) points to the ways in which current technology, such as sperm or ovarian banking, creates opportunities for transgender people to have children following surgery.

Conclusion

The themes discussed in this chapter raise significant implications for future social and family policy and, in particular, indicate the importance of developing policies that recognise the diversity of contemporary family structures. Moreover, the issues discussed in this chapter indicate that the incorporation of transgender practices of partnering and parenting into studies of family practices and intimacy facilitates a richer understanding of the dynamics of contemporary 'life experiments' (Weeks et al, 2001). Notions of agency and choice are apparent within the accounts discussed here, illustrating that complex decisions around gender transition are negotiated within the context of partnering relationships and family commitments. Narratives suggest that the meanings and experiences of sexual identity and sexual desire and practice may shift in relation to the performance of gender diversity. The boundaries between sexual intimacy and friendship are traversed as emotional support and care are emphasised within current partnering relationships and in relationships with ex-partners.

Many participants reflexively explore the impact of gender transition upon parenting relationships, and the notions of openness and honesty are stressed as important responsibilities within practices of parenting. Participants suggest that, from their experience, children are more able to accommodate the complexities within their changing situation if open dialogue takes place. Further, transgender parents identify a range of additional factors including the age of the child, the relationships between parents after divorce or separation, the gender of the parent, and the role of mediating agents as being significant to practices of transgender parenting. The narratives discussed in this chapter illustrate that transgender practices of partnering and parenting are amenable to complex shifts in meaning and expression. Gender transition can often be seen to enable an 'intimacy of the self' (Jamieson, 1998), which is built around mutual disclosure.

While these partnering and parenting narratives articulate personal creativity and agency, I suggest that the experiences discussed here speak not only about individual change over time, but that they speak also of sociohistorical changes in the diversification of meanings and experiences of gender and the impact of these shifts upon intimate lives and social frameworks. While not wishing to exaggerate the social acceptance of gender diversity, nor deny the continuing existence of transphobia, in the main, this research optimistically suggests that relationships with partners and children may be sustained or renewed within the context of gender transition. Additionally, findings illustrate the possibilities for the formation of new partnering relationships after gender transition. Stacey (1996) proposes that we are witnessing the 'queering of the family' as the meanings and expressions of 'family' diversify. The incorporation of transgender intimate practices into analyses of contemporary patterns of social life further illustrate how 'the family', as a social institution and as a process of lived experiences, is subject to ongoing contest, negotiation and innovation.

SEVEN

Kinship and friendship

From polemic that denotes a crisis in family life, bemoaning the loss of the 'traditional' family, to suggestions of increased agency in the creation of 'families of choice' (Weston, 1991), contemporary familial relationships provoke much public and sociological debate. While the impact of gender transition on relationships with parents, siblings and extended family differs with individual circumstance, to present instances of positive interaction and of disconnection the process of transition will always take place to some extent within the social framework of kinship. With this point in mind, the first section of this chapter explores gender transition within the context of kinship relationships. Initially I address the significance of support and care from parents and other family members for people beginning gender transition. The section then moves on to explore the narratives of participants whose transition led to fractured relationships with their family of origin.

As discussed in Chapter Two, various studies have shown that friendship is increasingly significant within contemporary practices of intimacy (Altman, 1982; Rubin, 1985; Nardi, 1992; Weeks, 1995; Weeks et al, 2001; Roseneil, 2003; Roseneil and Budgeon, 2004). Friends are seen to be as important as partners or family members and, for many lesbians and gay men in particular, friends are positioned *as* family (Nardi, 1992). The latter part of the chapter situates friendship as a significant site through which to address altered dynamics of intimacy within the context of gender transition. Here the concept of 'friends as family' is considered in relation to previous discussions of fractured familial relationships. Finally, the chapter explores practices of friendship in terms of the impact of gender transition upon existing friendships and in relation to discussions about the significance of friendships with other transgender people.

Kin relationships

Support of family

The support of family members, and particularly parents, can be seen to affect significantly both the decision to begin and the experiences of gender transition. For younger people, parental support is particularly significant. In the following quotation, for example, William (age 25) discusses how the support of his family gave him the confidence to begin transition as a teenager:

> I kind of bumbled through with my parents and they were always with me. I've lived with them for 25 years and they've always been there throughout my transition as I've lived at home. And they've always supported me. At the beginning they didn't think I'd go through with anything, but when they knew I would they supported me and they've been amazing. They've always believed what I've had to say. They always took me very seriously. My mum was the first to realise that I was very unhappy and so she got the help for me because I didn't know how to get it for myself, 'cos I was only 15. So she was the catalyst in getting me to see the right people. That was great. And I went with my mum for a while and then I went with my dad, which was really nice. And my brother's been great and so it's all been really, really supportive.

In sourcing information about relevant support services and care procedures for young transgender people, William's parents ensured that he was referred to a gender counsellor for young people. Moreover, both William and his parents became involved with Mermaids, a support group for transgender teenagers and their parents, and later began to offer support to other young people considering or beginning gender transition. This suggests a link between receiving and giving support, which will be explored further in the next chapter on transgender care networks.

As William was young and lived at home, his parents were continually involved throughout the various stages of his transition. For participants who are older and living away from their family, the decision to transition is largely arrived at independently and subsequently discussed with family members. Nevertheless, family support is significant, as Philip (age 42), who transitioned in his 30, shows:

> Well, by and large, I have had a positive reaction. Lots of people have said I'm not surprised, and even my dad said he wasn't surprised. My aunt said 'congratulations', my cousin said 'good for you', my sister said 'well, you've always been

very male even when you're in a frock'. Things like that,
very positive and important.

Philip's narrative indicates that support from parents and close family
members is important in affirming self-identity. In the following
quotation, Melanie (age 41) similarly discusses the importance of her
close relationship with her mother:

> We all want to be loved and we look to them for acceptance
> and it does matter. I couldn't say that I would have the same
> outlook if my mother didn't accept me. It does matter. The
> relationship with parents will be very different for younger
> people than for those of the older generation. Older-
> generation parents will find it much, much more difficult
> to accept to the same degree of the younger generation.
> And that makes a huge difference.

Here Melanie suggests that social attitudes to gender and sexuality
are undergoing significant change across the generations, and that
is benefiting younger people. Findings from this research largely
support Melanie's assertion that the generation of both transgender
people and of their family effect levels of acceptance and support,
demonstrating that the families of younger participants are more
likely to be sympathetic to their decision to transition than those of
older participants. However, as Lynne's (age 67) story shows, this is not
invariable. Lynne was in her 60s when she decided to transition and
her parents were in their 80s:

> My parents were great. I wasn't going to tell them but I
> thought 'I can't go on like this.' And they would say 'What
> the hell is going on in your life and why are you divorced
> twice?' and I couldn't tell them at the time. And in the
> end Dad was 82 when I told him and I thought 'they're
> going to live forever', so I told them. I told Mum first and
> she said 'Well, are you going to tell your dad, 'cos I'm not'
> [laugh] and I said 'I'll tell him.' So every time I went up
> there she'd say 'Have you told your dad?'. And in the end
> I told him and so I explained as basically as I could what
> was happening in my life and he just turned round and
> looked at me, and I was expecting a right punch up, and
> he just turned round and said 'Well you've been a good
> son, I'm proud of everything you've achieved, but if this is

what makes you happy then it's best you go for it'. I could have hugged him, he was great. And he was great for two and a half years and everybody knew by then. I was going up and doing the shopping and it was a place I went to school and for quite a long time I'd go as female and then I'd have to get changed into nondescript sort of unisex style of dress, still with the nails [laugh] 'cos my mum couldn't bear going into the village with me. And then one day she said 'Oh don't bother getting changed, I think everybody knows now anyway.'

For Lynne, being open about transitioning has had a positive impact upon her relationship with her parents. This is also the experience of other participants, such as Dionne (age 40): "My mum's been brilliant. She has been so supportive. For years we've been at loggerheads 'cos I haven't been able to talk to her about things and now there are no more secrets and I can talk to her and its fantastic." In Dionne's narrative, experiences of gender transition are linked explicitly to closer familial relationships. Greg's (age 44) discussion of his relationship with his partner's family also shows that greater intimacy can develop through open dialogue: "It actually opened up a new level of intimacy within her family. So her sister told me about her struggles and problems, and so the quality of our relationships has really changed because of me being honest about this."

Dionne and Greg's discussions of the positive outcomes of discussing transition with family members indicate an emerging environment of intimacy in which problems may be mutually shared and discussed; connecting with Giddens' (1992) notion of intimacy as an outcome of disclosing relationships. Although Dionne's (age 40) relationship with her mother became closer, her discussion of the reactions of other family members shows that familial support may not always be even: "My brother doesn't want to know. There wasn't that much of a relationship anyway. My brother and I never really got on. I'm not bothered too much about that. It would be nice to get on with him and his family but it's something that has never been there anyway so it's no loss." In emotionally distancing herself from her brother, Dionne is able to accept her brother's negative reaction to her transition. As I will explore in the next section, such pragmatism can be more difficult for those whose transition has led to a breakdown in relationships with parents.

Fractured families

For several participants in this research, gender transition impacted badly upon their relationships with parents and other family members. Although Bernadette (age 71) attempted to talk to her parents as a child about her gender discomfort, her parents were unable to understand her feelings:

> They didn't believe it. My father went to enormous lengths to [pause]. I was made to use carbolic soap and all sorts of curious things like that. I was bought Christmas presents that were so wrong for me. It didn't make sense at all. Whereas my mother couldn't cope, I mean my mother was a business woman, a very successful one, she couldn't make head nor tail of it, so she immediately employed her stepmother as my full-time nanny. If I had just been subject to my parents it would have been miserable. My mother didn't want to know. My mother, who was a typical product of the late 19th, early 20th century, felt that there was no distinction between gender anomaly and being homosexual, and she once announced to the world that if her son had been homosexual, he should have died.

Though Bernadette's childhood narrative is positioned within the context of the 1930s, the experiences of some younger participants indicate that hostile attitudes towards gender diversity may continue to be of consequence. In the following quotation, Tony (age 39) discusses how his relationship with his parents broke down once he told them of his decision to transition: "Family was what I was afraid of 'cos I knew what would happen and that was the hardest. Haven't seen them, haven't had contact with them for four years. As far as they're concerned, I'm dead." Amelia (age 47) expresses sadness at the breakdown of her relationship with her parents:

> I think my one regret is that I made a terrible mess of telling my parents and I haven't seen them from that day to this. The fault was on both sides, I think, partly mine and partly theirs. I told them, and that was that. One might say, whatever happened to unconditional love? I believe that my parents will simply not talk about me.

For Amelia, then, familial hostility has negatively impacted upon her otherwise positive experience of transition. Yet the narratives of others who have experienced strained familial relationships indicate that relationships with family members may be re-established over time. Despite having a problematic relationship with her mother throughout most of her life, Bernadette (age 71) shows that familial bonds may be developed anew: "Later on she came to terms with it all, in her 80s and 90s, surprisingly. She died at 93, not terribly long ago."

For others, discontinuities within relationships with parents are more short-lived, and difficulties with family members were overcome. Amanda (age 45), for example, says: "I lost my dad for a bit, for about a year. He decided that he couldn't handle the new me but by the end of last year he'd introduced me to his doctor in hospital when I visited him as his daughter for the first time." Like Amanda, Paul (age 34) had a period of time when he was out of contact with his parents:

> I've always been very kind of stubborn and determined, you know, I was going to do it. If I felt it was right that was enough, I was going to do it anyway. So I never felt I needed to go and sit them down and say 'Is this OK?' But I think my sister must have relayed it back to them and at the time I was actually quite distanced from my mother particularly, because she was insistent in calling me by my female name and that would have totally undermined the identity I was trying to create for myself. I just had to stay away for a while.

Paul's narrative suggests that time apart from family members is sometimes necessary within the process of identity formation. His discussion also articulates the difficulties that may arise with the linguistic shifts that accompany changed gender identity. The reluctance of parents to address their child by their new name and to adopt the corresponding pronoun is also articulated in the narratives of Anna and David. Anna (age 28) says:

> They won't call me 'Anna'. And we talk about it and I say 'Maybe when I've been "Anna" for 28 years, maybe then you'll change' and they agreed that they would after that length of time. Bloody hell [laugh]. I think there will come a point when calling me my previous name will be ridiculous looking the way I do and they'll go 'whatever'.

Similarly David (age 26) says:

> I kept giving them literature and saying, 'Do you want to read this? It will help.' [...] But it's been about five and a half years and it's only just now that they are starting to comfortably call me 'David' in my presence or just out of my presence in earshot. It's only just now that they do that.

David's discussion of preparing his parents by giving them literature to read about the process of gender transition points to the mutuality of emotional care and support. In discussing the negotiation of gender transition with family members, and particularly parents, several participants spoke of supporting their parents through the process. Greg (age 44), for example, says:

> It's a very long process, and it's a very difficult first year. You're trying to deal with all that's coming at you through treatment, trying to live a normal life in the other gender and then trying to gradually tell people when you're at your most vulnerable. And you have to literally put all your energy into helping other people. Whereas if you'd suddenly been diagnosed with multiple sclerosis all the people you loved would rally round and support you. But it's an unusual situation and it's shocking for people, and they need support and information from you.

These narratives indicate that transgender people are frequently the providers of support to family members, performing active 'kin keeping' (Williams, 2004: 44) as they attempt to explain the process of transition to the people close to them. This research thus identifies the provision of support to family members as a practice of care by transgender people. This connects with the research findings of the ESRC research project 'Care, Values and the Future of Welfare' (CAVA), which suggest that contemporary family life is often characterised by "the practical ethics of attentiveness to others' situations, accommodating one's own needs to those of others [...]" (Williams, 2004: 55). The narratives of David and Greg also indicate that it is often the marginalised people that are responsible for putting the dominant at ease. Thus an ethic of care is evident in the emphasis placed upon mutual understanding and emotional reciprocity. The practice of caring for others is also evident in narratives of friendship, where emotional support is again articulated as a mutual process.

Friendship

An ethic of friendship

Within these narratives of intimate relationships, a 'friendship ethic' (Weeks et al, 2001) is evident. Relationships with friends are articulated as being central to intimate lives and friendship is located as a key site of emotional care. Del and Melanie, for example, draw explicitly upon the role of support when discussing the significance of their friendship networks. Del (age 44) says: "My friends are my community, my family. I'm fairly independent but I have a close group of friends who are my support system, who when I'm in trouble I would call." While Melanie (age 41) says: "Friendships have always been important to me throughout my life and I've been very lucky that the friends I've made have been always there for me. My female friends are my main support network. It's very important to invest in those relationships."

Friendship may take on a particularly significant role in the lives of transgender people if gender transition has led to fractured relationships with members of their family of origin. Dan and Tony's relationships with their parents have been strained since they told them of their decision to transition. Dan (age 37) says: "Things have been difficult with my parents and in many ways, my partner, my son and my friends are my family now." Whereas Dan positions his friends alongside his other key intimate relationships, as a single person, Tony (age 39) locates his friends as the main providers of emotional support: "My friends have been my main means of support and they still are. My friends have effectively become my family."

In her work on the meanings of friendship for lesbians and gay men, Nardi (1992) speaks about friends 'as family' – emphasising the role of friendship for lesbians and gay men in the absence of familial support. Thus, in the face of limited or absent approval of their intimate relationships from families of origin, lesbians and gay men look to friendship networks for social, emotional and practical support. Likewise, friends can be seen to take the role of family for transgender people when kinship ties are disturbed or broken through transition. Moreover, in the absence of support from family members, Dan and Tony locate their friends as central sources of emotional support to connect with the notion of 'families of choice' (Weston, 1991; Nardi, 1992; Dunne, 1999; Weeks et al, 2001).

Friendships can be particularly significant in the early stages of transition, when the need for emotional support and self-validation is enhanced. Few participants knew other transgender people before they considered embarking upon gender transition and so existing friendship networks were drawn upon for support. Yet many participants had not discussed their feelings around gender with their friends before making the decision to transition. In the following quotation, Tony (age 39) talks about the positive reactions of his friends when he told them that he was about to transition:

> My friends have been absolutely brilliant. I couldn't fault them in any way. None of my friends ever turned round and said anything negative. In fact, for most of them it made sense. I think in a way it almost took pressure off them, 'cos I think they'd been sort of treading on egg shells, 'cos I was very, very secretive, and I think people didn't know who I was, what was going on. And then since transition I've been so much more relaxed and me, without having to play the role all the time. I can just be me now.

Tony thus suggests that telling his friends about his decision to transition has been mutually beneficial. As well as providing him with a support network, his disclosure has had a beneficial impact upon his friends. For Dan (age 37), it was also important to maintain existing friendships and, in the following quotation, he discusses how some friendships may take on a new significance after transition:

> When you meet a woman you develop a certain intimacy and you're able to talk about certain things. And as a man, women relate to you totally differently and I found it so difficult not to be able to get through that wall and be kept at arm's length. And that's one reason why it's been really important to me to keep all my previous female friends, 'cos I have a closeness and an intimacy with them that I don't have with women I've met since. Because I'm a man they're treating me as a man. And it was really strange 'cos you expect to go straight through into the clique and it's like 'you can let me in, I understand, I'm different'. I've got one friend who still goes into toilet talk, he still goes to the women's toilet sometimes. They are the best talks and he misses them so much. And he identifies as a gay man, so it's not like he's even got a female partner to have those intimate talks with, so he goes into the loo with his women friends [laugh].

In discussing the gendered nature of intimacy, Dan positions friendship within changing experiences and expectations of gender identity, which links back to previous discussions in Chapter Four. Although the close friends of many research participants were supportive of their decision to transition and were accepting of the shift in gender relationships, for others, such as Dionne and Karen, some friends were less accepting than others. Dionne (age 40) says: "I used to have a lot of mates who I went out with. But they were just mates and they aren't now. Out of all that came a few friends and we have got closer and those people have stayed with me all the way." Likewise, Karen (age 31) says: "Some of them [previous friends] I've lost, but I don't count them as friends, they were just people to go out with, to get drunk with, whatever. But a lot of them I've kept and they are good friends."

In discussing rejection by particular friends, both Dionne and Karen distinguish between 'mates' and 'good friends'. Thus it is suggested that differing levels of intimacy existed between the friends who supported their transition and those who did not. Distinct meanings of friendship are further articulated within discussions of the significance of building and maintaining friendships with other transgender people.

Transgender friendship networks

Many participants stressed the significance of their friendships with other transgender people. This can be seen to be particularly significant when first considering gender transition. In this way, the formation of friendships with transgender people is often discussed as an important moment in itself within the process of transition. In the following quotation, Bernadette (age 71) discusses the important role a close friend played in her decision to transition.

> I knew one transgendered person before I took the decision myself whose life was not unsimilar to mine. She was in the army as a colonel and was a big landowner and farmer. She transitioned in her 50s and she and I got on wonderfully and she was tremendously helpful to me and said all the right things at the right time. She was the one leading light that I had that gave me the confidence that things would be all right because they had been all right for her. That was very important to me at that time and we still meet for a coffee and a girlie chat every now and again.

While Bernadette emphasises the significance of having one close transgender friend, Dan (age 37) found friendship and emotional support during the early stages of transition within collective transgender networks:"There were a lot of us who transitioned together after *The Decision* [a television documentary about female-to-male transition], a lot of whom have also got children so we understood each other at a lot of levels and that was very good." Likewise, Cheryl (age 45) locates her friendships with other transgender women in terms of understanding and acceptance:"I've found a whole new circle of friends. I've met so many people and it's so good to talk to other people who know what you're going through."

For Dionne (age 40), areas of commonality and levels of understanding are the defining features of her closest friendship:

> She [her closest friend] has been so good. She'll sit down and talk to me for hours. It's been brilliant; she's always been there if ever I've needed a chat. It's been very important having a friend who has been through the same experiences. […] She's been the only support for a long time. Now I've come out there are those close friends that I've still got, but Amanda [another of the research participants] is the one that I can really talk to and now her friends as well, 'cos we've all got things in common. And it's mutual; they ask me for support as well. She's been a very close friend, she's been my counsellor. Because I haven't had any of that, been offered any of that, on the National Health, so the only counselling I get is from my friends, from talking to my friends.

In Dionne's narrative, friendships with other transgender people fill the gap created by a lack of counselling provision within health service care. William (age 25) also discusses the importance of being able to talk about issues of concern with friends who are experiencing similar changes within the early stages of gender transition:"In the beginning I think the people I felt I had most in common with were the people who were going through the stages exactly as I was and at exactly the same times, and so you could kind of talk about where you're at; which is very important."

Here similar experience and shared knowledge are articulated as key movers of close friendships. As participants progress through transition, however, shared experience may be less necessary within friendships. In the following quotation, William illustrates how wider areas of commonality have come into play within the formation of friendships.

> And now I think it's different when I make friends, it's more about their personality 'cos there's a guy that I've probably known for about five years now. We used to see each other quite a lot. Nice guy, but we kind of haven't talked for a long time, not because we stopped liking each other, but just that we don't have that much in common. You know, it would be really nice to see him, but I don't need to see him as much as before because we don't have that process to talk about, which is all-consuming.

In contrast to the changing nature of this particular friendship, William talks about reconnecting with someone he previously knew through a support group for transgender men:

> I bumped into this guy recently from some group and I actually thought, you know, 'you're a really nice guy', but I hadn't really kept in touch and maybe I should make more of an effort. But that's got nothing to do with, you know, we don't talk constantly about the process because it's changed. I'd like to know him because I like him.

William's narrative shows that the meanings of friendship are subject to temporal shifts, so that elements of similarity and notions of commonality are contingent upon changing circumstance. For other participants who have progressed through transition, however, the differentiation between individual friendships and community ties is less distinct. Amanda (age 45), for example, talks about her continuing friendships with women she met through transgender support groups:

> I feel very protective of my friends. And I do help a lot of people transition. I don't want them to have some of the problems I've had and a lot of the people I've helped out have become good friends and there are a lot of good friendships that have come out of that.

For Amanda, meanings of friendship and community belonging are combined to suggest fluidity between friendship networks and community organisation, a theme that will be further explored in the subsequent chapter on transgender care networks.

Conclusion

Rather than suggesting that gender transition gives rise to the demise of family relationships, the narratives considered in this chapter suggest that kin relationships maintain a significant place within intimate lives. This brings a challenge to Beck and Beck-Gernsheim's notion of individualisation whereby social bonds outside the couple relationship "seem too tenuous or unreliable" (1995: 24). Rather, there are many positive accounts of continuing support and care within participants' narratives of relationships with family members, and family support is experienced as important. While for some participants, the decision to begin gender transition led to rejection from family members, there is an apparent suggestion that these relationships were already strained. Moreover, other narratives show that difficulties within family relationships may be overcome so that family bonds can be re-formed or formed anew over time.

Bozett (1987) has challenged the assumption that families are defined by biology; while Franklin and Ragone's (2001) work on reproductive technologies has explored the changing relationship of biology and kinship. Similarly, Nardi's (1992) discussion of friends as family brings new meaning to the concepts of 'friendship' and 'family', moving beyond a biological definition of the family. Butler draws attention to legislative changes around lesbian and gay adoption and partnering rights to think about non-normative kinship relations that are able to transgress the "ideological function of marriage and the family as the normalised and privileged domain of sexuality" (1994: 14). As I suggested in the previous chapter, practices of gender transition also sever gender and sexual identities from biological understandings of identity formation. I would like to add to this that transgender practices of intimacy provide another illustration of 'families of choice', to illustrate how biological perceptions of kinship may be thought of anew as family networks negotiate transgressions of gender.

Friendship is identified as a key site of personal meaning and emotional support, the significance of which can be seen to run alongside or above that of kinship. Friendships can be seen to take on different meanings in relation to the distinct stage or time span of transition. Further, the significance of close relationships within both old and new friendship networks, and with transgender and non-transgender people, are reflexively considered. An 'ethic of friendship' is apparent in participants' discussions of the care and support given and received through their intimate networks. These narratives indicate that many family members and long-standing friends are willing to adjust to changes of gender identity, and are able to offer emotional care and support through the processes of transition. As Rebecca (age 55) says:

> The reaction of family and friends has, I suppose, been the most rewarding aspect of me taking the courage to move forward in this direction. What had always held me back was the fear of rejection by friends, family, and the world in general. And it was a great surprise, but maybe in retrospect not surprising, that people have been so accepting of me.

Participants' narratives of kinship and friendship often articulate a "practical ethic of compassionate realism" (Williams, 2004: 55), where adapting to new identities is seen as key to enabling commitment to continue. While not discounting the pain of rejection, overall, participants' narratives of family and friendship optimistically imply that, in many instances, these relationships are dynamically situated, and may be sustained or renewed within the context of gender transition.

EIGHT

Transgender care networks, social movements and citizenship

This chapter begins by considering practices of care within transgender support and self-help groups. Here I am extending the meanings of care discussed in Chapter Two to look beyond care as something that is given or received within an intimate context of family or friendship networks in order to examine care practices in relation to self-help groups and social movements.

Social movements have been explored in relation to contemporary processes of social change. Giddens (1991) has discussed social movements as a significant form of 'life politics', while Beck (1992) discusses the realm of 'subpolitics' whereby disenfranchised groups participate in the reconstruction of social life. Social movement theory has traditionally focused upon the structural claims of social movements around the redistribution of wealth and social inequality (Martin, 2001). More recently, Fraser (1995), Mellucci (1996), Williams (1999) and Williams et al (2002) have brought attention to the ways in which social movements represent struggles over social recognition and difference. Williams et al suggest that social movements are made up of 'collective actors' and "consist of subterranean networks of people and groups embedded in everyday life" (2002: 9). In broadening the study of social movements beyond a structural analysis, Williams (1999) follows Fraser (1995) and Honneth (1996) in using a 'politics of recognition' to account for the diversity of welfare struggles around difference.

In considering practices of care within transgender support groups, the aim of this chapter is to incorporate transgender community self-help groups into studies of social movements. The first part of the chapter draws on research into transgender care and then moves on to discuss the main transgender support and self-help groups in the UK, addressing the specific kinds of care these groups provide. The second part of the chapter explores the significance of support groups in relation to the notion of shared experience, and looks at the values that matter to transgender people in relation to the giving and receiving of care within support groups. The next section considers the extent to which transgender support groups fill the gaps left by a deficit of professional care. Finally, the chapter considers the complexities of

involvement in support groups in relation to a politics of transgender
visibility and issues of transgender citizenship and recognition.

Transgender care and support groups

The most comprehensive study of care within UK transgender
communities comes from a survey by Johnson (2001) undertaken for
the transgender support group, the Beaumont Society. Overall, the
report stresses a severe dissatisfaction with community methods of care
beyond the transgender community, and findings show that community
care for older, ill and disabled transgender people is undertaken in the
most part within the "social circle that exists around the care receiver"
(Johnson, 2001). Johnson discusses the importance of education and
training about transgender issues for all carers of transgender people.
Importantly, she emphasises the need to see transgender people who
are care recipients as active agents: "transgendered people could have
fought (in one way or another) all their lives for rights, justice and
medical care. Rather than being 'passive' in old age they are more
likely to be 'activists'" (Johnson, 2001). In conclusion, the report warns
against generalising the care needs of transgender people and indicates
that transgender communities identify care as a key area of importance.
One of the major objectives of transgender organisations is to provide
practical support and care for transgender people, for example, through
contact networks, self-help and voluntary organisations and information
lines. Yet such services remain largely voluntary, funded by transgender
organisations and individuals themselves. The care experiences and
needs of transgender people remain marginalised – leading some
transgender people to fall through both formal and informal care
networks – and the issue of public funding for transgender people as
a community of care providers and recipients is not addressed within
social policy. Conversely, welfare policy makers and practitioners
remain largely unaware of the distinct care needs of transgender people.
From empirical research into health care for transgender people in the
US, Singer (2006) claims that poor care arises from an unfamiliarity
and incomprehension of non-normative bodes among health care
professionals. Singer thus writes of the importance of training health
care workers to go beyond their "conceptual limit" (2006: 616) so
as to "recognize the legibility and meaning of trans identities and
bodies" (2006: 616). Good health practice thus demands an imaginary
leap on behalf of medical and health care practitioners. In turn this
would enable "[...] bodies that literally and metaphorically exceed

two-dimensional medical images [to] step into a new social context, and make new ethical claims" (Singer, 2006: 616).

Transgender communities have developed practices of care and support that correspond with the agency enacted by communities initially affected by the HIV/AIDS epidemic. Likewise, the significance of support networks for transgender people links to the importance placed upon support networks within lesbian and gay communities (Altman, 1982; Rubin, 1985; Weston, 1991; Nardi, 1992; Weeks, 1995; Roseneil, 2000; Weeks et al, 2001). In making this comparison, however, I do not wish to conflate the identities of lesbians, gay men and transgender people. Nor am I suggesting any unitary characteristics of care for either group. Indeed, such comparisons could equally be drawn between transgender communities and a number of previously marginalised groups who, due to social exclusion and a lack of resources, have found it necessary to build their own social networks and practices of care. When discussing care issues for transgender people, then, it is necessary to reflect upon the experiences of individuals who, though connected through the broad category of 'transgender', occupy various other distinct identity positions. These points link the themes of identity, intimacy and care to issues of citizenship and recognition.

There are five main support organisations in the UK. The first of these groups, the Beaumont Society (BS), was founded in the late 1960s. With over 4,000 members, the BS is the UK's largest transgender support group (www.beaumontsociety.org.uk/history.htm). The BS acts as a contact service for transgender people; providing an information line, regular social events and a separate group for female partners of transgender people. The BS defines itself as an "association of transvestites and transsexuals" and seeks to "provide a means of help and communication between members, in order to reduce the emotional stress, eliminate the sense of guilt and so aid better understanding for them and their families and friends" (www.beaumontsociety.org. uk/constitution.htm). The BS's constitution is unusual in its aim to link transvestite and transsexual people as two groups who do not always sit easily alongside each other. The constitution also sets out to provide support for family and friends of transgender people. The BS's objective of 'eliminating guilt' links with the goals of the lesbian and gay movement in the late 1960s and early 1970s, which enabled "an affirmation of a positive sense of self and of the collective means of realising this" (Weeks et al, 2001: 14).

Affirming a positive sense of self in the light of social stigma is also the aim of transgender support groups Gendys and the Gender Trust. Gendys is a network for "all who have encountered gender identity problems personally, transsexuals, transgendered people and gender dysphoric people of either sex, and for those who provide care, both professional and lay" (www.gender.org.uk); while the Gender Trust is a registered charity that provides a "caring support and an information centre for anyone with any question or problem concerning their gender identity, or whose loved one is struggling with gender identity issues" (www.gendertrust.org.uk). The two other main support groups, Mermaids and the FtM Network, offer support to more specific groups of transgender people. The former is a support group for transgender people under the age of 19 and their families and carers, while the latter is a contact and support group for transgender men. Within each of these groups, 'care' is understood and practised through the notion of shared experience, which, as the chapter moves on to explore, is articulated as especially significant in the beginning stages of gender transition.

Shared experience

Weston's (1991), Weeks' (1995; Weeks et al, 2001) work has shown how shared experience is drawn upon by lesbians and gay men in their 'coming out' stories, which, as Weeks describes, "told of discovering the self, achieving a new identity, finding others like yourself, and gaining a new sense of belonging" (Weeks et al, 2001: 14). This research indicates that these elements are also apparent in the 'coming out' experiences of transgender people. Out of all the participants, Cheryl (age 45) was at the earliest stage of her transition when our interview took place. She says: "The Beaumont chatline on the internet was my lifeline between November and Christmas. It was my only outlet and way of keeping in touch with other people and finding other people who were like me."

Greg (age 44), who transitioned 18 years ago, also remembers the significance of meeting other transgender people and, specifically, other transgender men: "There are shared experiences [...]. If I talk to another female-to-male you can nearly always find agreement about experiences, emotional experiences, along the journey." For many participants, contact with transgender support groups alleviated feelings of isolation. Georgina (age 29), for example, says: "Before I knew about the groups, for about a year, I just felt that I was the only person who was going through this. It was brilliant when I found out I wasn't the only one."

The social marginalisation of transgender cultures, then, can be seen to have led to particular practices of care and methods of self-help, which place a strong emphasis upon shared experience. There are direct links here with Weston's (1991) work on the significance of 'community' for lesbians and gay men. The importance of shared experience is also reflected in a diversity of studies into self-help and support groups. The ESRC research group CAVA explored community self-help groups for parents, for example, and found that "the groups often gave their members a sense of belonging and security [...]" (Williams, 2004: 69). In the following quotation, Paul (age 34) reflects on these themes:

> You lack confidence because you're not confident in your own body, and some people are almost paralysed by it and have trouble making friends, being open. It can be quite lonely and you feel you can't be honest with people, so those sort of people suddenly find a whole new set of friends and they've got something in common and I guess they kind of forge trust with other people that they didn't have before.

These discussions suggest that the principle of trust is held as a key value in the provision of care by support groups. Thus several participants talked about the significance of being able to be 'open' and 'honest', and of being able to 'trust' the people they met through support groups. Moreover, the principle of trust is often linked to reciprocity. As the next section will explore, there is a fluid demarcation between receiving and giving care through support groups.

Giving something back

The intersections of care-giving and receiving are articulated through participants' understandings of their involvement in support groups as a means of 'giving something back' to the communities and groups from which they had received support. In this way, many participants became involved in the running of the groups they had first contacted for support. Greg (age 44), for example, says: "Quite soon I took various roles within the self-help group myself. It meant that I was meeting other people who were like me, if you like. So since then I've always stayed involved. I've done lots of different things."

Several participants were formally involved in giving care and support to other transgender people. Christine, for example, is chairperson of the Gender Trust, while Emma is variously involved in transgender support groups as chairperson of GIRES – a transgender information service – as a local contact for the Gender Trust and as a qualified counsellor who specialises in gender identity issues. Others gave support in less formal ways. Rebecca (age 55), as a member of a support group, offers informal support to other transgender people at the start of their transition:

> People ring me up and want advice, as I'm a member of Gender Trust. I have had a lot of engagement with the Gender Trust because there is no one in this area. One of the problems here is that there are only two psychologists and it's a part-time service, once a week, and the waiting list is horrendous. It takes two years, and people are in crisis and I know exactly what that is like [...]

In discussing her role as a care-giver as well as a care recipient, Rebecca, like other participants, suggests a framework of care that identifies the values of choice, mutual interest and reciprocity in community practices (Williams et al, 2002).

William (age 25), who transitioned as a teenager, got support from Mermaids. In the following quotation, he talks about his present role as an organiser of this support group for young transgender people and their families:

> Mermaids is where my parents used to go 'cos it actually started as a parents' group and then it became a charity and I kind of went along for support and then my parents stopped going and I went on the committee. And I do other things for them as well as sitting on the committee. I went to a school, a girls' school and talked to the sixth form, like a group of psychology students, and some of the questions were absolutely brilliant and they were brilliant. Educating people who are in education, young people, is vital, absolutely vital.

Here William identifies education as a central means through which to change cultural perceptions of transgender people. Like William, Dan (age 37) has given talks to young adults; as he describes in the following quotation:

> I've done quite a lot of talks to evening classes doing sociology and so on, to talk to them about transgender issues and there have been some brilliant ones, some of them have been so good. Education and awareness is important.

Especially when I'm just introduced as a visiting lecturer with no background, and that is so powerful. One that I did – they were doing about membership to different groups – and I talked about being a single parent, that I was in a relationship, that I was white, that I'd been brought up as an Anglican but had lapsed, and a whole load of other things about myself and my education that I just threw in. And then I said 'Right, let's see if you have perceptions about the groups in society that I belong to.' And then on a flip chart I got them to give me feedback on perceptions about my ethnic background, my religion, my sexuality, my gender, my marital status. And so they came back and went 'white, male, heterosexual, divorced but cohabiting', and then I challenged them about how did they know that I was male? How did they know I was heterosexual? How could they assume these things about me? And then it was 'Well, you're a man' and I asked them 'How do you know I'm a man? Have I got a willy? Can you see my willy?'. And then I said 'I'm transsexual' and they went absolutely quiet and one of the girls said 'Oh, I really fancied you' and I said 'So, you can still fancy me.' And it was fantastic. It totally blows people's perceptions.

Both William and Dan articulate a framework of values in which education is central. Likewise, all of the transgender support groups discussed at the start of this chapter perform an educating role as well as existing as contact and social groups. Here the distinction between care, support and education is blurred as the social marginalisation of transgender people is identified on both an individual and a societal level. Thus support groups aim to alleviate cultural stigma and associated social isolation by providing contact among transgender people, while also attempting to eliminate the social discrimination that creates these components through broader educational initiatives. These points resonate with Noddings' (2002) discussions of education from a care perspective. Noddings proposes that education – "a constellation of encounters, both planned and unplanned, that promote growth through the acquisition of knowledge, skills, understanding and appreciation" (2002: 283) – is central to the development of caring in society. She argues for the importance of caring as an educational goal and identifies caring as a crucial pedagogical activity. In emphasising the importance of personal, social and life education, Noddings sees education as much more than training for economic life. Rather, education is located as an ethic of care.

Education as an ethic of care

The need for greater education about transgender issues is a major theme within narratives of care. This is apparent across a range of contexts. Johnson's (2001) study identifies the need for greater education about the particular needs of transgender people for their carers in both a home and a residential setting. The narratives of participants in this research discussed so far articulate the importance of teaching young people about transgender issues within an educational setting. As this section will move on to explore, a further theme concerning the importance of education relates to practices of care within medical professions.

The care of transgender people is delivered as part of a standardised system that is guided by the Harry Benjamin Association's 'Standards of Care' (2001). The first port of call for people who are having anxiety about their gender identity is usually their GP. When speaking about care, several participants spoke of their GP's lack of knowledge about procedures of care for transgender people. Sam (age 32), for example, says: "I went to my GP years ago and he looked at me like I was crazy. He didn't know what I was talking about at all." A deficit of care for transgender people thus arises from a lack of understanding at a general practitioner level. Accordingly, several participants believed that GPs needed comprehensive training about gender diversity issues. In the following quotation, Paul (age 34) takes this point further and articulates the need for training in the NHS on a broader level to combat discrimination against transgender people:

> I think there's still some discrimination against transsexuals, even though the nurses and doctors aren't supposed to take a stance. I mean, I was in hospital recently and I thought they didn't treat me as they ought because I was transsexual. [...] And sometimes there's ignorance or bias towards you. [...] So I do think that there is prejudice. And so I think there should be training, basic training, for nurses. I mean, again, if they had, maybe, a transsexual coming to talk to them. I don't know whether this is a good parallel or not, but like the police are recruiting more minorities and dedicated lesbian and gay officers to deal with and to understand that part of the community. In the same way it would be

good to see some transsexual doctors and transsexual nurses, someone in hospital you can talk to. I mean, I'd love to see a transsexual doctor, 'cos I think only a transsexual doctor can understand. It's like all things really; if you've been through it you can understand [...]

In discussing the importance of training in transgender issues for health professionals, participants again suggest that education is central to the provision of better care. A key theme to emerge from this research, then, is that education is significant across a range of sites – for care workers, within schools, colleges and universities, and for medical and health professionals. Thus education can be identified as an ethic of care. For Noddings an 'ethic of care' describes the ways in which care is a basic facet of human life and is the foundation for ethical decision making. Ethical caring is discussed as "a state of being in relation, characterized by receptivity, relatedness and engrossment" (Noddings, 2002: 11), factors all apparent in Paul's discussion of good care as practised through sensitivity, understanding and knowledge. Yet the development of ethical caring is further complicated by the extent to which the medical system shapes the lives of transgender people. Psychiatrists form a central part of the standardised medical system of care and, as Purnell argues, psychiatrists are "pivotal decision makers concerning access to treatment" (Purnell, in Monro, 2005: 54). Key here is the issue of regulation, which is fundamental to the transgender experience and not well addressed in the UK literature on care.

Towards an individual system of care

The notion of 'gender dysphoria' is central to the standardised system of care for transgender people. Typically, a GP will request a psychiatric referral, which will consider manifestations of 'gender dysphoria'. A diagnosis of 'gender dysphoria' enables access to surgery, which is understood within medical discourse and practice as the appropriate 'treatment' for 'gender dysphoria'. Thus those who conform to medical understandings by articulating the 'condition' of 'gender dysphoria' are granted gender reassignment, while those who question medical discourse, and/or articulate more ambiguous and complex gender identities and presentations are denied surgery. In performing the role of gatekeepers to 'treatment', medical practitioners and psychiatrists work as regulators within a system that largely continues to pathologise transgender experiences. It is not surprising, then, that the experience of the psychiatric system of many transgender people is largely negative. Dan (age 37), for example, says:

> Most psychiatrists are absolutely barking, absolutely out of their trees, you know, they need to see a psychiatrist [laugh]. While you do have to be checked to see that you're not suffering from a mental condition or any delusions, and I can understand that there has to be care to make sure you are who you say you are, I don't think that people should be made to jump through hoops.

While not rejecting the medical system outright, Dan suggests a move away from a standardised system. In contrast to the current standardised medical model of care, many participants in this research argue for an individualised system that would be more receptive to the diverse care needs of transgender people. In this way, Greg (age 44) says:

> There needs to be a good caring and informed relationship between psychiatrists and patients [...] I think the process should be an individual decision between the patient and the people making that clinical judgement *with* the patient. Because for some people it might be good to have surgery within six months or a year and for other people it won't. I think it should be more individual rather than prescriptive. What is best for you is not necessarily what is best for someone else.

Many participants spoke of their dissatisfaction with the length of contact time with psychiatrists. Dionne (age 40), for example, says:

> You get an appointment about once every three months at first, it's very sparse, and you don't get any counselling. You get a three-monthly visit with the psychiatrist for 20 minutes at first and the next one is four months and the next five months. They rush you in and out, it's a production line. They've offered me no group sessions or anything. They haven't offered me anything like that but I'd go if it was offered. My friends have been my counsellors. I don't think the Health Service is very helpful. I feel that on the whole it's done begrudgingly. Because I haven't had any counselling on the National Health, the only counselling

I get is from my friends, from talking to my friends who I've met through groups.

In discussing the lack of counselling provided within the current system of care, Dionne relates explicitly to the ways in which support groups and friendship networks fill the gap left by professional care services.

Filling care gaps

Many participants have pointed to a systematic lack of support for transgender people. Support groups are subsequently identified as vital for providing advice and information that is lacking within medical care. This can be seen to be particularly significant at the start of transition; as indicated by Paul (age 34):

> I think the important thing for me was having contact with transsexuals who were several years down the line from me, and that's the support now that I provide to other people. I man the FtM support network phoneline from time to time, and it's only then that you realise how vital you are to people like that, who are the same stage that you were, or where I was – needing someone to chat with or to work out what to do – 'cos more than the doctors, they're more experts, anyone who's been through it.

Paul's comments illustrate the ways in which support groups may challenge expert opinion by providing distinct practices of care based on shared experience. Themes here again resonate with CAVA's findings on support groups for parents, which suggest that:

> [...] becoming an 'expert-by-experience' was one way of claiming the importance of lay knowledge and expertise which professionals did not have. People said they wanted a more 'holistic' or integrated approach. Also many groups saw themselves not simply as receivers and distributors of information but, importantly, through sharing and developing information, as the *providers* of expertise and new knowledge. (Williams, 2004: 68–9, italics in original)

Additionally there are links here with the ethics of disability movements that have challenged a paternalist model of care that provides care on behalf of disabled people (Williams et al, 2002).

New forms of care provision can also be seen in the ways in which some participants build on the methods of care they have received within their local communities. After being involved with the London based FtM Network, Dan (age 37), for example, set up a support group to fill the gap in care for transgender men in the west of England:

> Western Boys, which we're just in the process of starting, would like to grow to serve the southwest in the same way that FtM London serves the wider community in the southeast and further away. We want it to be a support and a social group. We've got a safe meeting place so that people can come safely without any worries of being outed and for them to be in a safe environment. We want to develop that and we want to mix with the MtF community.

For Dan, the new support group fills a geographical gap in care for transgender men that has previously been organised from the south of England. It is also important to Dan to overcome the polarity between communities of transgender men and women. While he sees his new group as providing specific support for transgender men, he also wants to make links with groups who provide care for transgender women. In the following quotation, Dan talks about a novel plan to bridge these gaps:

> One of the goals we're setting ourselves with Western Boys is that we make contact with an MtF group in this area so that we can learn and share more. We could do clothes exchanges, which is one of the first things that I did with someone – with an MtF. We were of quite a similar build, though she was a bit taller, and we had one evening where I went to her house and our clothes fitted each other perfectly. I came back with a brand new fantastic wardrobe. Despite the fact that my wardrobe wasn't at all feminine, she was thrilled with her wardrobe. And links like that would definitely be useful.

Once more there are comparisons between initiatives of care and support by and for transgender people, and the practices of care developed by and for communities affected by HIV and AIDS in the 1980s and 1990s (Adam, 1992; Weeks et al, 2001). Such practices of care show how marginalised communities develop as a site of identity and resistance (Weeks et al, 2001). Moreover, these practices of care and support reflect a community ethics of care through which caring is valued and respected. There are also strong comparisons with Weeks et al's (2001) points about the caring practices of lesbians and gay men, Weeks et al found care to be central to the concept of commitment and the negotiation of responsibilities. Traditional caring institutions were viewed unfavourably, and were seen to limit personal and collective agency. Rather, linking back to the themes of the previous chapter, friendship networks were found to be of great importance in times of illness and for older respondents, and these 'informal' practices of care were valued above traditional caring institutions.

Transgender support and self-help groups can be understood as a social movement in which themes of social recognition and difference are key to the project of reshaping cultural understandings and social practices. Yet, as the next section moves on to explore, while many participants articulated a strong commitment to the involvement in support groups after transition, others saw community groups as less significant post-transition, and some felt that support groups held little or no importance.

Moving on

For some transgender people, support groups become less significant after the early stages of transition. Although William (age 25) remains an active member of Mermaids, believing that it is important to continue to offer support to other young transgender people, other support groups are less significant for him as a care receiver now that he is several years post-transition:

> It's still important for me to be part of the FtM London group but sometimes I just get thoughts like 'well, I don't really need to be doing that any more'. I do go to the group but I haven't been to for a long time because I've just had other things to do. But if I'm free on a Saturday, on the Saturday once a month whenever it is, I go. Whereas before I used to make a real effort because I really used to like it and I like the people, but now I just have lots of other people to see. But it's nice to go sometimes, just to catch up.

Like William, Amanda (age 45) suggests that while she maintains social contact with members of a support group whom she met at the start of her transition, her personal level of investment in these social events has shifted:

I go to a few of the London clubs. But I'm not really into little clubs. I'm not saying I've outgrown it, but there was a time for that and it's not really now. But then again if I want to see people I need to go to those places. And I'll go and I love it but I don't want to do it all the time. And I've met some good friends through those things and I met Cheryl [her partner]. So, yeah, I socialise wherever things are going on but I'm not really into going to what I see as transvestite groups. That's not applicable to me now. If that's their thing then fine, but it's not me anymore.

While, post-transition, William and Amanda still socialise in transgender environments, others, such as Tony (age 39), have little social contact with other transgender people:

I stay a member of FtM and do give my money to them because if it weren't for them I wouldn't be here. There was a lot of support and I have a lot of respect for them, immense respect. But I don't really see myself as part of that group. [...] I don't want to not be aware but at the same time I very much feel that if we're not careful we might alienate ourselves if we constantly only mix within our own kind. And I feel personally that's a danger. But if something happens in your life it's useful to know there's someone there. You know, teachers have got their unions; well, it's kind of like my union.

Though Paul (age 34) has more involvement with support groups than Tony, he too suggests that he has little personal investment in these groups since transitioning:

I couldn't see myself ever going on, you know sort of youth hostelling sort of things and stuff like that. Just 'cos I wouldn't want to be in a place full of transsexuals, and also, you know, that's the only thing you would have in common so it doesn't necessarily mean you're going to get on with them. But that said, I always go to the FtM Network get together every year because it was really important to me, it was quite sort of pivotal in convincing me that I could do it, you know, if these guys can look like this so can I, whatever it was, eight or nine years ago, and so I think it's important for me to be there.

Here, Tony and Paul relate to the contentious issue of assimilation, which was discussed in Chapter Three. Rather than expressing a desire to move away from transgender communities entirely, however, Tony and Paul suggest different degrees of identification with the term 'transgender' or 'transsexual', and varied degrees of investment in community organisations and support groups throughout the stages of transition. As David (age 26) illustrates, though, some transgender people do seek to move away from a transgender identity:

> **D:** I know there are groups on the internet and if I need advice I can go and get advice, but I don't feel the need to get actively involved because I don't think of myself as a transsexual. But I do think that more awareness and education in society as a whole is important, education and awareness just that there are transsexuals. I wouldn't do talks or things but it's for selfish reasons in that I want to move on. And I am very protective of it, of people knowing [...]. And I think that is very important and I know that's only going to come from people speaking out.
>
> **S:** But you don't because of the personal repercussions?
>
> **D:** Yeah.

Thus while David articulates the importance of visibility in relation to increased societal awareness, his reluctance to be vocal paradoxically prevents him from speaking out. This resonates with Taylor's findings that self-help movements are "heavily cultural, and revolve around disputed meanings and contested identities" (Taylor, quoted in Williams et al, 2002: 9). Issues of community involvement and visibility link to questions around a transgender politics of recognition and citizenship.

Politics of recognition and citizenship

Nadia's role in *Big Brother 5*, which was discussed in the Introduction, highlights the tensions apparent in questions of transgender citizenship. Nadia found a place in the *Big Brother* house following her openness about gender transition during auditions for the show. Yet, though programme makers, the media and *Big Brother* viewers knew about her recent transition, Nadia did not speak of transitioning to her housemates. Nadia was clearly aware that the public would be interested in her gender experience, explicitly coming out as a transgender woman in her audition video. Yet, in the *Big Brother* diary room and in subsequent media interviews, she spoke of her decision not to tell her housemates in terms of being accepted as a woman:

> I wanted to enjoy it, embrace the world. I didn't want to sit around and have deep conversations or anything like that [...] I don't want to tick a box and say I'm transgender. I don't understand why people want to categorise themselves like that [...] Rather than consider themselves transgender they [transgender women] should just let their personalities shine. We are women. I am a woman. If you want to get into that, you're going to be stuck most of the time talking about what you've been through, and that is the last thing I want. (Nadia Almada, quoted in *Observer*, 22 August 2004)

Some participants in this research also articulated individual, rather than transgender identities. In answer to my question 'is the term transgender relevant to you?', Tony (age 39), for example, says: "I've never thought of myself as transgender. I'm just a bloke who's gone through one or two shit things but that's all I've ever been."

Narratives of moving beyond a transgender identity are characteristic of 'claims to citizenship'. Weeks et al (2001) suggest that recent social movements, particularly feminism and the lesbian and gay movement, are characterised first by moments of transgression and second by claims to citizenship. Transgression is defined as: "[...] the constant invention and reinvention of new senses of the self, and new challenges to the inherited institutions and traditions that hitherto had excluded these new subjects" (Weeks et al, 2001: 91). The moment of transgression is followed by the claim to citizenship: "[...] the claim to equal protection of the law, to equal rights in employment, parenting, social status, access to welfare provision, and partnership rights and same sex marriage" (Weeks et al, 2001: 91). The moment of citizenship mirrors the goals of many transgender organisations and, importantly, was the lynchpin of the 2004 Gender Recognition Act (GRA).

Legislative changes brought by the GRA, however, show the complexities of 'claiming citizenship' for some transgender people. For married people the legislation is problematic as marriages have to be annulled before a change of birth certificate is permitted. Bernadette transitioned from male-to-female 15 years ago and remains married to her wife of 40-plus years. The GRA means that Bernadette now has to choose between legal recognition as female, and her long-standing marriage. One option for Bernadette and her wife is divorce and register for a same-sex civil partnership. However, since neither Bernadette nor her wife considers themselves to be in a lesbian relationship, this is a problematic choice. Press for Change (PfC) lobbied unsuccessfully to overturn this requirement of the GRA. Claire McNab, vice-president of PfC, summarises the outcome:

> We were left with the consequences of the government's coldly symmetrical logic: that marriage was for opposite-sex couples and civil partnerships for same-sex couples, with no exception even for the hundred or so couples about to move from one category to the other. A harsh logic, requiring people to change their legal relationship just for logical neatness [...] (McNab, 2004)

As Chapter Two suggested, transgender practices of intimacy indicate that partnering and parenting relationships are amenable to complex shifts in gendered meaning and expression. Such transformations show how intimate relationships, more broadly, are subject to ongoing contest, negotiation and innovation.

While these intimate narratives speak of sociohistorical changes in the diversification of meanings and experiences of gender, they are muted by legislation that denies the storyteller the recognition and rights of citizenship. Weeks et al state that "[...] without the claim to full citizenship, difference can never be fully validated" (2001: 91). Yet, although the GRA aims to enable transgender people to claim citizenship, it reinforces inequality for those who are married. Such a paradox supports Williams' claim that "[...] moves to recognise diversity may sometimes expose or reinforce inequality" (2004: 82). Moreover, if a 'moment of citizenship' is conceived out of the desire for inclusion, we must also bring a more radical voice into the frame.

Transgressing citizenship

Downplayed in discussions about claims to citizenship are the sections of social movements that place more import on the moment of transgression than the moment of citizenship. From this perspective, the wisdom of soliciting validation is questioned. Such a position preserves the celebration of difference, and questions the merits of normativity and assimilationism. Radical gender and sexual movements such as Queer Nation and Transsexual Menace act as a cautionary reminder of the dangers of a whole-hearted liberal approach to citizenship claims. Hence those who remain 'different' are frequently constructed as 'difficult' and become further marginalised. Aizura's (2006) work on transgender rights and discourses of nationalism in Australia is significant here in illustrating how other factors – in Aizura's case 'race' and culture – can impact on the rights afforded to gender-diverse people. Juang (2006) has similarly commented upon the ways in which transphobia is cut through with racial and ethnic discrimination. Boyd's (2006) work is also relevant here in showing how transsexual bodies may trouble historical narratives of identity and thereby fracture national geographies. These studies show the importance of developing an intersectional analysis of transgender, which considers (trans)gender experiences alongside other social and cultural identities: "Indeed, accuracy demands that we attend to the different origins, histories, and consequences of structures of oppression" (Juang, 2006: 707).

In discussing a moment of citizenship it must not be forgotten that most recent social movements divide on the desirability of citizenship as a political goal, with many arguing that such a route inevitably leads to the subjugation of difference and transgression. This debate is apparent within transgender communities on the question of 'passing'. While some transgender people see 'passing' as a prerequisite for social acceptance and inclusion, others argue against assimilating into an incomprehensible binary gender system (Stone, 1991; Feinberg, 1992, 1999; Bornstein, 1994; Wilchins, 1997). For some research participants, such as Del (age 44), it is also important to articulate gender fluidity:

> I don't think it's linear. I think it's more like if you have [Del draws diagram]. Here we have our source and that's whoever we are and it shoots out in a more kind of radial way, so it's more like a kind of colour chart and you can pick all the different colours.

Following the GRA, the law now allows for movement *across* the binary of male/female, however, the spectrums *in between* male and female, such as transgendered, intersexed, bi-gendered and androgynous, remain outside current frameworks of citizenship. The Act thus further marginalises those who cannot, or will not, define as 'man' or 'woman', and, as such, is unable to account for the full spectrum of gender diversity. For Boyd, some transgender bodies are intrinsically 'outlaw bodies', "[...] unruly, unreadable, inconsistent [...]" (2006: 431). Further:

> [...] while most bodies, even transgendered bodies, fit neatly
> or fold back into the body politic as readable, comprehensible,
> and intelligible, some retain or reclaim a fleeting moment
> of social, cultural unintelligibility, inhabiting a queer space
> [...] outside, beyond, invisible to, and perhaps, as a result, in
> confrontation with the state. (Boyd, 2006: 431)

Although the law now concedes that gender identity may change across
the lifespan, its narratives of identity remain spatially fixed. Rather than
seeing gender transition as an end-point, however, many participants
discussed how their understandings and experiences of gender shifted
through transition. Yet an understanding of gender as intertextual and
precarious is at odds with current concepts of citizenship. In this way,
people who rebuff the gender binary by refusing to dovetail gender
presentation and gender identity neatly – for example, bi-gendered
trans people, butch trans lesbians, camp trans men, cross-dressers, and
drag kings and queens – continue to be excluded from the rights
and recognition of citizenship. In rejecting the surgical route, then,
transgender people fall outside the domain of the 'deserving' citizen
(Richardson, 1998).

Weeks et al discuss debate around recognition within lesbian and gay
communities as "[...] one based on boundary-defenders who argue for
a social movement based on a collective identity, and boundary-strippers
who argue for the deconstruction of identity and binary categories
[...]" (2001: 192). Although similar themes are apparent in debates
around recognition and assimilation within transgender communities,
the tensions around a transgender politics of identity are more complex
in that the 'boundary strippers' of gender may simultaneously act as
'boundary defenders' in arguing for the importance of a transgender
(rather than transsexual) identity that denotes gender difference.
Moreover, some trans theorists (Wilchins, 1997; Prosser, 1998) have
cautioned against a tendency towards transgression within transgender
politics. Thus Wilchins (1997) discusses a hierarchy of transgression
wherein: "a voice that originated from the margins began to produce
its own marginalized voices" (2002: 59). For Wilchins (2002), all
political movements based on identity are flawed; Wilchins proposes that
movements should be issue based. There are, then, conceptual problems
as well as civil inequalities in recent moves to grant transgender people
citizenship. Constructed upon a gender binary model, the GRA is
unable to recognise the diversity of new (trans) masculinities and
femininities as they are variously constructed and experienced. Hence,

rather than broadening the realm of citizenship in relation to gender diversity, the Act works to reinforce a normative gender model.

Conclusion

Transgender support groups and self-help groups are challenging both the meanings and the practices of care provision for transgender people. A medically based standardised system of care is critiqued and many transgender people stress the need for a framework of care that is responsive to a diversity of individual needs. In often moving between being the receivers and providers of care, many transgender people articulate the importance of shared experience, and challenge the notion of expert care as based upon objective knowledge. Transgender support groups often fill the gaps in care left by professional organisations, and many transgender people identify areas of discrimination in the care system and, in particular, argue for a more comprehensive system of training for medical professionals. Moreover, education is recognised as an important issue in relation to increasing awareness of transgender issues and eliminating discrimination. Education can thus be identified as an ethic of care.

Transgender communities largely exist as marginalised subcultures in terms of the normative frameworks that guide social and welfare provision. Support groups offer a key source of care within transgender communities and can be understood as a social movement that is articulating a distinct framework of social values around the care of transgender people. Mobilised from a collective grass-roots level, this social movement poses a critique to gendered binary understandings of social inclusion, citizenship and welfare provision. In this respect, the increasing visibility of transgender communities is not only important in terms of social inclusion, citizenship and welfare provision, but is also key to social and cultural understandings of the diversity of shifting practices of identity, intimacy and care in contemporary society.

Discussions in this chapter indicate that involvement in support groups is not evenly practised and that concerns over visibility impact upon involvement within community support groups. There are, then, investments in competing discourses around a politics of transgender visibility. The last part of the chapter examined issues of recognition and transgender citizenship. Representing the civil recognition of gender transition, the GRA marks an important change in attitudes towards transgender people and aims to end social exclusion. Yet while the 'claims to citizenship' of some trans people – those who have undergone surgery or who articulate 'gender dysphoria' – may be facilitated through the new framework of rights, the enduring influence of a medical model upon social and legal understandings of transgender mean that those who 'transgress' – married trans people who choose not to divorce and those who construct identities outside the gender binary – remain on the margins of citizenship, residing as 'non-citizens'. My findings here support Richardson's (1998) argument that social change sought through the notion of 'citizenship' tends to emphasise 'sameness' rather than equality of 'difference'. Thus the current framework of transgender citizenship still fails to account for gender diversity.

This chapter suggests that while some transgender people articulate individualism and are reluctant to position themselves as members of a collective transgender culture, others present distinct transgender identity positions that are consciously created in opposition to traditional ways of thinking about gender. These latter gender identity practices offer a challenge to political goals of assimilation, signposting a radical politics of gender transformation in which 'difference' is positioned as a site of importance and celebration in its own right.

In their discussion of sexual citizenship, Bell and Binnie argue that "[…] to disidentify – to remain as non-citizens – will maintain systems of exclusion and discrimination that brings real material harm to many people" (2000: 146). Along these lines, the GRA must be welcomed for its aim to remedy exclusionary systems for transgender people. However, as this chapter has shown, although some transgender people are benefiting from recent UK policy developments, other practices of gender transformation have become further marginalised. The complexities of transgender identity positions and identity politics that have been discussed in previous chapters thus mean that transgender citizenship is an uneven and contested terrain.

NINE

Conclusions: (re)theorising transgender

Towards a queer sociology of transgender: implications for (trans)gender theory

Conceptually, this book has mapped out a queer sociological approach to transgender. A queer sociology of transgender sits on the intersections of deconstructive analyses and empirical sociological studies of identity formations and practices. The theoretical starting point of the book was a critique of medical perspectives on transgender. Over the last century, medical perspectives have occupied a dominant position that has significantly affected how transgender is viewed and experienced within contemporary Western society. Although contemporary medical approaches represent a more complex understanding of transgender practices than was previously offered, I have argued that there remain serious problems in the correlation of transgender and biological and/or psychological pathology. A medical model remains tied to a binary understanding of gender that fails to take account of the many gender identity positions that fall between or beyond the categories of male/female. Moreover, medical approaches to transgender continue, in the main, to work within a heteronormative framework that is unable to account for the complexities of transgender sexualities. A range of alternative theoretical perspectives – ethnomethodology; historical and anthropological studies; radical, pluralist, poststructuralist and postmodern feminism; queer theory; and transgender studies – were drawn upon to explore the varied ways in which social and cultural theory has critiqued medical discourse on transgender.

From this diverse body of work, I identified pluralist, poststructuralist, and postmodern feminist approaches, queer theory and transgender studies as significant for the development of a queer sociological analysis of transgender. Pluralist feminist approaches offer a theoretical framework of gender and sexuality that is able to account for non-normative identities and practices, enabling an analysis of divergent gender expressions that are unfixed to the 'sexed' body. Importantly, poststructuralist and postmodern feminism emphasises the discursive formation of gender and sexuality, bringing an understanding of gender as distinct from biological 'sex'. In bringing attention to 'difference', these perspectives encourage feminism to move beyond a singular and an essential conceptualisation of 'woman'. I have argued, however, that some strands of poststructuralism and postmodern thinking are problematic for a sociological theory of transgender as they neglect the role of embodiment within gender identities and expressions and fail to account for material conditions. Moreover, these perspectives have tended to focus upon transgender as a symbolic site of gender deconstruction, which leaves transgender subjectivities under-explored. I proposed that MacDonald's (1998) model of a grounded postmodern theory is significant for a queer sociology of transgender as it stresses the importance of analysing the ways in which social structures and corporeality impact upon the formation of distinct (trans)identity formations. This theoretical model is valuable in its understanding of gender as socially relational *and* performatively constructed.

I have suggested that the intervention of queer theory has led to three significant shifts in the analysis of transgender. First, the deconstruction of identity categories and the analysis of gender and sexual identities as fluid pose a strong challenge to a medical model that pathologises gender diversity and works to reinforce a gender binary system. Second, queer theorists have criticised the strands of lesbian and gay theory and political activism that have been exclusive towards those whose gender and sexual identities and practices fall outside the configuration of female/lesbian and male/gay – a homonormative binary. This marks a significant shift from the suspicious gaze with which transgender people have been viewed within many lesbian and gay communities, and challenges the positioning of the transgender individual as 'outsider' within strands of lesbian and gay writing. Rather, queer theory has positively embraced difference and has argued against the representation of sexual identity categories as authentic. Third, queer theorists have challenged the correlation of gender identity and 'sex' that lies at the heart of radical feminist hostility to transgender people, and which significantly effected the dominant feminist position on transgender throughout the 1980s and early 1990s. Through this sociobiological approach 'sex' is largely dependent upon chromosomes and thus is secured at birth. From this perspective, gender is also linked to biological 'sex'. In contrast, queer theorists have sought to untie gender and 'sex'. Queer theory's deconstruction of an inside/outside binary significantly detracts from essentialising hierarchies that marginalise those who, through factors of structure and/or agency, inhabit gender borderlands.

Yet I have argued that queer theory has also neglected the material and embodied contours of transgender lives and has failed to account for diverse and competing transgender subjectivities. Here I concur with other scholars (MacDonald, 1998; Monro, 2005; Namaste, 2000; Stryker, 2006; Whittle, 2006), whose arguments I discussed in Chapter One, who caution against adopting poststructuralism as *the* analytical framework through which to theorise transgender. These issues are important for a sociological analysis of transgender. I have suggested that work from transgender studies offers a way through this dichotomy. In Chapter One, and through subsequent chapters, I have drawn upon work by transgender theorists (Stone, 1991; Feinberg, 1992, 1999; Bornstein, 1994; Califia, 1997; Halberstam, 1998, 2005; Namaste, 2000) that makes apparent divergent understandings of gendered and sexual, social and embodied identities. Transgender studies articulate the importance of a grounded theory that not only celebrates the deconstruction of identities and the emergence of difference, but which is also attentive to the lived experiences of multiple subjective positions. Interventions by theorists such as Stone (1991), Bornstein (1994), Califia (1997), Feinberg (1999) and Halberstam (1998, 2005) show that a queer imaginary does not have to run counter to a material analysis.

The intersections of transgender studies and queer theory offer a theoretical space in which to conceptualise a queer sociological approach to transgender. Throughout this book, I have proposed that a queer sociological approach is important for developing new understandings of transgender. A sociological turn enables queer theorisations of transgender to move beyond their current limitations by paying greater attention to specificity. Thus, in accounting for material and embodied experiences, a queer sociological framework enhances understandings of the diversities of transgender experiences, allowing for a more nuanced analysis of gender and sexual transformations. I have subsequently suggested that a queer sociological framework facilitates the grounding of transgender experiences within social practices and discourses. Moreover, this allows for both the celebration and the critical analysis of gender diversity. A queer sociological approach to transgender thus encourages departure from theorising transgender practices as either wholly deviant or transgressive.

Recognising gender diversity: implications for studies of intimacy, care and citizenship

The book moved on to consider sociological studies of changing practices of intimacy, care and citizenship. I suggested that this body of work was important to the premise of this book as it has, from different theoretical sites, challenged gender essentialism and heteronormativity. Work on non-normative practices of intimacy and care usefully draws attention to the divergent meanings and experiences of intimacy and care, thus offering an understanding of the ways in which these practices operate within different social contexts. Recent analyses of non-normative practices of intimacy and care have broadened sociological understandings by bringing to light the creative affective practices within same-sex relationships and 'families of choice'. I have argued, however, that this body of work continues to work within a gender binary framework that is unable to account for transgender practices of intimacy and care.

Moving beyond a gender binary model is important for an understanding of the meanings and experiences that transgender people bring to intimacy and care. I proposed that this could be developed through consideration of transgender practices of intimacy and care within the dynamic of 'families of choice' (Weston, 1991; Weeks et al, 2001). Moreover, I have suggested that such an analysis departs from the theorisation of transgender as a medical issue, bringing it into the 'public' realm. Yet, in making this alliance, it is important to be aware that inequalities in relation to social structures and cultural resources mean that not all families have the same choices (Taylor, 2007). Moving away from understanding transgender as a privatised medical issue would also bring transgender into dialogue with the theoretical frameworks of 'intimate citizenship' and an 'ethic of care', both of which seek to bridge the private/public divide and aim to take account of marginalised gender and sexual practices. I proposed that studies of intimacy and of care develop in ways that take account of transgender practices. This move is significant not only to a politics of inclusivity – here incorporating transgender practices into studies of intimacy and care – but is also key to enabling this field of study to broaden its analysis of contemporary non-normative affective and caring practices.

Current debates on sexual citizenship point to the compromises that 'claims to citizenship' entail for members of lesbian and gay communities (Richardson, 1998; Bell and Binnie, 2000). In this way, assimilation is a condition of citizenship. While common themes run through issues of intimate, sexual and transgender citizenship, I have suggested that work on sexual citizenship needs to theorise beyond a gender binary in order to address the specificities pertinent to transgender citizenship. Moreover, developing a conceptual framework of citizenship that transgresses a gender binary enables a richer understanding of the intersecting subject positions from which contemporary citizens speak. In turn, this enables a closer analysis of the ways in which social formations interconnect.

Imagining beyond binaries: a sociology of transgender

In this book I have explored a number of substantive questions about transgender practices of identity, intimacy, care and citizenship. To this end the book has drawn on, and made links with, a range of studies from within and outside the UK that have explored transgender identity formations and experiences, and transgender practices of intimacy and care. The book has empirically considered MtF (male-to-female) and FtM (female-to-male) transgender practices and those that are located between and beyond these categories. The scope of address suggests both commonalties and diversities within and between transgender individuals and communities. Transgender communities represent a diverse constituency and, rather than articulating a common experience, transgender narratives suggest a range of competing discourses. While some participants articulated fluidity of gender identity, others spoke of moving between fixed points. There are, then, tensions between notions of identity as fluid or fixed. Though some participants spoke of the importance of claiming a transgender identity, others articulated the desire to move beyond this subject position.

Debates within transgender communities around the implementation of the 2004 Gender Recognition Act reflect similar concerns about the desirability of assimilation within lesbian and gay communities following the 2004 Civil Partnerships Act. While some interviewees considered gender assimilation to be both desirable and necessary for the protection of transgender civil rights, others offered a challenge to the notion of assimilation, proposing a (trans)gender politics in which difference is considered as a site of importance and celebration in its own right.

These debates link to the issues raised in relation to transgender identities and experiences explored in Chapter Three. While some participants constructed distinct transgender identity positions, consciously created in opposition to traditional ways of thinking about gender, sexuality and transition, others articulated individualism and were reluctant to position themselves as members of a collective transgender culture. As some participants spoke of the pleasures of gender transition, positioning (trans)gender identity as fluidly situated and practised, others talked of the immutable formation of (trans)gender identity. Nevertheless, the corporeal body figures large in these narratives and the body is experienced, managed and modified through subjective understandings and social positionings of (trans)gender. Bodily narratives thus suggest that transgender identities are constructed and negotiated through, and in opposition to, a range of factors: medical discourse and practice, gender, sexuality, social class, age, affective relations and social, cultural and political understandings and networks.

In Chapters Four and Five, I suggested that an analysis of feminism and lesbian, gay, bisexual and queer (LGBQ) movements is important for an understanding of transgender identities and experiences. Participants' narratives have indicated that transgender men and women encounter distinct feminist challenges and experience different levels of acceptance within feminist and/or lesbian, gay and bisexual communities. In particular, many transgender men and women spoke of rejection from second-wave feminism, but told more positive stories about their relationships with contemporary feminism. Similarly, many narratives of sexuality suggest problems with lesbian and gay identity politics, and participants have spoken of negativity from some lesbian and gay communities. Yet queer politics and theory have encouraged a more pluralistic outlook that, in turn, is more welcoming to transgender people. Participants' understandings and experiences of sexual desire, identity and practice suggest that transgender sexualities are often fluidly and contingently situated alongside gender and gender transition. The large numbers of non-heterosexual participants within this research speaks of the complex interactions between gender and sexuality. However, there are both commonalities and distinctions between transgender and non-heterosexual identities and practices. Debates around the significance of linking transgender politics with a LGBQ lobby has shown that there are strongly divided views within transgender communities about a politics of coalition.

Chapters Six and Seven suggested that the impact of gender transition upon parenting and partnering, and kinship and friendship, indicates that complex decisions about gender transition are often reflexively negotiated and practised within the context of intimate relationships and commitments. Here I proposed that the incorporation of transgender practices of parenting and partnering and kinship and friendship into studies of family practices, intimacy and care enables a richer understanding of contemporary social life.

In Chapter Eight, I argued that transgender support groups and self-help groups challenge the meanings and practices of care for transgender people. Many participants challenge a standardised medical system of care, proposing a framework of care that is responsive to a diversity of needs. The practices of transgender support groups fill the gaps left by professional systems of care. Some participants identified existing discrimination against transgender people in the care system and discussed the importance of education and the training of health professionals for increasing the awareness of transgender issues and ending discrimination. Yet involvement in support groups was uneven, and there existed competing discourses around politics of transgender visibility and recognition. Such complexities led me to read transgender citizenship as an uneven and disputed landscape.

So the themes of the book are taken full circle, indicating again the diversity of transgender identities and pointing to both the similarities and differences between categories of transgender experience. The subjective and collective nuances and tensions that have been explored in this book thus lend support to Halberstam's (1998) argument that diversity *in itself* does not equate to radicalism. This highlights the importance of developing grounded analyses of intimacy, care and citizenship, which are conceptually and empirically developed beyond the binaries of gender (man/woman) and sexuality (homo/hetero).

In the introduction to the book, I discussed media attention to transgender following the prominent role of Nadia Almada in the reality television show *Big Brother 5*, which I returned to in Chapter Eight. Nadia's situation is useful for summarising the tensions within a politics of transgender identity that have been apparent throughout this book. Social, cultural and legislative shifts indicate an increased interest in transgender, and – to a certain degree – a greater tolerance of some practices of gender diversity, in contemporary British society. In turn, this may enable easier access to transgender identities. Yet, as I explored in Chapter Eight, Nadia's desire to move beyond a transgender identity is reflected in the narratives of some of the participants in this book. Moreover, Nadia's comments link with the narratives of participants who seek to fit into a society that, although marked by an increased tolerance of difference, remains structured through a gender binary and heteronormativity. The reluctance to claim a transgender identity can thus be seen to be indicative of the permeations of gender and sexual normativity. Nevertheless, on learning of the positive reaction from transgender organisations at the end of the series of *Big Brother*, Nadia reflected "I'm glad if I can educate people about my experiences" (Nadia Almada, quoted in *Observer*, 22 August 2004). Similarly, a wholly assimilationist position was not the norm of the majority of people whose narratives have been considered in this book and, to different degrees, most stressed the importance of a transgender identity and of transgender communities.

The intricacies of transgender identities and subjectivities indicate the importance of developing a sociological theory of gender diversity that is generated from empirical study. Further, a theoretical model that fuses social and cultural theories of identity is relevant for understanding the emergence and the experiences of contemporary transgender practices. This book, then, aims to bridge the gap between social theories and poststructuralist accounts of gender identity formation. Social theories of identity (Giddens, 1991, 1992; Beck, 1992; Bauman, 1996) are concerned with the historical development of self–identity, while cultural theory (Weedon, 1987; Butler, 1990, 1993) has problematised identity categories. Bridging this dichotomy lends sway to a conceptual framework that accounts for the complex and processual nature of identity formation and recognises the multiple and fluid elements within identity positions, while also acknowledging subjective accounts that suggest a more determined experience of identity. A further way in which (trans)gender theory may be taken forward is through the development of grounded intersectional analyses that account for the ways in which gendered experiences and practices are constructed through divergent subject positions and social structures. This relies on future studies being mindful of how variables, such as gender, sexuality, age and generation, 'race' and ethnicity, social class, and geographical location, work in tandem and in resistance to produce lived experience(s).

At the close of Chapter One, I contextualised this book in relation to UK sociological studies of gender diversity (Ekins, 1993, 1997; King, 1993; 2003; Ekins and King, 1996, 1997, 2006; Hird, 2000, 2002a, 2006; Monro, 2000, 2003, 2005, 2006a). These studies engage with, revise and develop poststructuralist analyses of transgender. They stress how practices of gender diversity are social processes; constructed by, through and in opposition to dominant modes of being and seeing. This body of work provides the intellectual home of this book. With the aim of contributing to, and further developing, sociological analyses of transgender, this book thus argues for the importance of theorising gender diversity in relation to social structures, discursive formations, subjective understandings, embodied corporalities and cultural (and subcultural) practices.

Notes

Introduction

[1] 'Trans' is an umbrella term that is short for 'transgender' and covers all transgender people.

Chapter One

[1] *Berdache* is a term developed by European colonisers to refer to indigenous people of North America who took on social roles not usually associated with their gender.

Chapter Two

[1] This is not to deny that non-nuclear models of community have always existed, for example, in non-Western cultures and in many working-class cultures in the UK.

Chapter Three

[1] Ekins' work (1993) on the experiences of transitioning from male to female; King's (1993) work, which uses empirical case studies to distinguish between transvestite and transsexual identities, and Monro's work on transgender politics (2005) and the experiences of young trans people (2006b) are important exceptions here.

[2] The 'real-life experience' is defined as the full adaptation of a new gender role. Clinicians assess a person's real-life experience by reviewing the following criteria:

1   to maintain full or part-time employment;
2   to function as a student;
3   to function in community-based volunteer activity;
4   to undertake some combination of items 1–3;
5   to acquire a (legal) gender-identity-appropriate first name;
6   to provide documentation that persons other than the therapist know that the patient functions in the desired gender role.

(Harry Benjamin International Gender Dysphoria Association, 2001)

Chapter 5

[1] It is important to note that I did not include partners in my sample and therefore did not formally interview partners of participants.

Chapter 6

[1] It is important to note that the children in question were not interviewed and to acknowledge that children may offer different accounts.

Research notes

The research

The empirical material on which this book draws comes from two research projects. The first research project – 'Transgender Identities, Intimate Relationships and Practices of Care' – was completed for doctoral study (2000–04). The research was funded by the ESRC research project 'Care, Values and the Future of Welfare' (CAVA) at the University of Leeds. The second project – 'Transgender Practices of Identity, Intimacy and Care' – was funded by an ESRC postdoctoral fellowship at the University of Leeds (2004–5). The aim of the project was to conduct detailed further analysis of the previous research in light of the 2004 Gender Recognition Act.

Communication was first established with transgender community, self-help and campaigning groups. A range of transgender organisations that publish regular newsletters and journals agreed to carry an outline of my research and a call for participants. Further access to sources came from placing requests for participants on transgender websites. I had two personal contacts that put me in contact with other people. I also made contact with academics working within transgender studies. Over a period of several months prior to interviewing, I visited a range of transgender spaces, such as self-help groups, social events, workshops and community meetings. I also made use of internet transgender discussion forums to talk about the research. In selecting people to interview, I used a theoretical sampling strategy (Weston, 1991; Weeks et al, 2001) whereby participants were purposively selected in relation to a range of variables (gender, sexuality, age, occupation, geographical location, partnering and parenting status, and transitional time span) in order to maximise diversity of the sample group. However, research findings do not presume to be representative of transgender people as a whole group.

The research was carried out in a UK setting and research on non-UK, and particularly non-Western, transgender cultures would have produced different findings. Time limitations of the research meant that I was unable to interview all the people who were interested in participating in the project. I am aware that the people who contacted me are connected, to varying degrees, with a wider transgender 'community', or, at least, subscribe to transgender newsletters, journals or email mailing lists where I placed the requests for participants. This is not the case for many transgender people who have no contact with other transgender people and transgender groups. The voices of the unknown number of such people are not to be found within this research. Further limitations of the study relate to the complex ways in which 'race' and ethnicity impact upon transgender experiences. These are important areas for future social analyses of transgender. Though I aimed to maximise diversity of the sample group in terms of 'race' and ethnicity, I was unsuccessful in this; it proved very difficult to make contact with organisations for racially and ethnically diverse transgender people. 'Informal' discussions highlighted the specific difficulties faced by transgender people from minority ethnic communities and addressed the complexities between transgender, ethnicity and 'race', which represents a greatly under-researched area (Roen, 2001).

My position as a non-transgender researcher will have affected the findings of the research on which this book draws, although it is not possible to know to what extent. Common experiences between researcher and participants have been seen to affect levels of trust positively and thus to impact significantly upon the emerging data (Dunne, 1997; Oakley, 2000). A transgender researcher may have benefited from an 'insider' position to build trust with potential participants. This could have given her/him access to people who might not have replied to my requests for participants, which clearly stated my position as a non-transgender person. A transgender researcher might also have had 'inside' knowledge that could have led her/him to ask different questions. Two personal contacts were invaluable in providing a 'way in' on occasions where I contacted particular participants directly, thus acting as a starting point for the development of trust in these instances. Weeks et al (2001) importantly caution against overemphasising areas of commonality between respondents and researchers, and follow Edwards (1993) and Song and Parker (1995) in addressing how other differences are always at play. Yet I recognise that the research on which this book draws is partial and that my non-transgender status is built into that partiality.

Data was generated through two-stage, semi-structured, in-depth interviews. Thirty interviews were conducted; 13 of the sample group had, variably, transitioned from male to female, 13 from female to male, and 4 identified as bi-gendered. Fourteen members of the sample group identified as heterosexual, 10 as bisexual, 4 as lesbian, 1 as gay and 1 as queer. Eighteen participants were in relationships, while 12 were single; 3 members of the sample group remained married to their pre-transition partners, 7 participants were parents. A little under half of the sample lived in rural towns or villages, while just over half lived in cities. The age range of the sample group was from 25 to 71 years old. While the occupations of participants were mixed, the sample included a significant number of participants employed in professional occupations, and several working within creative industries as writers, musicians and artists, suggesting a higher representation of middle-class participants than working-class. Participants were at different stages of transition, and the sample included people who use hormone therapy and/or a range of surgical modifications and those who reject such interventions. All of the participants were white and all resided in the UK. While some participants selected to use pseudonyms, others chose to be known by their own names. Biographies of the research participants are provided in the pen portraits below.

Interviews took between one and three-and-a-half hours. Most interviews took place in participants' homes. Interviews were used as a means through which to explore the social world of participants (Blaikie, 2000). Rather than approaching the interview method as a means to a 'fixed' text, which reveals 'true' meaning, I followed Plummer (1995) in viewing narratives as socially constructed and sociohistorically specific. I was influenced by Hollway and Jefferson's (2000) 'narrative approach', which moves beyond a 'question-and-answer' interview style and allows the interviewer to respond flexibly to the narrator. One of the central characteristics is that questions are open ended so that 'stories' may be told.

The participants[1]

Amanda is a 45-year-old transsexual woman. She is white British and lives in a city. She is bisexual and lives with her girlfriend. She is a security officer for a police force.

Amelia is a 47-year-old woman. She is white European and lives in a town. She is heterosexual and lives with her boyfriend. She is a historian, researcher and writer.

Anna is a 28-year-old who describes her gender as 'fuzzy'. She is white British and lives in a city. She says that 'there is no word' to describe her sexuality. She is single and shares a flat with a couple she is not close to. She is an architect.

Bernadette is a 71-year-old transsexual woman. She is Celtic and lives in a village. She is heterosexual and lives with the woman she has been married to for 40 years. She has two stepchildren. She is a retired physicist and chairperson of her local council.

Cheryl is a 45-year-old transsexual female. She is white English and lives in a city. She is bisexual and is living temporarily with her girlfriend. She has two children. She is a craft technician.

Chris is a 41-year-old FtM. He is white British and lives in a town. He is bisexual and single. He is a customer service adviser.

Christine is a 60-year-old woman. She is white and lives in a village. She does not want to categorise her sexuality. She lives with the woman she married 30 years ago. She has two children. She is a retired chartered accountant and trustee of a number of charities.

Dan is a 37-year-old FtM. He is white British and lives in a town. He is heterosexual and lives with his girlfriend. He has one child. He is a civil engineer.

Dave is a 46-year-old trans man. He is Celtic and lives in a village. He is heterosexual and lives with his female partner. He is a voluntary worker.

David is a 26-year-old man. He is white Scottish and lives in a city. He is heterosexual and lives with his girlfriend. He is a graphic designer.

Del is 44-years old and describes himself as queer or FtM, 'depending on who I'm talking to'. He is white American and lives in a city. He is queer/pansexual and is single. He is a photographer and filmmaker.

Dionne is a 40-year-old woman. She is Jewish white European and lives in a town. She is bisexual and is single. She is a bus driver.

Emma is a 54-year-old woman. She is white British and lives in a village. She is heterosexual. She lives with the woman she has been married to for 30 years. She is a company secretary and a support worker.

Gabrielle is a 45-year-old trans woman. She is Anglo-Jewish and lives in a city. She is a trans lesbian and lives with her girlfriend. She is a musician.

Georgina is a 29-year-old trans woman. She is Jewish and lives in a city. She is a lesbian and single. She is a student.

Greg is a 44-year-old man. He is white English and lives in a village. He is heterosexual and lives with his wife, whom he married in an Anglican service of blessing. He is an artist.

Jackie is a 29-year-old trans woman. She is white British/European and lives in a city. She is bisexual and lives with her boyfriend. She is a designer.

Karen is a 31-year-old woman. She is white British and lives in a city. She is bisexual and lives with the woman she married three years ago. She is a nurse.

Lee is a 55-year-old trans man. He is white British and lives in a city. He is bisexual and lives with his female partner. He is a mature student.

Lynne is a 67-year-old trans female. She is white English and lives in a town. She is a lesbian and is single. She has three children. She is a retired aircraft fitter for the Royal Air Force.

Melanie is a 41-year-old woman. She is Scottish and lives in a town. She is heterosexual and lives with her girlfriend. She has one child. She is a company manager.

Paul is a 34-year-old female-to-male transsexual. He is white British and lives in a town. He is heterosexual and lives with his girlfriend. He is a writer for a public relations company.

Philip is a 42-year-old trans man. He is white British and lives in a city. He is gay and single. He is a student, care worker and sex worker.

Rebecca is a 55-year-old bi-gendered woman. She is white British and lives in a city. She does not believe that there is a word that describes sexuality, though the 'object of [her] desire is female'. She is single. She has one child. She is an employment adviser.

Sam is 32 years old and is bi-gendered. S/he is white British and lives in a town. S/he is heterosexual and single. S/he is a computer analyst.

Sophie is a 32-year-old bi-gendered woman. She is white British and lives in a city. She is heterosexual and single. She is a computer software designer.

Steve is a 38-year-old FtM. He is white British and lives in a town. He is bisexual and single. He is a care worker.

Svar is a 41-year-old man. He is white British and lives in a city. He is queer/bisexual and lives with his girlfriend. He is a sculptor.

Tony is a 39-year-old man. He is white British and lives in a town. He is heterosexual and is single. He is a teacher.

William is a 25-year-old trans man. He is Jewish and lives in a city. He is bisexual and lives between his girlfriend and his parents. He is an advertising designer.

Research analysis and validity

Weeks (2004) has recently talked about how social concepts are reflected back to researchers by their interviewees. This, Weeks suggests, is representative of the ways in which we live 'reflexive lives'. These points resonate strongly with my experiences during this research. Many participants had a deep knowledge of theoretical debates around transgender. Several participants had been interviewed by journalists for newspaper articles, some had been appeared in television documentaries, and two participants had been guests on television chat shows. Moreover, one participant had written an autobiography, while two others were artists whose focus of work was on transgender. In analysing the data, I became aware that, in many cases, I had accessed 'rehearsed narratives' that had been constructed and reconstructed through their telling and retelling.

These narratives, however, were not rehearsed in the same ways and can be broadly understood as following two different strands: 'a medically approved' narrative and a 'queer' narrative. In the former, the focus was on the psychological and embodied manifestations of gender discomfort – a transsexual narrative – while the latter stressed gender as a continuum to reject the notion of a gender binary system – a transgender narrative. Nevertheless, there was not always a strict demarcation between these two narrative strands and transsexual narratives frequently rejected traditional ways of conceptualising transgender as symptomatic of a 'wrong' body experience, while, conversely, transgender narratives often reflected the significance of the material body. I was also aware that the people who wanted to participate in the research were likely to have the most positive stories to tell about gender transition and that people with less positive stories were not as likely to contact me.

Through both the interview and analytical phases of the research, then, I approached the data as socially constructed and situated at a particular moment in time. However, as Plummer (1995) suggests, rejecting the idea that narratives represent an essential 'truth' may seem to deem individual narratives to be 'untruths'. Thus I follow Plummer in using Spence's distinction between 'historical truth' and 'narrative truth'. In contrast to the positivist underpinnings of 'historical truth', 'narrative truth' focuses upon "what people say in the here and now: the work of stories in the living present" (Plummer, 1995: 171).

Plummer's understanding of how stories work in the here and now links to the ways in which the narratives of this research are grounded in a particular moment in time. While this is the case for a wide range of social science research projects that explore feelings, values and experiences, it seemed to me to hold particular resonance for narratives of transition. Moreover, these narratives *of* transition are told while *in* transition, although transitory to different degrees. My final interview question asked 'do you think transition has an end point?'; for most participants there was not one end point, but rather different closing moments that, in turn, led to new starting points. In this way, many of the participants would have had different experiences to draw on if I had interviewed them at a future time. Yet viewing this as a problem of longitudinal value only arises if research is viewed as offering a fixed, timeless 'truth', or if it is deemed to be factual. Instead, this research addresses narratives, rather than 'facts', and all narratives are of their moment. As Plummer has argued, the 'sociological phenomena' (Plummer, 1995: 167) of storytelling shows how stories are part of social changes and sociopolitical discourses. Moreover, the wider themes to arise from the research in terms of considerations for social policy have implications for the future. Thus temporal considerations relate both to the moment of individual narratives of transition and to sociohistorical time.

The question of validity was addressed by inviting the respondents to read their interview transcriptions. This allowed participants to validate or correct data and to offer further information (Wright, 1997).

Ethical considerations

In the course of the research, I asked people about some of the most intimate aspects of their lives. Sexuality was a key topic, and I also asked about bodily changes and surgery. I asked questions about participants' close relationships, which, for some, touched on difficult experiences with friends, families, partners and children. Ethical considerations were thus paramount throughout the research. I followed Hollway and Jefferson's criteria for social researchers in which "the ethical principles of honesty, sympathy and respect would be central" (2000: 102). I was aware that the particularly sensitive nature of researching transgender issues demanded that I remain 'extra aware' of ethical considerations. Transphobia leads to violence, hostility and the loss of jobs, homes and custody of children. While all participants were open about their identities to some extent (if they had not been they would not have agreed to be involved in the research), this differed in degrees. On the ethics of researching transgender, I was influenced by Griggs (1998) and Cromwell (1999), who stress the importance of avoiding misrepresentation. The ethical issue of researching transgender issues as a non-transgender person carried the additional concern of misrepresentation. In this respect, I followed the guidelines laid out by Hale (1997) for non-transgender people working on transgender.

As a non-transgender researcher, I had anticipated difficulty in gaining access to participants. This was not the case, however, and I was unable to interview all the people who contacted me (30 people were selected out of a potential sample group of 100). The large response to requests for participants led me to wonder, and to ask, why people had wanted to participate. The most common reason concerned the social awareness of transgender issues and experiences. The representation of transgender people – especially in popular media and journalism – was associated with misconceptions of 'who' transgender people 'were' and, in turn, to discrimination on both a social (ie hostility on the street) and a political (ie lack of legal recognition of gender of choice) level. Involvement in the research was linked to dynamics of social and political change as participants spoke of 'speaking out' and of 'putting the record straight'. Here there is an understanding of knowledge as a vehicle for social change. This corresponds with Plummer's (1995) discussion of storytelling as a political process and illustrates how storytelling may be used by previously disenfranchised communities to assert their growing strength. In this way, it is significant that the timing of the research design coincided with legislative proposals representing the civil recognition of transgender people (the Gender

Recognition Bill). Plummer's model for understanding the social construction of storytelling incorporates the 'cultural and historical level', which denotes the specific historical moment in which a story is told and heard. Plummer notes that "many stories are in silence – dormant, awaiting their historical moment" (1995: 35). Perhaps the large response to this research, then, can be read as an indication that the 'historical moment' has arrived for some transgender individuals.

Note

[1] These are the descriptions the participants gave of themselves. Ages were given at the time of interviews, which took place in 2002.

Bibliography

Adam, B. (1992) 'Sex and Caring Among Men', in K. Plummer (ed) *Modern Homosexualities: Fragments of Lesbian and Gay Experience*, London: Routledge.

Adu-Pou, S. (2001) 'Envisioning (Black) Male Feminism: A Cross Cultural Perspective', *Journal of Gender Studies*, vol 10, no 2: 157-67.

Aizura, A. (2006) 'Of Borders and Homes: The Imaginary Community of (Trans)sexual Citizenship', *Inter Asia Cultural Studies*, vol 7, no 2: 289-389.

Altman, D. (1982) *The Homosexualization of America, the Americanization of the Homosexual*, New York, NY: St Martin's Press.

Altman, D. (1993) *Homosexual: Oppression and Liberation*, New York, NY: New York University Press.

Aminzade, R., Meyer, D. and Taylor, V. (eds) (1994) *Social Movements: Protest and Contention*, Minnesota: University of Minnesota Press.

Arber, S. and Gilbert, N. (eds) (1993) *Women and Working Lives: Divisions and Change*, London: Macmillan.

Back, L. and Solomos, J. (2000) *Theories of Race and Racism: A Reader*, London: Routledge.

Bailey, J.M. (2003) *The Man who Would be Queen: The Science of Gender Bending and Transsexualism*, Washington, DC: Joseph Henry Press.

Bauman, Z. (1996) 'From Pilgrim to Tourist – or a Short History of Identity', in S. Hall and P. du Gay (eds) *Questions of Cultural Identity*, London: Routledge.

Bauman, Z. (2003) *Liquid Love: On the Frailty of Human Bonds*, Cambridge: Polity Press.

Beck, U. (1992) *Risk Society: Towards a New Modernity*, London: Sage.

Beck, U. and Beck-Gernsheim, E. (1995) *The Normal Chaos of Love*, Cambridge: Polity Press.

Beck, U., Giddens, A. and Lash, S. (eds) (1994) *Reflexive Modernization*, Cambridge: Polity Press.

Begum, N. (1992) 'Burden of Gratitude: Women with Disabilities Receiving Personal Care', *Feminist Review*, no 40: 70-80.

Bell, D. and Binnie, J. (2000) *The Sexual Citizen: Queer Politics and Beyond*, Cambridge: Polity Press.

Benhabib, S. (1994) 'Feminism and the Question of Postmodernism', in *The Polity Reader in Gender Studies*, Cambridge, Polity Press.

Benjamin, H. (1953) 'Transvestism and Transsexualism', *International Journal of Sexology*, vol 7.

Benjamin, H. (1966) *The Transsexual Phenomenon*, New York, NY: Julian Press.

Berridge, V. and Strong, P. (eds) (1993) *AIDS and Contemporary History*, Cambridge: Cambridge University Press.

Bhalla, A. and Blakemore, K. (1981) *Elders of the Minority Ethnic Groups, All Faiths for One Race (AFFOR)*, Report for Birmingham City Council, Birmingham: Birmingham City Council.

Billings, D.B. and Urban, T. (1982) 'The Socio-medical Construction of Transsexualism: An Interpretation and Critique', *Social Problems*, vol 29: 266-82.

Bindel, J. (2004) 'Gender benders beware', *Guardian*, 31 January.

Binnie, J. (2004) *The Globalisation of Sexuality*, London: Sage.

Blaikie, N. (2000) *Designing Social Research*, Cambridge: Polity Press.

Blumstein, P. and Schwartz, P. (1983) *American Couples*, New York, NY: William Morrow.

Bockting, W.O. (2005) 'The Man who Would be Queen', http://en.wikipedia.org/wiki/The_Man_Who_Would_Be_Queen

Bockting, W.O. and Coleman, E. (eds) (1992) *Gender Dysphoria: Interdisciplinary Approaches in Clinical Management*, New York, NY: The Haworth Press.

Bolin, A. (1994) 'Transcending and Transgendering: Male-to-Female Transsexuals, Dichotomy and Diversity', in G. Herdt (ed) *Third Sex, Third Gender: Beyond Sexual Dimorphism in Culture and History*, New York, NY: Zone Books.

Bolin, A. (1998) *In Search of Eve: Transsexual Rites of Passage*, South Hadley: Bergin and Garvey.

Bordo, S. (1993) *Unbearable Weight: Feminism, Western Culture and the Body*, Berkeley, CA: University of California Press.

Bornstein, K. (1994) *Gender Outlaw: Men, Women and the Rest of Us*, New York, NY: Routledge.

Boyd, N.A. (2006) 'Bodies in Motion: Lesbian and Transsexual Histories', in S. Stryker and S. Whittle (eds) *The Transgender Studies Reader*, New York and Abingdon: Routledge.

Bozett, F.W. (1987) *Gay and Lesbian Parents*, New York, NY: Praeger.

Brake, M. (1976) 'I May be Queer But at Least I am a Man', in D.L. Barker and S. Allen (eds) *Sexual Divisions and Society: Process and Change*, London: Tavistock.

Bristow, J. (1997) *Sexuality*, London: Routledge.

Broad, K.L. (2002) 'GLB+T?: Gender/Sexuality Movements and Transgender Collective Identity (De) Constructions', *International Journal of Sexuality and Gender Studies*, vol 7, no 4: 241-64.

Burke, P. (1996) *Gender Shock: Exploding the Myths of Male and Female*, New York, NY: Doubleday.

Burns, C. (2004) www.bigbrother.digitalspy.co.uk

Bussmaker, J. and Voet, R. (1998) 'Citizenship and Gender: Theoretical Approaches and Historical Legacies', *Critical Social Policy*, vol 18, no 3.

Butler, J. (1990) *Gender Trouble: Feminism and the Subversion of Identity*, New York and London: Routledge.

Butler, J. (1993) *Bodies that Matter: On the Discursive Limits of Sex*, New York, NY: Routledge.

Butler, J. (1994) 'Against Proper Objects', *Differences*, vol 6, nos 2 and 3.

Butler, J. (2001) 'The End of Sexual Difference?', in E. Bronfen and M. Kavka (eds) *Feminist Consequences: Theory for the New Century: Gender and Culture*, New York, NY: Columbia University Press.

Butler, J. and Scott, J.W. (eds) (1992) *Feminists Theorize the Political*, New York, NY: Routledge.

Calhoun, C. (1995) *Critical Social Theory*, Oxford: Blackwell.

Califia, P. (1981) *Samois: Coming to Power: Writings and Graphics on Lesbian S/M*, Berkeley, CA: Samois.

Califia, P. (1997) *Sex Changes: The Politics of Transgenderism*, San Francisco, CA: Cleis Press.

Carabine, J. (1996) 'Heterosexuality and Social Policy', in D. Richardson (ed) *Theorising Heterosexuality: Telling it Straight*, Buckingham: Open University Press.

Castells, M. (1997) *The Information Age: Economy, Society and Culture. Volume II: The Power of Identity*, Oxford: Blackwell.

Cauldwell, D.O. (1949) *What's Wrong With Transvestism?*, Kansas: Haldeman-Julius.

Clare, D. (1984) 'Transhomosexuality', Unpublished paper presented to the Annual Conference of the British Psychological Society, Warwick, UK.

Cohen, E. (1991) 'Who Are "We"?: Gay "Identity" as Political (E)motion (A Theoretical Rumination)', in D. Fuss (ed) *Inside/Out: Lesbian Theories, Gay Theories*, New York, NY: Routledge.

Connell, R.W. (1987) *Gender and Power*, Oxford: Blackwell.

Connell, R.W. (1995) *Masculinities*, Cambridge: Polity Press.

Cooper, D. (1995) *Power Struggle: Feminism, Sexuality and the State*, Buckingham: Open University Press.

Crompton, R. (1998) *Class and Stratification: An Introduction to Current Debates*, Cambridge: Polity Press.

Cromwell, J. (1999) *Transmen and FTMs: Identities, Bodies, Genders and Sexualities*, Champaign, IL: University of Illinois Press.

Daly, G. and Cowen, H. (2000) 'Redefining the Local Citizen', in L. McKie and N. Watson (eds) *Organising Bodies*, London: Macmillan.

Davis, K. (ed) (1997) *Embodied Practices: Feminist Perspectives on the Body*, Thousand Oaks, CA: Sage.

De Sutter, P. (2006) 'Gender Reassignment and Assisted Reproduction: Present and Future Reproductive Options for Transsexual People', *Human Reproduction*, vol 16, no 4: 612-14.

Denzin, N. and Lincoln, Y. (1998), *Handbook of Qualitative Research*, Thousand Oaks, CA: Sage.

Devor, H. (1987) 'Gender Blending Females', *American Behavioural Scientist*, vol 31.

Devor, H. (1989) *Gender Blending: Confronting the Limits of Duality*, Bloomington, IN: Indiana University Press.

Devor, A.H. and Matte, N. (2006) 'One Inc. and Reed Erickson: The Uneasy Collaboration of Gay and Trans Activism, 1964–2003', in S. Stryker and S. Whittle (eds) *The Transgender Studies Reader*, New York, NY, and Abingdon: Routledge.

Duggan, L. and Hunter N.D. (1995) *Sex Wars: Sexual Dissent and Popular Culture*, New York, NY: Routledge.

Dunn, J.L. (2001) 'Innocence Lost: Accomplishing Victimization in Intimate Stalking Cases', *Symbolic Interactionism*, vol 24: 285-313.

Dunne, G. (1997) *Lesbian Lifestyles: Women's Work and the Politics of Sexuality*, London: Macmillan.

Dunne, G. (1999) 'A Passion for "Sameness" Sexuality and Gender Accountability', in E.B Silva and C. Smart (eds) *The New Family: The New Practices and Politics of Family Life*, London: Sage.

Dworkin, A. (1987) *Intercourse*, London: Arrow Books.

Edwards, R. (1993) 'An Education in Interviewing: Placing the Researcher and the Research', in C.M. Renzetti and R.M. Lee (eds) *Researching Sensitive Topics*, London: Sage.

Ekins, R. (1993) 'On Male Femaling: A Grounded Theory Approach to Cross-Dressing and Sex-Changing', *Sociological Review*, vol 41: 1-29.

Ekins, R. (1997) *Male Femaling: A Grounded Theory Approach to Cross-Dressing and Sex-Changing*, London and New York: Routledge.

Ekins, R. and King, D. (1996) *Blending Genders: Social Aspects of Cross-Dressing and Sex-Changing*, London: Routledge.

Ekins, R. and King, D. (1997) 'Blending Genders: Contributions to the Emerging Field of Transgender Studies', *International Journal of Transgenderism*, vol 1, no1, at www.symposion.com/ijt/ijtc0101.htm

Elkins, R. and King, D. (1999) 'Towards a Sociology of Trangendered Bodies', *Sociological Review*, vol 47: 580-602.

Ekins, R. and King, D. (2001) 'Transgendering, Migrating and Love of Oneself as a Woman', *International Journal of Transgenderism*, vol 5, no 3, at www.symposion.com/ijt/ijtc0101.htm

Ekins, R. and King, D. (2006) *The Transgender Phenomenon*, London: Sage.

Ellen, B. (2004) 'The More People Criticised, The Stronger I Became', *Observer*, 22 August.

Elliot, P. and Roen, K. (1998) 'Transgenderism and the Question of Embodiment: Promising Queer Politics?', *Journal of Lesbian and Gay Studies*, vol 4, no 2: 231-69.

Ellis, H. (1938) *1928 Studies in the Psychology of Sex*, vol 7, New York, NY: F.A. Davis & Co.

Epstein, J. (1995) *Altered Conditions: Disease, Medicine and Storytelling*, London: Routledge.

Epstein, J. and Straub, K. (1991) *Body Guards: The Cultural Politics of Gender Ambiguity*, New York, NY, and London: Routledge.

Estlund, D.M. and Nussbaum, M.C. (eds) (1997) *Sex, Preference and Family: Essays on Law and Nature*, New York, NY, and Oxford: Oxford University Press.

Evans, D. (1993) *Sexual Citizenship: The Material Construction of Sexualities*, London: Routledge.

Fausto-Sterling, A. (1993) 'The Five Sexes: Why Male and Female are not Enough', *The Sciences*, vol 33, no 2.

Fay, B. (1975) *Social Theory and Practice*, London: Allen and Unwin.

Featherstone, M., Hepworth, M. and Turner, B.S. (1991) *The Body: Social Processes and Cultural Theory*, London: Sage.

Feinberg, L. (1992) *Transgender Liberation: A Movement Whose Time Has Come*, New York, NY: World View Forum.

Feinberg, L. (1993) *Stone Butch Blues*, Ithaca and New York, NY: Firebrand Books.

Feinberg, L. (1996) *Transgender Warriors: Making History From Joan of Arc to Dennis Rodman*, Boston, MA: Beacon Press.

Feinberg, L. (1999) *Trans Liberation: Beyond Pink or Blue*, Boston, MA: Beacon Press.

Feinberg, L. (2006) 'WWP's Support for Early Gay Liberation: Lavender and Red', at www.workers.org/2006/us/lavender-red-81/

Felski, R. (1996) 'Fin de Siecle, Fin de Sexe: Transsexuality, Postmodernism and the Death of History, *New Literary History*, vol 27, no 2: 137-53.

Fenstermaker, S., West, C. and Zimmerman D. (1991) 'Gender Inequality: New Conceptual Terrain', in R. Lesser-Blumberg (ed) *Gender, Family and Economy: The Triple Overlap*, Newbury Park, CA: Sage.

Finch, J. (1989) *Family Obligations and Social Change*, Cambridge: Polity Press.

Finch, J. and Groves, D. (1980) 'Community Care and the Family: A Case for Equal Opportunities?', *Journal of Social Policy*, vol 9, no 4.

Finch, J. and Groves, D. (eds) (1989) *Labour of Love: Women, Work and Caring*, London: Routledge.

Fisk, N. (1973) 'Gender Dysphoria Syndrome. (The How, What, and Why of a Disease)', in D. Laub and P. Gandy (eds) *Proceedings of the Second Interdisciplinary Symposium on Gender Dysphoria Syndrome*, Stanford, CA: University of California Press.

Flax, J. (1997) 'Postmodernism and Gender Relations in Feminist Theory', in S. Kemp and J. Squire (eds) *Feminisms*, Oxford: Oxford University Press.

Foucault, M. (1977) *Discipline and Punish: The Birth of the Prison*, Harmondsworth: Penguin.

Foucault, M. (1978) *The History of Sexuality, Volume 1: An Introduction*, New York, NY: Random House.

Foucault, M. (1980) *Power/Knowledge: Selected Interviews and Other Writings 1972–1977*, New York, NY: Pantheon.

Foucault, M. (1986) *The Care of the Self: The History of Sexuality Volume Three* (trans. R. Hurley), London: Penguin Books.

Franklin, S. and Ragone, H. (eds) (2001) *Reproducing Reproduction: Kinship, Power and Technological Innovation*, Pennsylvania: Pennsylvania University Press.

Fraser, N. (1995) 'Rethinking Recognition: Overcoming Displacement and Reification in Cultural Politics', in B. Hobson (ed) *Recognition Struggles and Social Movements: Contested Identities, Agency and Power*, Cambridge: Cambridge University Press.

Fraser, N. (1999) 'Classing Queer: Politics in Competition', *Theory, Culture and Society*, vol 16, no 2: 107-31.

Freud, S. (1923) 'The Ego and the Id', in S. Freud (1953–65) *The Standard Edition of the Complete Psychological Works of Sigmund Freud* (trans. J. Strachey) London: Hogarth Press.

Freud, S. (1953–65) *The Standard Edition of the Complete Psychological Works of Sigmund Freud* (trans. J. Strachey) London: Hogarth Press.

Fuss, D. (ed) (1991) *Inside/Outside: Lesbian Theories, Gay Theories*, New York and London: Routledge.

Gabb, J. (2001) 'Desirous Subjects and Parental Identities: Constructing a Radical Discourse on (Lesbian) Family Sexuality', *Sexualities*, vol 4, no 3: 333-52.

Gagne, P. and Tewksbury, R. (1997) 'Coming Out and Crossing Over: Identity Formation and Proclamation in a Transgender Community', *Gender & Society*, vol 11, no 4: 478-508.

Gagnon, J.H. and Simon, W. (1974) *Sexual Conduct: The Social Sources of Human Sexuality*, London: Hutchinson

Garber, M. (1992) *Vested Interests: Cross-Dressing and Cultural Anxiety*, New York, NY: Routledge.

Garfinkel, H. (1967) *Studies in Ethnomethodolgy*, Englewood Cliffs, NJ: Prentice Hall.

Geertz, C. (1998) *Works and Lives: The Anthropologist as Author*, Stanford, CA: Stanford University Press.

Giddens, A. (1991) *Modernity and Self Identity: Self and Society in the Late Modern Age*, Cambridge: Polity Press.

Giddens, A. (1992) *The Transformation of Intimacy: Sexuality, Love and Eroticism in Modern Societies*, Cambridge: Polity Press.

Giddens, A. (1994) *Beyond Left and Right: The Future of Radical Politics*, Cambridge: Polity Press.

Gilligan, C. (1982) *In a Different Voice*, Cambridge, MA: Harvard University Press.

Glasser, B. and Strauss, A. (1967) *The Discovery of Grounded Theory*, Chicago, IL: Aldine.

Glick, E. (2000) 'Sex Positive: Feminism, Queer Theory and the Politics of Transgression', *Feminist Review*, vol 64: 19-45.

Goffman, E. (1979) *Gender Advertisements*, New York, NY: Harper & Row.

Graham, H. (1983) 'Caring: A Labour of Love', in J. Finch, and D. Groves (eds) *A Labour of Love: Women, Work and Caring*, London: Routledge and Kegan Paul.

Graham, H. (1990) 'Feminist Perspectives of Care', in J. Bornat, C. Pereira, D. Pilgrim and F. Williams (eds) *Community Care: A Reader*, London: Macmillan.

Grant, C. (1996) 'Queer Theorrhea (And What It Might Mean For Feminists)', in S. Jackson and S. Scott (eds) *Feminism and Sexuality: A Reader*, Edinburgh: Edinburgh University Press.

Green, J. (2006) 'Look! No Don't! The Visibility Dilemma for Transsexual Men', in S. Stryker and S. Whittle (eds) *The Transgender Studies Reader*, New York and Abingdon: Routledge.

Green, R. (1978a) 'Definition and Synopsis of Etiology of Adult Gender Identity', at www.gires.org.uk/Text_Assets/Etiology_Definition. pdf

Green, R. (1978b) 'Sexual Identity of 37 Children Raised by Homosexual or Transsexual Parents', *Journal of Psychiatry*, vol 692: 692-7.

Green, R. (1998) 'Transsexuals' Children', *International Journal of Transgenderism*, vol 2, no 4, at www.symposion.com/ijt/ijtc0601. htm

Green, R. and Money, J. (eds) (1969) *Transsexualism and Sex Reassignment*, Baltimore, MD: Johns Hopkins University Press.

Greer, G. (1999) *The Whole Woman*, London: Random House.

Griggers, C. (1993) 'Lesbian Bodies in the Age of (Post)mechanical Reproduction', in M. Warner (ed) *Fear of a Queer Planet: Queer Politics and Social Theory*, Minneapolis, MN: University of Minneapolis Press.

Griggs, C. (1998) *S/He: Changing Sex and Changing Clothes*, Oxford: Berg.

Grosz, E. (1994) *Volatile Bodies: Towards a Corporal Feminism*, Bloomington and Indianapolis: Indiana University Press.

Gunaratnam, Y. (1990) 'Breaking the Silence: Asian Carers in Britain', in J. Bornat, C. Pereira, D. Pilgrim and F. Williams (eds) *Community Care: A Reader*, London: Macmillan.

Gutierrez, A. (1989) 'Must We Deracinate Indians to Find Gay Roots?', *Outlook*, no 4.

Halberstam, J. (1998) *Female Masculinity*, Durham, NC: Duke University Press.

Halberstam, J. (2005) *In a Queer Time and Space: Transgender Bodies, Subcultural Lives*, New York and London: New York University Press.

Halberstam, J. and Lagrace, D. (1999) *The Drag King Book*, London: Serpent's Tail.

Hale, J. (1997) 'Suggested Rules for Non-Transsexuals Writing about Transsexuals, Transsexuality, Transsexualism, or Trans', at www. sandystone.com/hale.rules.html

Hale, J. (1998) 'Tracing a Ghostly Memory in my Throat: Reflections of Ftm Feminist Voice and Agency', in T. Digby (ed) *Men Doing Feminism*, New York and London: Routledge.

Hall, S. and du Gay, P. (eds) (1996) *Questions of Cultural Identity*, London: Sage.

Harry Benjamin International Gender Dysphoria Association (2001) 'Standards of Care for Gender Identity Disorders, Sixth Version', at www.pfc.org.uk/medical/soc2001.htm

Hausman, B. (1995) *Changing Sex:Transsexualism,Technology, and the Idea of Gender*, Durham, NC, and London: Duke University Press.

Hearn, J. (1989) 'Reviewing Men and Masculinities – Or Mostly Boys' Own Papers', *Theory, Culture and Society*, vol 6, no 4: 665-89.

Hedges, W. (1997) 'Queer Theory Explained', Department of English, SOU, at www.sou.edu/English/hedges/sodashop/RCenter/Theory/Explained/queer.htm

Hennessy, R. (1995) 'Queer Visibility in Commodity Culture', in L. Nicholson and S. Seidman (eds) *Social Postmodernism: Beyond Identity Politics*, Cambridge: Cambridge University Press.

Herdt, G. (ed) (1994) *Third Sex,Third Gender: Beyond Sexual Dimorphism in Culture and History*, New York, NY: Zone Books.

Heyes, C.J. (2000) 'Reading Transgender, Rethinking Women's Studies, *NWSA*, vol 9, no 2: 170-80.

Hird, M.J. (2000) 'Gender's Nature: Intersexuals, Transsexuals and the "Sex"/"Gender" Binary', *Feminist Theory*, vol 1, no 3: 347-64.

Hird, M.J. (2002a) 'For a Sociology of Transsexualism', *Sociology*, vol 36, no 3: 557-95.

Hird, M.J. (2002b) 'Out/Performing Our Selves – Invitation for Dialogue' *Sexualities*, vol 5, no 2: 337-56.

Hird, M.J. (2004) *Gender, Science and Technology*, Houndmills, Palgrave.

Hird, M.J. (2006) 'Animal Trans', *Australian Feminist Studies*, vol 21, no 49: 35-48.

Hirschauer, S. (1997) 'The Medicalization of Gender Migration', *International Journal of Transgenderism*, vol 1, no 1, at www.symposion.com/ijt/ijtc0104.htm

Hirschfeld, M. (1910) *Die Transvestiten*, Berlin: Pulvermacher.

Hollibaugh, A. (1989) 'Desire for the Future: Radical Hope in Passion and Pleasure', in C.Vance (ed) *Pleasure and Danger: Exploring Female Sexuality*, London: Pandora.

Hollway, W. and Jefferson, T. (2000) *Doing Qualitative Research Differently: Free Association, Narrative and the Interview Method*, London: Sage.

Honneth, A. (1996) *Struggle for Recognition:The Moral Grammar of Social Conflicts*, Cambridge: Polity Press.

Irwin, S. (1999) 'Resourcing the Family: Gendered Claims and Obligations and Issues of Explanation', in E. Silva and C. Smart (eds) *The New Family?*, London: Sage.

Jackson, P. (2003) *Dear Uncle Go: Male Homosexuality in Thailand*, Thailand: Bua Luang Books.

Jackson, S. (1996) 'Heterosexuality, Power and Pleasure', in S. Jackson and S. Scott (eds) *Feminism and Sexuality: A Reader*, Edinburgh: Edinburgh University Press.

Jackson, S. (1999) *Heterosexuality in Question*, London: Sage.

Jackson, S. and Scott, S. (eds) (1996) *Feminism and Sexuality: A Reader*, Edinburgh: Edinburgh University Press.

Jamieson, L. (1998) *Intimacy: Personal Relationships in Modern Society*, Cambridge: Polity Press.

Jeffreys, S. (1997) 'Transgender Activism: A Feminist Perspective', *Journal of Lesbian Studies*, vol 1, no 3/4: 55-74.

Johnson, S. (2001) 'Residential and Community Care of Transgendered People', at www.beaumont society.org.uk/res&comcare.htm.

Jones, L. (2004) *Observer*, 8 August (see www.pfc.org.uk).

Juang, R. (2006) 'Transgendering the Politics of Recognition', in S. Stryker and S. Whittle (eds) *The Transgender Studies Reader*, New York and Abingdon: Routledge.

Katz, J. (1976) *Gay American History: Lesbians and Gay Men in the U.S.A*, New York, NY: Thomas Y. Crowell.

Kaveney, R. (1999) 'Taking Transgender Politics', in K. More and S. Whittle (eds) *Reclaiming Genders: Transsexual Grammars and the Fin de Siecle*, London and New York, NY: Cassell.

Kellner, D. (1992) 'Popular Culture and the Construction of Postmodern Identities', in S. Lash and J. Freeman (eds) *Modernity and Identity*, Oxford: Blackwell.

Kemp, S. and Squire, J. (1997) *Feminisms*, Oxford: Oxford University Press.

Kessler, S.J. (1990) 'The Medical Construction of Gender: Case Management of Inter-Sexed Infants', *Signs*, vol 16, no 1: 3-26.

Kessler, S.J. and McKenna, W. (1978) *Gender: An Ethnomethodological Approach*, New York, NY: Wiley.

Kessler, S. and McKenna, W. (2000) 'Who Put the "Trans" in Transgender? Gender Theory and Everyday Life', *International Journal of Transgenderism*, vol 4, no 3.

King, D. (1993) *The Transvestite and the Transsexual: Public Categories and Private Identities*, Aldershot: Avebury.

King, D. (2003) 'Gender Migration: A Sociological Analysis (or the Leaving of Liverpool)', *Sexualities*, vol 6, no 2: 173-94.

Koyama, E. (2000) *Whose Feminism is it Anyway?: The Unspoken Racism of the Trans Inclusion Debate*, at http://eminism.org/readings/pdf-rdg/whose-feminism

Koyama, E. (2003) 'Transfeminist Manifesto', in R, Dicker and A. Piepmeier, (eds) *Catching a Wave: Reclaiming Feminism for the 21st Century*, Lebanon: Northeastern Press.

Kulick, D. (1998) *Travesti: Sex, Gender and Culture among Brazilian Transgendered Prostitutes*, Chicago, IL: University of Chicago Press.

Lash, S. (1994) 'Reflexivity and its Doubles: Structure, Aesthetics, Community', in U. Beck, A. Giddens and S. Lash (eds) *Reflexive Modernization*, Cambridge: Polity Press.

Lawler, S. (2000) *Mothering the Self: Mothers, Daughters, Subjects*, London and New York, NY: Routledge.

Leeds Revolutionary Feminists (1981) *Love Your Enemy?: The Debate Between Heterosexual Feminism and Political Lesbianism*, London: Onlywomen Press.

Lewins, F. (1995) *Transsexualism in Society: A Sociology of Male-To-Female Transsexuals*, South Melbourne: Macmillan Education.

Lewis, G. (ed) (1998) *Forming Nation, Framing Welfare*, London: Routledge.

Lister, R. (1996) 'Citizenship Engendered', in D. Taylor (ed) *Critical Social Policy: A Reader*, London: Sage.

Lister, R. (1997) *Citizenship: Feminist Perspectives*, Basingstoke and London: Macmillan.

Lorber, J. (1994) *Paradoxes of Gender*, New Haven, CT: Yale University Press.

MacCowan, L. (1992) 'Re-collecting History, Renaming Lives: Femme Stigma and the Feminist Seventies and Eighties', in J. Nestle (ed) *The Persistent Desire: A Femme-Butch Reader*, Boston, MA: Alyson Publications.

MacDonald, E. (1998) 'Critical Identities: Rethinking Feminism through Transgender Politics', *Atlantis*, vol 23, no 1.

Mackenzie, G.O. (1994) *Transgender Nation*, Bowling Green, OH: Bowling Green State University Press.

MacKinnon, C. (1982) 'Feminism, Marxism, Method and the State: An Agenda for Theory', *Signs: Journal of Women in Culture and Society*: 515-44.

McIntosh, M. (1978) 'The State and the Oppression of Women', in A. Kuhn and A.M. Wolpe (eds) *Feminism and Materialism*, London: Kegan Paul.

McNab, C. (2004) 'Married Trans People and Civil Partnerships: Where Next?', at www.pfc.org.uk/pfclists/news-arc/2004q3/msg00044.htm

McNay, L. (2000) *Gender and Agency*, Cambridge: Polity Press.

Maltz, R. (1998) 'Real Butch: The Performance/Performativity of Male Impersonation, Drags Kings Passing as Male and Stone Butch Realness', *Journal of Gender Studies*, vol 7: 273-86.

Marshall, T.H. (1950) *Citizenship and Social Class*, Cambridge: Cambridge University Press.

Martin, G. (2000) 'New Social Movements, Welfare and Social Policy: A Critical Assessment', ESRC research group on Care, Values and the Future of Welfare, University of Leeds, Workshop Paper 20, Workshop 5, 'Conceptual Developments', at www.leeds.ac.uk/cava/papers/paper20greg.htm

Martin, G. (2001) 'Social Movements of Care', ESRC research group on Care, Values and the Future of Welfare, University of Leeds, Workshop Paper 23, Workshop 6, 'Conceptual Developments', at www.leeds.ac.uk/cava/papers/paper20greg.htm

Mason, J. (1996) *Qualitative Researching*, London: Sage.

Mason-Schrock, D. (1996) 'Transsexuals' Narrative Construction of the "True Self"', *Social Psychology Quarterly*, vol 59: 176-92.

Matisons, M.R. (1998) 'The New Feminist Philosophy of the Body', *European Journal of Women's Studies*, vol 5, no 1: 33-45.

Melluci, A. (1996) *The Playing Self: Person and Meaning in the Planetary Society*, Cambridge: Cambridge University Press.

Merleau-Ponty, M. (1962) *The Phenomenology of Perception*, London: Routledge, Kegan Paul.

Monro, S. (2000) 'Theorizing Transgender Diversity: Towards a Social Model of Health, *Sexual and Relationship Therapy*, vol 15, no 1: 33-45.

Monro, S. (2003) 'Transgender Politics in the UK', *Critical Social Policy*, vol 23, no 4: 433-52.

Monro, S. (2005) *Gender Politics: Citizenship, Activism and Sexual Diversity*, London: Pluto Press.

Monro, S. (2006a) **'Growing Up Transgender: Stories of an Excluded Population'**, in C. Leccardi and E. Ruspini (eds) *A New Youth? Young People, Generations and Family Life*, London: Ashgate.

Monro, S. (2006b) 'Transmuting Binaries: The Theoretical Challenge', *Sociological Research Online*, vol 12, no 1.

Monro, S. and Warren, L. (2004) 'Transgendering Citizenship', *Sexualities*, vol 7, no 3: 343-62.

More, K. and Whittle, S. (eds) (1999) *Reclaiming Genders: Transsexual Grammars and the Fin de Siecle*, London and New York, NY: Cassell.

Morgan, D. (1999) 'Risk and Family Practices: Accounting for Change and Fluidity in Family Life', in E. Silva and C. Smart (eds) *The New Family?*, London: Sage.

Morris, J. and Lindow, V. (1993) *User Participation In Community Care Services*, Leeds: Community Care Support Force.

Namaste, K. (1996a) 'The Politics of Inside/Out: Queer Theory, Poststructuralism, and a Sociological Approach to Sexuality', in S. Seidman (ed) *Queer Theory/Sociology*, Oxford: Blackwell.

Namaste, K. (1996b) 'Tragic Misreadings: Queer Theory's Erasure of Transgender Subjectivity', in B. Beemyn and M. Eliason (eds) *Queer Studies: A Lesbian, Gay, Bisexual and Transgender Anthology*, New York, NY, and London: New York University Press.

Namaste, K. (2000) *Invisible Lives: The Erasure of Transsexual and Transgendered People*, Chicago, IL: University of Chicago Press.

Nardi, P. (1992) 'That's What Friends are For: Friends as Family in the Lesbian and Gay Community', in K. Plummer (ed) *Modern Homosexualities, Fragments of Lesbian and Gay Experience*, London: Sage.

Nasir, S, (1996) '"Race", Gender and Social Policy', in C. Hallett (ed) *Women and Social Policy: An Introduction*, Hemel Hempstead: Harvester Wheatsheaf.

Nataf, Z. (1996) *Lesbians Talk Transgender*, London: Scarlet Press.

Nestle, J. (ed) (1992) *The Persistent Desire: A Femme Butch Reader*, Boston, MA: Alyson Publications, Inc.

Noddings, N. (1983) *Caring, a Feminine Approach to Ethics and Moral Education*, Berkeley, CA: University of California Press.

Noddings, N. (2002) *Starting at Home: Caring and Social Policy*, Berkeley, CA: University of California Press.

Oakley, A. (2000) *Experiments in Knowing: Gender and Method in the Social Sciences*, Cambridge: Polity Press.

O'Connell, S.P. (1999) 'Claiming One's Identity: A Constructivist/ Narrativist Approach', in G. Weiss (ed) *Perspectives on Embodiment*, New York, NY: Routledge.

Oudshoorn, N. (1994) *Beyond the Natural Body: An Archaeology of Sex Hormones*, London: Routledge.

Pahl, R. and Spencer, L. (2004) 'Personal Communities: Not simply Families of "Fate" or "Choice"', *Current Sociology*, vol 52, no 2: 199-221.

Parliamentary Forum on Transsexualism (1996) 'Transsexualism: The Current Medical Viewpoint', at www.pfc.org.uk/medical/mediview.htm

Pateman, C. (1989) *The Disorder of Women: Disorder, Feminism and Political Theory*, Cambridge: Polity Press.

Pauly, I.B. (1969) 'Adult Manifestations of Male Transsexualism', in R. Green and J. Money (eds) *Transsexualism and Sex Reassignment*, Baltimore, MD: Johns Hopkins University Press.

Phillips, A. (1993) *Democracy and Difference*, Cambridge: Polity Press.

Plummer, K. (1992) *Modern Homosexualities: Fragments of Lesbian and Gay Experience*, London: Routledge.

Plummer, K. (1995) *Telling Sexual Stories: Power, Change and Social Worlds*, London: Routledge.

Plummer, K. (1998) 'The Past, Present and Future of the Sociology of Same-Sex Relations', in P. Nardi and M. Schneider (eds) *Social Perspectives in Lesbian and Gay Studies*, London: Routledge.

Plummer, K. (2000) *Documents of Life 2: An Invitation to Critical Humanism*, London: Sage.

Plummer, K. (2003) *Inventing Intimate Citizenship: Personal Decisions and Public Dialogues*, Seattle, WA: University of Washington Press.

Price, J. and Shildrick, M. (1999) *Feminist Theory and the Body: A Reader*, Edinburgh: Edinburgh University Press.

Prosser, J. (1998) *Second Skins: The Body Narratives of Transsexuality*, New York, NY: Columbia University Press.

Raymond, J. (1980) *The Transsexual Empire*, London: Women's Press.

Raymond, J. (1994) *The Transsexual Empire* (2nd edn), New York, NY: Teachers' Press.

Raymond, J.G. (1996) 'The Politics of Transgenderism', in R. Ekins and D. King (eds) *Blending Genders: Social Aspects of Cross-Dressing*, London: Routledge.

Rich, A. (1979) *On Lies, Secrets and Silence: Selected Prose, 1966–1978*, New York, NY: Norton.

Richardson, D. (1998) 'Sexuality and Citizenship', *Sociology*, vol 32: 83-100.

Richardson, D. (2000) 'Constructing Sexual Citizenship: Theorizing Sexual Rights', *Critical Social Policy*, vol 20, no 1: 105-35.

Riddell, C. (1980) *Divided Sisterhood: A Critical Review of Janice Raymond's 'The Transsexual Empire'*, Liverpool: News from Nowhere.

Riddell, C. (1996) 'Divided Sisterhood: A Critical Review of Janice Raymond's *The Transsexual Empire*', in R. Ekins and D. King (eds) *Blending Genders: Social Aspects of Cross-Dressing*, London: Routledge.

Roen, K. (2001a) '"Either/Or" and "Both/Neither": Discursive Tensions in Transgender Politics', *Signs: Journal of Women in Culture and Society*, vol 27, no 2: 501-22.

Roen, K. (2001b) 'Transgender Theory and Embodiment: The Risk of Racial Marginalisation', *Journal of Gender Studies*, vol 10, no 3: 253-63.

Roscoe,W. (ed) (1988), *Living the Spirit:A Gay American Indian Anthology*, New York, NY: St Martin's Press.

Roseneil, S. (1995) *Disarming Patriarchy: Feminism and Political Action at Greenham*, Buckingham: Open University Press.

Roseneil, S. (1996) 'Transformations and Transgressions: Experience, Consciousness and Identity at Greenham', in N. Charles and F. Hughes-Freeland (eds) *Practising Feminism: Identity, Difference and Power*, London: Routledge.

Roseneil, S. (2000) 'Queer Frameworks and Queer Tendencies:Towards an Understanding of Postmodern Transformations of Sexuality', *Sociological Research Online*, vol 5, no 3.

Roseneil, S. (2003) 'We'd Rather be Friends', *New Statesman*, 15 December.

Roseneil, S. and Budgeon, S. (2004) 'Beyond the Conventional Family: Intimacy, Care and Community in the 21st Century', *Current Sociology*, vol 52, no 2: 127-34.

Roseneil, S. and Seymour, J. (1999) *Practising Identities: Power and Resistance*, London: Macmillan.

Roughgarden, J. (2004) *Evolution's Rainbow: Diversity, Gender and Sexuality in Nature and People*, Los Angeles, CA: University of California Press.

Rubin, G. (1989) 'Thinking Sex: Notes for a Radical Theory of the Politics of Sexuality' in C.Vance (ed) *Pleasure and Danger: Exploring Female Sexuality*, London: Pandora.

Rubin, G. (1992) 'Of Catamites and Kings: Reflections on Butch, Gender and Boundaries', in J. Nestle (ed) *The Persistent Desire. A Femme-Butch-Reader*, Boston, MA: Alyson Publications.

Rubin, H. (1996) 'Do You Believe in Gender?', *Sojourner*, vol 21, no 6.

Rubin, L. (1985) *Just Friends:The Role of Friendship in Our Lives*, New York, NY: Harper.

SAMOIS (eds) (1987) *Coming to Power:Writings and Graphics on Lesbian S/M*, Boston, MA: Alyson Publications.

Sandell, J. (1994) 'The Cultural Necessity of Queer Families', at www. popcultures.com/articles/queer.htm

Sarup, M. (1996) *Identity, Culture and the Postmodern World*, Edinburgh: Open University Press.

Schacht, S.P. and Ewing, D.W. (1998) *Feminism and Men: Reconstructing Gender Relations*, New York, NY: New York University Press.

Schrock, P. and Reid, L. (2006) 'Transsexuals' Sexual Stories', *Archives of Sexual Behaviour*, vol 35, no 1: 75-86.

Scott, J.W. (1992) 'Experience', in J. Butler and J.W. Scott (eds) *Feminists Theorize the Political*, New York, NY: Routledge.

Scott, S. and Morgan, D. (1993) *Body Matters: Essays on the Sociology of the Body*, London: Falmer Press.

Sedgwick, E.K. (1990) *Epistemology of the Closet*, Berkeley, CA: University of California Press.

Segal, L. (1997) 'Sexualities' in K. Woodward (ed) *Identity and Difference: Culture, Media and Identities*, London: Sage.

Seidler, V.J. (1989) *Rediscovering Masculinity: Reason, Language and Sexuality*, London: Routledge.

Seidman, S. (1993) 'Identity and Politics in a "Postmodern" Gay Culture: Some Historical and Conceptual Notes', in M. Warner (ed) *Fear of a Queer Planet: Queer Politics and Social Theory*, Minneapolis and London: University of Minnesota Press.

Seidman, S. (ed) (1996) *Queer Theory / Sociology*, Oxford: Blackwell.

Sevenhuijsen, S. (1998) *Citizenship and the Ethics of Care: Feminist Considerations About Justice, Morality and Politics*, London: Routledge.

Sharpe, A. (2002) *Transgender Jurisprudence: Dysphoric Bodies of Law*, London: Cavendish.

Shilling, C. and Mellor, P.A. (1997) *Re-Forming the Body: Religion, Community and Modernity*, New York, NY: Sage.

Silva, E. and Smart, C. (eds) (1999) *The New Family?*, London: Sage.

Singer, T.B. (2006) 'From the Medical Gaze to Sublime Mutations: The Ethics of (Re)Viewing Non-Normative Body Images', in S. Stryker and S. Whittle (eds) *The Transgender Studies Reader*, New York and Abingdon: Routledge.

Smart, C. and Neale, B. (1999) *Family Fragments?*, Cambridge: Polity Press.

Smart, C. and Neale, B. (2002) 'Caring, Earning and Changing: Parenthood and Employment After Divorce', Centre for Research on Family, Kinship and Childhood Working Paper Series, at www.leeds.ac.uk/family

Snow, D.A. and Anderson, L. (1987) 'Identity Work Among the Homeless: The Verbal Construction and Avowal of Personal Identities', *American Journal of Sociology*, vol 19: 1336-71.

Song, M. and Parker, D. (1995) 'Commonality, Difference and the Dynamics of Disclosure in In-depth Interviewing', *Sociology*, vol 29, no 2: 241-56.

Stacey, J. (1996) *In the Name of the Family: Rethinking Family Values in the Postmodern Age*, Boston, MA: Beacon Press.

Stein, A. and Plummer, K. (1996) '"I Can't Even Think Straight": "Queer" Theory and the Missing Sexual Revolution in Sociology', in S. Seidman (ed) *Queer Theory / Sociology*, Oxford: Blackwell.

Steiner, B.W. (ed) (1995) *Gender Dysphoria: Development, Research, Management*, New York, NY: Plenum.

Stoller, R.J. (1964) 'A Contribution to the Study of Gender Identity', *International Journal of Psycho-Analysis*, vol 45: 220-6.

Stoller, R. (1968a) 'Passing and the Continuum of Gender Identity', in J. Marmor (ed) *Sexual Inversion: The Multiple Roots of Homosexuality*, New York, NY: Basic Books.

Stoller, R. (1968b) *Sex and Gender, Vol I: The Development of Masculinity and Femininity*, New York, NY: Jason Aronson.

Stoller, R. (1975) *The Transsexual Experiment, Vol II: Sex and Gender*, London: Hogarth Press.

Stone, S. (1991) 'The *Empire* Strikes Back: A Posttranssexual Manifesto', in J. Epstein and K. Straub (eds) *Body Guards: The Cultural Politics of Sexual Ambiguity*, London: Routledge.

Stone, S. (1996) *The War of Desire and Technology at the Close of the Mechanical Age*, Cambirdge, MA: MIT Press.

Storr, M. (2003) 'Postmodern Bisexuality', in J. Weeks, J. Holland and M. Waites (eds) *Sexualities and Society: A Reader*, Cambridge: Polity Press.

Straub, K. (1992) *Body Guards: The Cultural Politics of Gender Ambiguity*, New York and London: Routledge.

Stryker, S. (1998) 'The Transgender Issue: An Introduction', *Journal of Lesbian and Gay Studies*, vol 4, no 2: 145-58.

Stryker, S. (2006) '(De)Subjugated Knowledge: An Introduction to Transgender Studies', in S. Stryker and S. Whittle (eds) *The Transgender Studies Reader*, New York, NY, and Abingdon: Routledge.

Stryker, S. and Whittle, S. (eds) (2006) *The Transgender Studies Reader*, New York, NY, and Abingdon: Routledge.

Stychin, C. (1998) *A Nation By Rights: National Cultures, Sexual Identity Politics and the Discourse of Rights*, Philadelphia, PA: Temple University Press.

Szasz, T. (1990) *Sex by Prescription*, New York, NY: Syracuse University Press.

Tatchell, P. (2004) 'Partners in Discrimination', at www.petertatchell.net/partnership/partnerdiscrimination.htm

Taylor, J. and Chandler, T. (1995) *Lesbians Talk Violent Relationships*, London: Scarlet Press.

Taylor, V. and Whittier, N. (1992) 'Collective Identity in Social Movement Communities: Lesbian Feminist Mobilization', in A. Morris and C. Mueller (eds) *Feminist Frontiers*, New York, NY: McGraw Hill.

Taylor, Y. (2005) 'The Gap and How to Mind It: Intersections of Class and Sexuality', *Sociological Research Online*, vol 10, no 3.

Taylor, Y. (2007) *Working-class Lesbian Life Experiences: Classed Outsiders*, Houndmills: Palgrave.

Towle, E.B. and Morgan, L.M. (2002) 'Romancing the Transgender Narrative: Rethinking the Use of the "Third Gender" Concept', *Journal of Lesbian and Gay Studies*, vol 8, no 4: 469-97.

Tronto, J. (1993) *Moral Boundaries: A Political Argument for an Ethic of Care*, New York, NY: Routledge.

Tully, B. (1992) *Accounting for Transsexualism and Transhomosexuality: The Gender Identity Careers of over 200 Men and Women who have Petitioned for Surgical Reassignment of the Sexual Identity*, London: Whiting & Birch.

Turner, B. and Hamilton, P. (eds) (1994) *Citizenship: Critical Concepts*, London: Routledge.

Ungerson, C. (1987) *Policy is Personal: Sex, Gender and Informal Care*, London: Tavistock.

Vance, C. (ed) (1989) *Pleasure and Danger: Exploring Female Sexuality*, London: Routledge.

Valentine, G. (1993) 'Hetero-Sexing Space: Lesbian Perceptions and Experiences of Everyday Spaces', *Environment and Planning D – Society and Space 9*, no 3: 395-413.

Walby, S. (1994)) 'Is Citizenship Gendered?', *Sociology*, vol 28, no 2: 107-21.

Walby, S. (1997) *Gender Transformations*, London: Routledge.

Warner, M. (ed) (1993) *Fear of a Queer Planet: Queer Politics and Social Theory*, Minneapolis, MN, and London: University of Minnesota Press.

Waugh, P. (1997) 'Modernism, Postmodernism, Gender: The View From Feminism', in S. Kemp and J. Squires (eds) *Feminisms*, Oxford: Oxford University Press.

Weedon, C. (1987) *Feminist Practice and Poststructuralist Theory*, Oxford: Blackwell.

Weeks, J. (1977) *Coming Out: Homosexual Politics in Britain from the Nineteenth Century to the Present*, London: Quartet.

Weeks, J. (1990) *Coming Out: Homosexual Politics in Britain from the Nineteenth Century to the Present* (revised and updated edn), London: Quartet.

Weeks, J. (1993) 'AIDS and the Regulation of Sexuality', in V. Berridge and P. Strong (eds) *AIDS and Contemporary History*, Cambridge: Cambridge University Press.

Weeks, J. (1995) *Invented Moralities: Sexual Values in an Age of Uncertainty*, Cambridge: Polity Press.

Weeks, J. (1998) 'The Sexual Citizen', *Theory, Culture and Society*, vol 15, no 3: 35–52.

Weeks, J. (2004) Keynote address (unpublished), 'Pleasure and Danger, Sexualities in the 21st Century' Conference, Cardiff University, 30 June – 2 July.

Weeks, J., Heaphy, B. and Donovan, C. (2001) *Same Sex Intimacies: Families of Choice and Other Life Experiments*, London and New York, NY: Routledge.

West, C. and Zimmerman, D. (1987) 'Doing Gender', *Gender & Society*, vol 1: 125–51.

Weston, K. (1991) *Families We Choose: Lesbians, Gays, Kinship*, New York, NY: Columbia University Press.

Whitehead, H. (1981) 'The Bow and the Burden Strap: A New Look at Institutionalized Homosexuality in Native North America', in S. Ortner and H. Whitehead (eds) *Sexual Meanings: The Cultural Construction of Gender and Sexuality*, New York, NY: Cambridge University Press.

Whittle, S. (1996) 'Gender Fucking or Fucking Gender? Current Cultural Contributions to Theories of Gender Blending', in K. Ekins and D. King (eds) *Blending Genders: Social Aspects of Cross-Dressing and Sex-Changing*, London: Routledge.

Whittle, S. (1998) 'Guest Editorial', *Journal of Gender Studies*, vol 7, no 3.

Whittle, S. (2000) *The Transgender Debate: The Crisis Surrounding Gender Identities*, Reading: South Street Press.

Whittle, S. (2006) 'Foreword', in S. Stryker and S. Whittle (eds) *The Transgender Studies Reader*, New York, NY, and Abingdon: Routledge.

Whittle S. and McMullen, M. (1995) *The Transvestite, the Transsexual and the Law* (3rd edn) London: Beaumont Trust.

Whittle, S. and Turner, L. (2006) '"Sex Changes"? Paradigm Shifts in "Sex" and "Gender" Following the Gender Recognition Act?', *Sociological Research Online*, vol 12, no 1.

Wieringa, S. and Blackwood, E. (eds) (1999) *Cultures, Identities, Sexualities*, New York, NY: Columbia University Press.

Wilchins, R.A. (1997) *Read my Lips: Sexual Subversion and the End of Gender*, New Yorlk, NY: Firebrand Books.

Wilchins, R.A. (2002) 'Gender Rights are Human Rights', in J. Nestle, C. Howell, and R.A. Wilchins (eds) *GenderQueer: Voices from Beyond the Sexual Binary*, Los Angeles, CA: Alyson Publications.

Williams, F. (1992) 'Somewhere over the Rainbow: Universality and Diversity in Social Policy', in N. Manning and R. Page (eds) *Social Policy Review 4*, Canterbury: Social Policy Association.

Williams, F. (1999) 'Good-Enough Principles for Welfare' *Journal of Social Policy*, vol 28, no 4.

Williams, F. (2000) 'Understanding the Dynamics of Social Change, Social Relations and Welfare Settlements: Towards an Analytical Framework', ESRC research group on Care, Values and the Future of Welfare, University of Leeds, Workshop Paper, at www.leeds.ac.uk/cava/papers/workshoppapers.htm#details

Williams, F. (2004) *Rethinking Families*, London: Calouste Gulbenkian Foundation.

Williams, F., Roseneil, S. and Martin, G. (2002) 'Collective Voices around Partnering and Parenting', Collective Interventions on the Terrain of Care and Intimacy: The CAVA Project, International Seminar Papers at www.leeds.ac.uk/cava/papers/intseminar4williamsroseneilmartin. htm

Williams, W.L. (1986) *The Spirit of the Flesh: Sexual Diversity in American Indian Culture*, Boston, MA: Beacon Press.

Wilson, E. (1977) *Women and the Welfare State*, London: Tavistock.

Wilson, M. (2002) '"I am the Prince of Pain, for I am a Princess in the Brain": Liminal Transgender Identities, Narratives and the Elimination of Ambiguities', *Sexualities*, vol 5, no 4: 425-48.

Wilton, T. (2000) 'Out/performing Our Selves: Sex, Gender and Cartesian Dualism', *Sexualities*, vol 3, no 2: 273-54.

Woodward, K. (ed) (1997) *Identity and Difference: Culture, Media and Identities*, London: Sage.

Woolf, N. (1991) *The Beauty Myth: How Images of Beauty Are Used Against Women*, New York, NY: Anchor.

Wright, E. (1997) 'Thoroughly Postmodern Feminist Criticism', in S. Kemp and J. Squires (eds) *Feminisms*, Oxford: Oxford University Press.

Index

Page references for notes are followed by n